P9-DDH-552

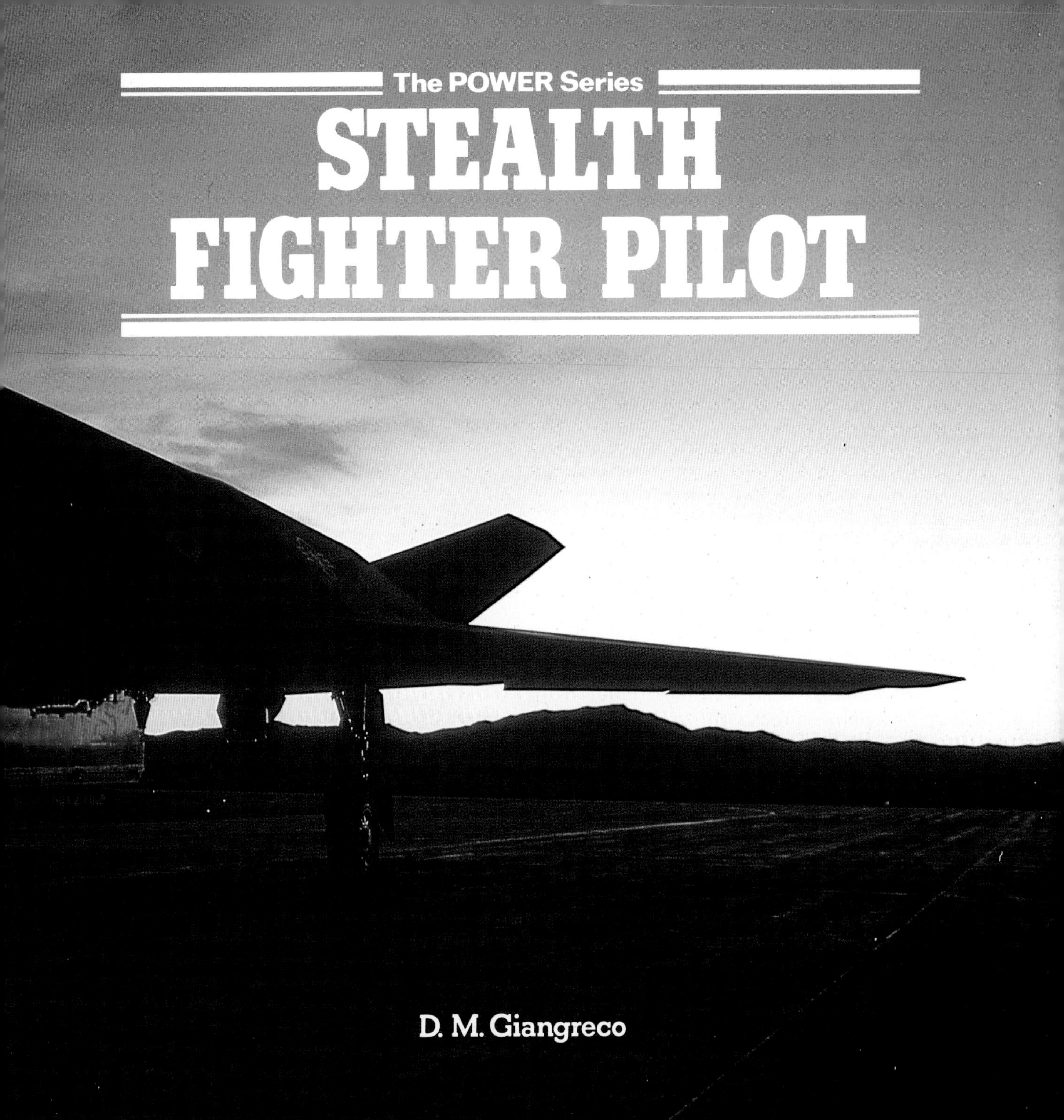

The POWER Series

STEALTH FIGHTER PILOT

D. M. Giangreco

Motorbooks International

First published in 1993 by Motorbooks International Publishers & Wholesalers, PO Box 2, 729 Prospect Avenue, Osceola, WI 54020 USA

Library of Congress Cataloging-in-Publication Data

Giangreco, D. M.
Stealth fighter pilot/D. M. Giangreco.
p. cm. — (The Power series)
Includes index.
ISBN 0-87938-716-5
1. F-117 (Jet fighter plane) 2. Fighter pilots —United States—History. I. Title. II. Series: Power series (Osceola, Wis.)
UG1242.F5G49 1993
358.4'383—dc20 93-30069

On the front cover: The multifunction display is reflected in the face plate of stealth pilot Jack Shaw. *USAF*

On the title page: A Lockheed F-117A at dusk. *Lockheed*

On the frontispiece page: A 2,000lb bomb is gently moved into position beneath Terry Foley's F-117A. *Lockheed*

On the back cover: Above, In the early days of the F-117 program, security was taken very seriously at the Tonopah base. Below, Jack Shaw in the F-117A cockpit simulator. *Lockheed*

Printed and bound in Hong Kong

Contents

Acknowledgments

I would like to thank the many people whose efforts added so much to this book: Guy Aceto at *Air Force Magazine;* Lockheed's Richard Stadler, Bob Mainert, Paul Martin and Denny Lombard; Lt. Col. F. T. Case and Col. Tom Cardwell of the Air Force Studies and Analysis Agency; S/Sgt. Kelly Godbey of the 350th Refueling Squadron; Jerome G. Peppers at Wright-Patterson AFB; Bob Bockman, DoD Public Affairs; Tony Geishauser of Texas Instruments; Bob Waller, DoD Still Media Records Center; Mike Bucannon of the 1361st Audio Visual Squadron; as well as S/Sgt. George R. Partelow and SM/Sgt. Robert Wickley of the 1352nd Audio Visual Squadron. The many individuals at Fort Leavenworth, Kansas, who lent their assistance include: Carol Ramke and Betty Bohannon at the Command and General Staff College Library; Janet Wray of the Public Affairs Office; Col. Dave Glantz, Dr. Graham Turbiville, and Lt. Col. Les "The Man" Grau (Ret) from the Foreign Military Studies Office; Brian Loy in the Threats Directorate; and, from the staff of *Military Review,* Cynthia L. Chacon, Belva Kaye Wilson and Lt. Col. William P. King.

A great many members of Team Stealth, who serve with the 49th Fighter Wing or belonged to the now deactivated 4450th Tactical Fighter Group and 37th Tactical Fighter Wing, lent generously of their time. They include M/Sgt. Bobby Shelton; M/Sgt. Al Mack, SM/Sgt. Vincent C. Breslin, SM/Sgt. Harold P. Myers (Ret); SM/Sgt. Gary Martin; Capt. Tim Veeder; Capt. Matt Byrd; Capt. Phil McDaniel; Capt. Mike Ritchie; Maj. Greg Feest; Maj. Jerry Leatherman (and his lovely wife Nancy); Maj. Earl Shellner; Lt. Col. Ralph Getchell; Col. Robert C. Huff; Col. Raleigh Harrington; and former wing commanders Col. Al Whitley and Col. Tony Tolin. Several former Team Stealth pilots who also granted me interviews under the condition that I use pseudonyms were originally listed in the footnotes as "Tom," "Dick," and "Harry" but, at the suggestion of "Dick," their names were changed to those of three World War I pilots in the 1938 movie classic *Dawn Patrol:* "Capt. Scott," "Capt. Courtney," and "Maj. Brand."

And, finally, I would also like to thank my wife, Kathy, who probably knows more about the development and fielding of the F-117A than most Air Force personnel after single-handedly transcribing and editing nearly 200 pages from taped interviews with Team Stealth members.

The views expressed in this book are those of the author and do not purport to reflect the position of the Department of the Army, the Department of Defense, or any other government agency.

Preface

On Sunday, August 19, 1990, Col. Anthony J. ("Tony") Tolin gazed across the tarmac at Langley Air Force Base (AFB), Virginia, at a sight he hadn't even been allowed to see when he recently commanded the highly classified unit that flew the plane: 22 F-117A stealth fighters lined up along a flight line in broad daylight.

For years, the ugly, bat-shaped plane had been kept under wraps. The previous decade had seen thousands of people work on the ultraclassified Senior Trend project to develop and field the aircraft, yet its secrets had been tenaciously guarded. Its secrets—but not the fact that the plane itself existed. Scattered articles had appeared in aviation and defense publications almost from the day the technology that spawned it began to be developed at Lockheed's Skunk Works, where such ground-breaking aircraft as the U-2 and SR-71 Blackbird spy planes had been born. A disgusted congressman had even held aloft a mass-produced replica of the top-secret jet in open congressional hearings while berating US Air Force (USAF) generals for having allowed such lapses in security that even a commercial company, catering to model-making hobbyists, could obtain blueprints. As the congressman would later learn in 1988, the sleek, rounded replica he held in his hands so victoriously in 1986 looked absolutely nothing like the aircraft that had been flying since 1981.

By holding fast to the stealthy jet's secrets long after its existence became known, the USAF ensured that even highly informed outside observers had only a vague idea of how well Lockheed and the USAF had succeeded in developing an aircraft that was practically invisible to radar. Moreover, simply observing its odd shape told one nothing about its key strengths, such as extreme bombing accuracy; its weaknesses, such as a limited usefulness in conditions of poor visibility; or of the razor-sharp professionals who flew it. Today, though, two dozen of these jets were lined up wing tip to wing tip for spy satellites and photographers to see, a public expression of America's will to risk one of its most valuable strategic assets to protect Saudi Arabia from an Iraqi army that had already swallowed its little neighbor Kuwait whole.

Would Iraq's strongman, Saddam Hussein, understand the significance of this scene? If he didn't, surely the Soviets would make it clear to him. Col. Tolin, now posted to Langley as the assistant deputy to the chief of staff, hoped that Hussein would get the message. But if he didn't, Tolin told reporters, the menacing-looking aircraft "give us an ability…to get in with the least amount of casualties and attack those important targets if necessary."

History has duly recorded that Hussein did not heed the warning given at Langley that day. Sixty-five stealth pilots were eventually deployed to Saudi Arabia and bombed Iraq in an air campaign that shattered Iraq's ability to defend itself. Before them, nearly a hundred more aviators took part in the development of the aircraft they fondly called the Black Jet, some losing their life or becoming badly injured in the process. This is their story.

F-117As at Langley AFB during the 37th TFW's deployment to Saudi Arabia. M/Sgt. Boyd Belcher, USAF

Prologue

Abdula Salam Mustafa was born the son of a Shuni herder in the Euphrates valley near Syria. The oldest of six children, Abu (Son of) Mustafa had journeyed to Baghdad, Iraq, with his father in 1976. The ancient capital was then a bustling, growing metropolis, renewed by the black gold pumping from a thousand wells, and Abu Mustafa's father hoped the carpentry skills he had learned in his youth would help him to obtain a job in one of the dozens of state building projects spreading outward along the banks of the Tigris. A bright, hard-working eight year old who ate little, Abu Mustafa would make the perfect carpenter's assistant. Besides, if Abu Mustafa's father could offer an employer four hands for the price of two, he might perhaps be picked ahead of other workers.

On this cold, clear winter night 15 years later, Jundi Awwal (Private, First Class) Mustafa finds his mind drifting back again and again to the events of his childhood. His fingers drum the control board just above the knobs flanking the radar scope's circular screen, and he forces himself to concentrate on his job: monitoring a P-15M early-warning radar system that scans the western approaches of Baghdad for low-flying American aircraft. The C-band system, nicknamed Squat Eye by the infidels, together with a shorter-range Low Blow system, comprise the eyes of a Soviet-made S-125 Pechora (SA-3 Goa) air defense missile system.

When the war opened two long weeks ago, on Thursday, January 17, 1991, Mustafa's mobile missile battalion was positioned about 6mi north of a key command bunker and 3/4mi west of a series of warehouses containing artillery shells of various calibers. From that position, the Pechora battalion could provide close-in defense of the munitions depot as well as protect the northern approaches of the bunker. For point defense, the bunker was also flanked by another Pechora battalion, a V-750 Dvina (SA-2 Guideline) battalion, capable of higher-altitude kills, and two batteries of 14.5-millimeter (mm) antiaircraft artillery (triple-A), which, unlike Mustafa's unit, were all deployed in a system of revetments and hardened shelters. A dummy Pechora battalion occupied a site 1 1/2mi southeast of the bunker.

In the early-morning hours of that first day of fighting, Mustafa was off-duty, talking with his friends in the communications van, when the land line to Baghdad suddenly went dead. This was a fairly unusual occurrence but didn't particularly interest Mustafa, who stepped down from the van to let the others sort it out. While he was zipping his British-patterned military jacket against the cold, something caught his eye. Flashes like distant lightning appeared beyond the northern horizon. At first, they seemed to be west of Baghdad's dull glow, then, they spread east to the city itself. Mustafa watched, transfixed, as his friends inside the van continued to chatter about the radio—then finally began yelling the alarm when flashes started to erupt at points all along his right. As soldiers tumbled bleary-eyed from their vans and tents, Mustafa dashed across to the control van, almost tripping over a trio of thick electrical cables. He bounded up into the guidance control room and asked the startled *arif* (sergeant) operating the I-band radar if he could see anything, even though Mustafa knew that the medium-range system might not yet detect any aircraft.

A Fan Song air defense radar destroyed by a HARM during the Gulf War. US Department of Defense (DOD)

The two men, joined by the Low Blow's D-band operator, stared intently at the screen as the pandemonium outside quickly drowned out the hum of the system. For an instant, Mustafa thought he saw a weak ghost of a blip appear among the normal ground clutter to the north, but it soon vanished and seemed inconsequential. Then, he heard it. Above the ruckus outside was the unmistakable sound of jet engines, yet a blank screen stared back at him. Bumping past the guidance control officer who had just burst into the van, Mustafa rushed to the open door, braced his hands on both sides, and craned his neck upward. Yes, it was a plane, but where? *How*? Others outside began looking up, too, and he called out for everyone to quiet down as the radar operator tried to explain to his commander that no targets existed.

The sound had almost trailed off to nothing, and people had begun to talk in hushed tones and move off to their duty stations, when two quick explosions tore the night air. Mustafa was returning to the screen when he heard the distant blasts. He immediately turned and stood as the van door framed a ball of orange flame rising into the air above the bunker.

That was Mustafa's first encounter with the F-117A, or *shaba* (ghost), as the men in his battalion called it. He could not say it disappeared into the night sky. Nothing had really been there to disappear, just a spot of dim light that flickered for a moment on a radar screen before the dull rumble of a jet engine rose and fell.

The events of that first night meeting seemed far away now, and the shaba had not returned—but many other American planes had visited the area. Jets from "Bush's navy" bombed the warehouses the next afternoon and escaped unharmed after destroying Mustafa's battalion's Low Blow before their first attack run. In this second attack, the guidance control officer, a *mulazim awwal* (first lieutenant), had done exactly as his Soviet teacher had instructed and tried to trick the American pilots by turning on the D-band missile guidance radar before he actually intended to fire. Once the Americans had launched an antiradiation missile to home in on the radar, the false signal was shut down and the supposedly now-unguided missile was expected to fall away and crash. However, the Americans' missile did something completely unexpected. Unlike the weapon used against the valiant defenders of Hanoi and Haiphong, who outwitted similar homing missiles that the infidels had used over North Vietnam, this new weapon apparently had some way of targeting a radar site even after it was shut off. The missile ripped into the unmanned Low Blow, and the resulting explosion not only wrecked the radar but killed eight soldiers even though they were outside of a high earthen revetment that surrounded the unit.

Mustafa's duty station was located at a different position within the battalion perimeter, nearly 200 yards from the destroyed radar unit. After that attack, with no guidance-tracking radar operational and no sites left to defend, Mustafa had settled down to watching the war unfold around him and concentrated on his job at the screen of his medium-range early warning radar. The Americans had appeared to have little interest in his C-band Squat Eye, since it was not designed to direct the battalion's deadly surface-to-air missiles, and even headquarters had seemed to have forgotten about him and his friends. Only sporadic contact had been maintained with the country's integrated air defense network because the land lines were inoperative, and the radios were frequently jammed. It had been whispered that many high-level commanders had been killed on the opening night of the war, and the scarcity of input from above to Mustafa's battalion for almost a week had seemed to confirm it. Finally, however, the battalion had received orders to move north to its current position near Baghdad.

Once in position, the battalion had received new equipment, replacements for its casualties, and much advice on how to fight off the Americans' relentless electronic warfare, which was rendering Iraq's Soviet-made radars useless. In the last week, the battalion had experienced jamming running throughout the full range of the ultrahigh frequency (UHF) signals available to its systems. Repeater jamming, which created false blips as targets, was alternately directed against Mustafa's C-band radar, the I-band tracking, and D-band acquisition radars, and sometimes all the systems at once. On other occasions, the repeater jamming would be combined with barrage jamming, which simply whited out every scope. Mustafa and the other operators had to gain their operating frequencies further and further down the waveband to escape the noise, until their radars were essentially useless.

After two weeks of war, morale in Mustafa's battalion is at rock bottom, and the men feel that all their training and all their efforts have been for nothing. "At least we're still alive," Mustafa thinks.

Even though it is a chilly January night, the door to the Squat Eye's control van remains wide-open. The inside temperature is uncomfortably high from the heat generated by myriad electronic systems. Still, Mustafa reflects, the van is infinitely cooler now than in the summer months when he would joke that his mother could use it to bake bread. Mustafa feels a drop of sweat roll down his back as he stretches and then leans forward again into the soft green light of the radar scope.

By now, he is reasonably familiar with the ground clutter pattern within the arc of the Squat Eye's 130mi beam. The radar's reach extends almost as far north as Kirkuk, as far west as the new Al-Asad Air Base (AB), and well into Iranian airspace to the east. As targets move closer, it is Mustafa's job to hand them off to the new Low Blow, located in the midst of the battalion's combat and command elements. The Low Blow uses an I-band fixed-direction tracking radar that reaches out nearly 50mi to encompass Al-Taqaddum AB within its cone of vision, and a short-range D-band guidance radar to engage target aircraft as far as 18mi from the battalion's four quad-rail missile launchers. As a practical matter, however, Mustafa has found that the *raid* (major) who commands the battalion seems more intent on preserving the Low Blow and just putting on a good show of firing his Pechora missiles in the ineffective optical mode, than on aggressively tracking the infidels' jets and risking death from above. The I-band radar is almost invariably powered down when an aircraft appears to be on a heading toward the battalion, and the D-band has been switched on only twice in the last week for tests to see if the system is working properly.

Peering intently into the radar scope, Mustafa sees that the built-up areas of Baghdad immediately to the east are a jagged mass of light that renders observation over the city virtually impossible with this type of radar system. Bright spots representing high points in the terrain—mostly made by human beings—dot the screen's field, and the rising lands to the west and north of Baghdad show up clearly in the outer areas of the screen running from eight o'clock to two o'clock. The general lines of the Tigris and Euphrates river valleys can also be made out because of the large number of communications towers and other tall structures in population centers and air bases.

Closer to the battalion's position, Mustafa's radar picks up the echoes of everything from brick kiln chimneys to the sophisticated network of huge towers at the Abu Ghurayb International Radio Communications complex to the control tower at the new Baghdad International Airport to the flagpoles adorning the bleachers of a nearby racetrack. The P-15M Squat Eye used by his air defense unit is designed to provide better low-level coverage than the original P-15 Flat Face still found in most of Iraq's 30 or more S-125 Pechora battalions, and, consequently, its radar scope displays considerably more ground clutter than the Flat Face. Mustafa was chosen to monitor the unit's C-band radar because of his uncanny ability to pick out the movement of even the most subtle pips, even when the passage of storm fronts plays havoc with the radar.

Yes, by the grace of Allah Al-Raheem (the Merciful), Jundi Awwal Mustafa is both a dedicated soldier of Islam and a topflight radar technician. On this January night, he is being allowed more time just to slow down and take it a little easy than on any other since the battalion's move north. Air activity seems to be at a much lower pace than normal and is mostly centered well to the south and west. He's also had to contend with virtually no jamming but knows that the night is still young. Mustafa's mind wanders from recollections of long-forgotten events in his childhood to thoughts of a young woman he met from Al-Quawayr, Iraq, and his own mortality. He smiles when he thinks about how ironic it is that the Ba'th lackeys in Baghdad had believed themselves immune from the infidels' assaults behind their vaunted wall of triple-A and missiles around the capital. The *shaba* he encountered the first night of the war had put an end to awed descriptions of Baghdad's "impregnable" defenses.

He's thought often of the *shaba* in the last two weeks. From the little he's been told of its technology, it seems that perhaps the lowest-frequency radars would have the best luck of making it show more clearly. Had Allah smiled on the P-12 Spoon Rest crews and allowed them to throw their *nur* (light) on the *shaba*? Analyzing his own P-15M radar, he doesn't believe that boosting its radiated power would accomplish much. Maybe expanding the aperture would work? No, it probably wouldn't be worth it. The narrowed beam would need a lot more time to sweep the sky, degrading its tracking of conventional aircraft. And besides, the radar would be dragging in all variety of noise: rising bubbles of hot air, radar reflections refracted by the atmosphere, even birds. The whole screen would become awash in false echoes like that one at ten o'clock.

False echo? Mustafa leans closer to the screen. The milky pip just north of the regular Euphrates clutter near Ar-Ramadi, Iraq, does not appear on the next western pass of the beam—or the next—but all of Mustafa's attention stays focused on the few square inches of screen where a subsonic jet, on an unknown heading, might reappear. It certainly seems to be nothing of any consequence, just another flake on a snowy screen, but some inner voice tells Mustafa not to take his eyes off the area.

Another! Can this be it again? A fairly strong return appears in the sky over the southern end of Ath-Tharthar Lake in Iraq. Mustafa opens up the direct phone link with the control van and tells the guidance control officer that he believes he has a target. "Yes!" A second pip flashes brightly over the lake. "I have two sweeps!" Then, he gives its heading, azimuth, and distance. His eyes remain riveted on the screen until his mental clock tells him that the now-invisible target has reached the clutter along the Tigris. That is the last he will see of the *shaba* for now, but he is certain that he caught a glimpse of it moving northeast across the lake, and surmises that if the earlier pip above Ar-Ramadi was the same *shaba*, then the aircraft is flying in an arc that will have it approaching Baghdad from the north. "Al-Wahhaab (the Bestower) be praised." Mustafa realizes that if the night had been more busy, he'd have never detected the aircraft.

Mustafa is ordered back to the control van, and after passing the radar scope off to the assistant operator, he leaps out the door of the hot radar van and feels a blast of winter as his sweating body plunges into the night air. He knows what is happening and sprints as fast as he can past darkened missile reload vehicles and quizzical soldiers who watch the madman race by.

Mustafa, the new guidance control officer, and several others have hatched a plan to try to bring down a *shaba* if presented with the right circumstances. If the infidel pilot flies over the battalion in the same general direction in which its batteries are aligned, they believe that perhaps one missile in a full battalion salvo might pass close enough to the *shaba* to activate the proximity fuse on the Pechora's Doppler radar. The resulting detonation might damage or even bring down the aircraft, although this possibility is very weak. To Mustafa and the others, though, trying for it is better than doing nothing at all. When the idea was originally brought to the battalion commander, however, he balked at the idea of "wasting" sixteen missiles in the forlorn hope of shooting down an invisible plane. It was one thing to shoot off five, six, or seven Pechoras a day at visible targets you might not hit, but this absurd scheme would only bring disgrace on the battalion—and him.

Mustafa, in concert with the others, is about to make one last try at convincing the *raid*. Reaching the headquarters van, he slows down to catch his breath and sees that he is walking into an argument. The new *mulazim awwal* (first lieutenant) and a *rais uraf* (staff sergeant) long experienced in target acquisition are alternately pleading with and threatening the commander to get him to turn the batteries southward from their westward orientation. If the *shaba* is moving south along the general line of the Mosul-Baghdad highway, it might be heard as it passes overhead and, for a brief moment, be vulnerable. Mustafa pushes his way past several worried-looking soldiers, but before he can add that they are fast running out of time, the *raid* orders a halt to any more discussion. Such insolence is unheard of, and every man is ordered to return to his post immediately.

Then, the sky a dozen miles to the north, above the huge Taji military complex, erupts into a mass of antiaircraft fire. A quick look at the I-band screen tells the men what they already knew. Only a *shaba* could have crept up unseen to bomb Al-Taji.

The commander immediately realizes that the echoes over Ath-Tharthar must have been real! He orders the Battery A launcher, which is already oriented slightly to the southwest, to rotate directly south. As he had two weeks before, Mustafa again calls out for quiet, but the small crowd that has gathered near the van door to hear the argument needs no prompting. In spite of the men's silence, though, the night has suddenly filled with sound: the hum of the radars is joined by the high-pitched whine of Battery A's launcher being turned, the dull racket up north, and now the warming up of Baghdad's triple-A.

Precious seconds are ticking by, and the din is picking up. Even if the infidel hasn't turned off on another heading, the noise of Baghdad's own defenses might prevent Mustafa from detecting the sound of the *shaba's* engines. When a soldier approaches the group asking what is up, Mustafa firmly motions for him to be quiet. Then he hears it. The *shaba* has returned, and its track appears to be some indefinable distance east of the battalion. A soldier calls out from the van that the I-band can see it almost overhead. The D-band acquisition radar was powered down, however, and its narrow beam is pointed uselessly to the west anyway. Everything is happening too fast.

"Twenty degrees more," Mustafa calls. "Twenty degrees more, then fire!" The quad-rail launcher again turns on its axis, and a pair of missiles is instantly fired off. The solid-fuel boosters light up the launching pad and cast stark shadows in the command areas as the missiles roar past to the southeast. In three seconds, the boosters are blown off when the liquid-fuel ramjets ignite and push the missiles higher and faster.

High above the Iraqi battery, the *shaba*'s pilot, Capt. Matt Byrd, is startled by the bright flash of the missiles' ignition and realizes that he has been somehow targeted. Trusting the technology that has brought he and the other F-117 pilots home each night of the war so far, he remains on course toward his next target and watches as the deadly SA-3s approach.

The soldiers around Mustafa cheer and clap. Mustafa, however, can only watch the two yellow jets of flame as they continue to climb without the jinks associated with command guidance, and slowly begin to separate. He hears himself commanding the rockets—"Strike it down; strike it down"—in a firm, steady voice.

After what seems like an eternity but is actually only 21 seconds from launch, the Pechoras explode almost simultaneously, adding their own notes to the chorus of antiaircraft weapons. Two soldiers are certain that the jet has been struck, and point at what they believe are flaming pieces of it falling from the sky. Mustafa looks over at them and quietly remarks that no, it was probably just part of the missiles' own rocket engines. He knew immediately that the Pechoras missed their mark, since the path of the unguided missiles was smooth and long—too long. They clearly overshot the aircraft, continued their flight, and automatically self-destructed when their fuel was expended.

Mustafa turns and starts back to his station, leaving behind small knots of soldiers discussing the events of the last few minutes. He wants to talk to no one, and walks in silence as Baghdad's air defenses continue to thunder and rattle with undiminished fury. "These fools," he thinks. "They're firing at nothing." The invisible invader has escaped. Mustafa stops, looks at the antiaircraft activity to the south, and wonders if the infidel has struck another target. "We'll meet again, *shaba*. In a week, in a year, or five years. We'll meet again, and, by the grace of Allah, I'll strike you down."

Chapter 1

Team Stealth

The 37th Tactical Fighter Wing—Provisional (TFW—P), or "Team Stealth," comprised 1,500 USAF personnel stationed at the King Khalid AB near the King Fisal Military Cantonment and the small Saudi Arabian city of Khamis Mushayt. Located in the Asir Mountains less than 50mi north of Yemen—one of Iraq's few cheerleaders in the region—King Khalid AB was the home of a Saudi F-15C Eagle-Tornado IDS wing. An extensive network of well-maintained aircraft shelters and support facilities was turned over to the arriving Americans, and as elements of the Saudi wing moved to forward bases near Iraq, even more of the base was made available to the growing US contingent. Less than half of the provisional wing's men and women at King Khalid—about 700—came from the 37th TFW's home at Tonopah Test Range (TTR), Nevada. The balance arrived from at least 36 US bases around the globe, and had never set eyes on an F-117A Black Jet before their arrival in Saudi.

Team Stealth's presence at King Khalid AB was a closely guarded secret during the prolonged US build-up, but at a live Central Command (CENTCOM) press briefing shortly after the first strikes on Baghdad, the world saw for the first time the culmination of over a decade's development and training. The commander of CENTAF, CENTCOM's air component, Lt. Gen. Charles A. Horner, pointed to an F-117's aerial video footage of his "counterpart's headquarters," and a stunned press corps watched its four walls explode outward.[1]

Over the Persian Gulf War's 43 nights of combat operations, the Black Jets routinely flew missions against the toughest targets in Iraq. Gen. Horner later stated, "The F-117 allowed us to do things that we could have only dreamed about in past conflicts. Stealth enabled us to gain surprise each and every day of the war. For example, on the first day of the air campaign the F-117s delivered the first bombs of the war against a wide array of targets, paralyzing the Iraqi air defense network. The attacks on radar sites and command and control bunkers used to control Iraqi defense allowed waves of conventional aircraft to strike with high effectiveness and very low losses.

"But F-117s did much more than that. They allowed us to strike the 'heart' of the enemy—downtown Baghdad—not only on Day 1, but night after night. Stealth allowed us to maintain continuous pressure on vital target sets regardless of the defenses—anywhere in Iraq. F-117s were the only aircraft that attacked 'downtown' Baghdad targets—by most accounts more heavily defended than any Eastern European targets at the height of the Cold War. They did it with impunity. Without the F-117 the fighter pilot losses and the civilian casualties would have been an order of magnitude higher."[2]

The members of Team Stealth, from wrench turner to pilot, felt justifiably proud of their accomplishments during Operation Desert Storm, and as they've moved on to other assignments, they've spread their experience and talent to hundreds of other units within the USAF, and even Great Britain's Royal Air Force (RAF). But as the war continues its inexorable slide into the past, many who served with the 37th TFW—P have found that their accomplishments in the Gulf are being twisted. The immensely successful stealth operations, and war as a whole, are being turned on their head and trumpeted as some sort of failure. For months after the close of hostilities, one would run across newspaper articles stating that stealth technology doesn't work. "Chinese radars appear to have detected the plane,"[3] "Czechoslovak [general] says system...could detect the radar-avoiding Stealth up to 250 miles away,"[4] and "Radar operators aboard Royal Navy destroyers...identified F-117s in the Gulf at ranges up to 40 miles"[5] are just a few of the statements to have appeared. The authors of these stories almost always had little, if any, understanding of low-observable (LO) technology or the ways in which that technology is applied in combat. In fact, in at least 1,280 combat sorties, where 1,669 bombs were dropped directly on target, not only were no aircraft shot down, but none were even hit.

However, figures like these elicit little more than yawns from critics of the F-117 who claim that the aircraft is just another example of wasteful government spending on an unnecessary war toy. They argue that, after all, not only the unstealthy F-15E and F-16C were used to drop laser-guided bombs (LGBs), but even the "decades-old" F-111 and antique Buccaneer S. Mk-2 bombers were similarly used, and that none of these aircraft were destroyed by the vaunted Iraqi air defenses. The most vocal critic in the US Congress, Representative Ronald V. Dellums of California, has frequently stated that the lack of F-117 losses during Desert Storm actually proves nothing about stealth technology's effectiveness, since loss rates for all Coalition aircraft were extremely low during the war: "Our loss rate was so low (less than four one-hundredths of one percent based on missions flown) that one could have predicted the F-117A force would have emerged unscathed."[6] Adding a clever effort at spin control, gadfly defense consultant Jeffrey Record opined that "Desert Storm may prompt a reassessment of the magnitude of the USAF's investment in stealth."[7] Record went on to say, "It is doubtful whether a significantly lower loss rate could have been achieved had every US and allied aircraft been completely stealthy."[8]

What remains mysteriously absent from such critiques is the recognition that the F-117 was repeatedly sent into the jaws of a sophisticated and deeply echeloned air defense system, so the risk to more vulnerable aircraft and their crew was greatly reduced throughout the entire theater of operations.

Although this aspect of the air campaign is consistently and conveniently overlooked by American critics, a studied lack of concern for *nevidimka* (un-

Lt. Gen. Charles Horner points to a strike video of an attack on the Iraqi Air Force Headquarters. DOD

Col. Alton C. ("Al," "The Boss") Whitley, Team Stealth commander.

observable) aircraft was also displayed by the Soviet, and now Russian, air defense establishment. A well-developed arms industry is one of the few generators of badly needed foreign currency among the states that comprised the former Soviet Union, and they have been understandably persistent in their efforts to downplay shortcomings in their military hardware. They assert that the air defense system set up in Iraq was not a factor in the defeat; rather, it was the radar operators and antiaircraft personnel. The commander of the Air Defense Radiotech-

Ralph Getchell

Jerry Leatherman

nical Troops, Lt. Gen. G. Dubrov, confidently stated that stealth aircraft can "indeed show up on the screens. More specifically," he continued, "we have established that some radars can in fact detect Stealth. At shorter ranges than in the case of other aircraft, to be sure, but they can do it. Work in this area continues, of course."[9] Reading from the same script, Alexander Reutov, deputy minister of the former Soviet Ministry of Radio (Radar) industry, also steadfastly maintained that "the problem of stealth is solved," adding, "The problem now is the distance of the interception....We are, of course, testing this."[10]

Hearing these comments—and their pointed disclaimers—Maj. Jerry ("Jap") Leatherman broke into a wide grin. Leatherman, who flew 21 combat missions in the Gulf War and was chief of the 37th TFW's mission planning cell, believed "that a lot of people who pooh-pooh Stealth do so because they have no counter to it. If you can convince [others that] it's no good, then the fact that you have no counter doesn't show a glaring error in your defenses."[11]

Low-observable technologies like those used in Lockheed's F-117 and F-22 as well as Northrop's B-2 are not intended to make an aircraft completely invisible to radar frequencies at all angles and distances. Every aircraft has engines that create heat and noise that can be detectable even after reduction by clever engineering. The passage of a plane through the air will generate heat on its body that a powerful infrared (IR) sensor could detect, and even condensation from the engine exhaust can increase vulnerability. Moreover, aircraft are physical objects that can be seen at night under certain atmospheric conditions and with the aid of powerful electro-optical sensors magnifying starlight.

Many of these potential vulnerabilities are, themselves, able to be countered by a variety of methods. For example, lights on the underside of an aircraft can be brightened or dimmed with computer assistance to simulate the visual effects of a clear or a cloudy sky, night or day, to limit the effectiveness of electro-optical sensors. But attempting to counter effectively every conceivable technological threat is neither financially feasible nor even necessary. The proper use of tactics to enhance a stealth aircraft's survivability in combat, by maximizing its strengths and minimizing its weaknesses, is the proper course—one that was followed with remarkable success during the Gulf War. Said one veteran of Desert Storm, "I don't care if the Iraqis got a glimpse of us [on radar]. They couldn't do anything about it."[12]

Jack Gordon, a Lockheed executive deeply involved in the development of the F-117, readily admitted that "under the right set of circumstances, the aircraft can be seen."[13] The problem for an enemy air defense system, however, is detecting it at a militarily useful distance. The most likely threat that an F-117 is likely to face is a Soviet- or Russian–made surface-to-air missile (SAM) system. According to Maj. Gen. I. Stassevich, a former Soviet air defense commander, "A precision-guided missile requires three to eight minutes in its firing cycle from reconnaissance detection to engagement. Air defense weapons have to move within this timeframe."[14] Stealth aircraft allow an opponent only a tiny fraction of that time to do its job. "We all realize that there are (observable) elements of stealth," said Vice-President Tom Burbage of Lockheed, "but the US government has wisely chosen to concentrate on the most problematic one...radar detection."[15]

While the government and contractors have steered clear of using the word *invisible* with regard to stealth aircraft and have openly stated that the various stealth aircraft are to some degree detectable. They have also stressed that the stealthy F-117 is only one part of a team whose elements work together to achieve air victories. During testimony before the House of Representatives Appropriations Committee on April 30, 1991, Gen. Horner displayed charts showing the number and types of conventional aircraft used in an unsuccessful January 19, 1991, raid on the huge Baghdad nuclear complex; the number of F-117s and supporting tankers that made a successful strike twonights later; and a projection of how many stealthy B-2 bombers it would take to achieve the same results.

To the USAF, which produced the charts, and the House committee, which approved the B-2 appropriation, it was a very straightforward assessment: one target, two back-to-back missions, and a conservative look at future capabilities. It wasn't long, though, before "knowledgeable defense sources," "informed sources," and "experts," worried that the success of the F-117 would continue to rub off on the much-fought-over B-2 program, surfaced to claim that the charts overemphasized stealth's effectiveness. USAF personnel, who throughout the testimony had repeatedly stressed that teamwork between the various air elements had been a key to victory, were flabbergasted to find that they had supposedly portrayed the F-117 as a "lone gunslinger."

Numerous references during the testimony showed that in certain combat situations, the stealthy aircraft had worked in combination with the EF-111 electronic-jamming Raven. Said Gen. Horner, "You have to bring a mix of tools, a mix of capabilities or else you force yourself into inefficient ways of doing business."[16] Apparently, though, critics began to circulate the story of the USAF's supposed lack of candor to willing reporters and stories began to appear under headlines such as "The myth of the lone gunslinger—In the Gulf, the Stealth fighter did not fly solo."[17] In a convoluted train of events, a "myth" was created by the media's inattention to detail and then "exposed" by the same media, which patted itself on the back for supposedly catching a duplicitous US government in yet another lie to a gullible US public.

It seems that no matter what the people who actually fought the war might say, their words often carry less weight than those of "spin doctors" who know how to work a news reporter's limited knowledge of defense matters to their advantage. Said Col. Whitley, "Politics seems to have greatly overshadowed the war fighters, but *c'est la vie*."[18]

To an F-117 jockey, electronic support is nice to have but is unnecessary in most scenarios. "You've got to remember," said one stealth pilot who flew in the Gulf, "microwave jamming helps everybody in the neighborhood, and when we're clever about how we apply it [to operations], it gives us more options."[19] His boss, Col. Ralph Getchell, who commanded the 37th's 415th Tactical Fighter Squadron (TFS) and flew 19 combat missions, added, "There were times when jamming support was particularly useful....They may not be able to see us, but they can see the jamming."[20]

Secretary Donald Rice of the USAF pointed out that it is not uncommon for a dozen or so conventional attack aircraft, striking just one target, to be supported by over twice their number of fighter es-

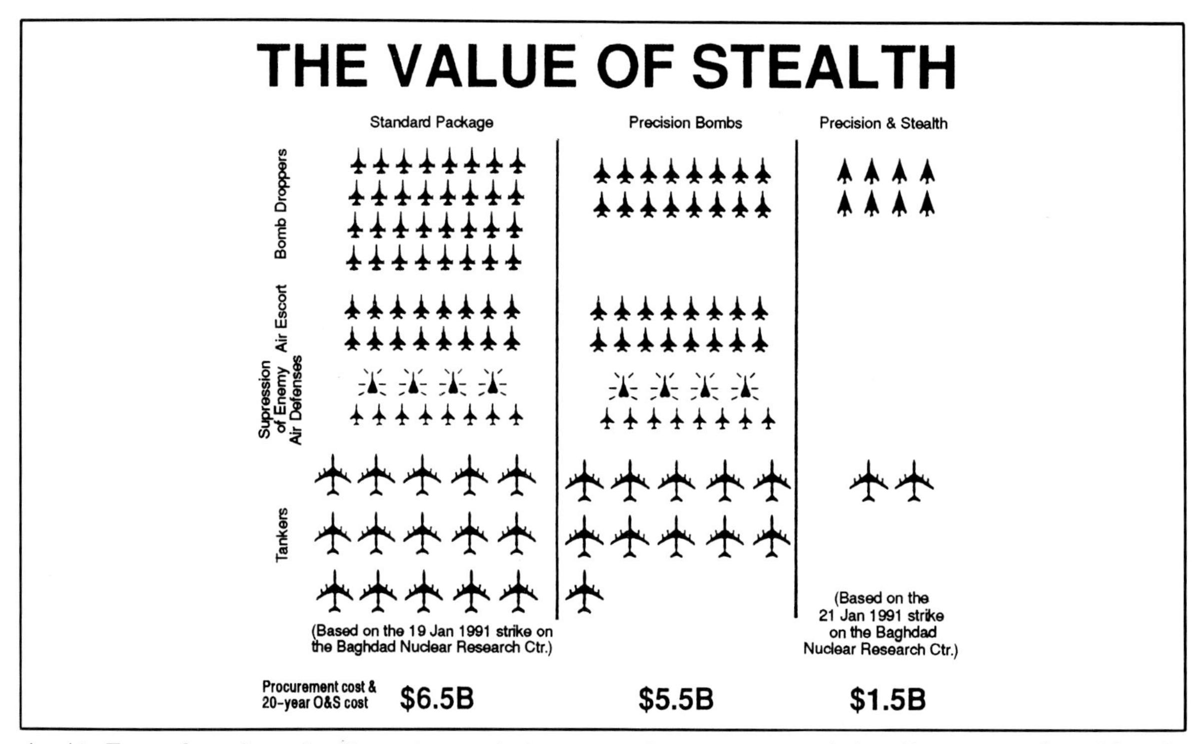

An Air Force chart from the House Appropriations Committee hearings. Critics said this and other charts exaggerated the effectiveness of stealth technology. DOD

corts, radar jammers, and defense-suppression aircraft, all of which quickly run up the number of tankers needed for aerial refueling. Contrast this with F-117 operations where a dozen aircraft will precisely deliver 24 2,000lb LGBs on nearly as many separate targets, all without any dedicated support aircraft other than tankers.

Several years after the war, the debate continued on why the F-117s of the 37th TFW—P were so remarkably successful. Was it the aircraft's well-known ability both to suppress and to deflect the Soviet-built radars, or was it, as critics maintain, the incompetence of a second-rate Iraqi air defense system? Was success a product of a brilliant campaign plan executed by a superbly trained team, or did the 37th just get real lucky? The most reasonable explanation is that Team Stealth benefited from all of these to some degree. It is interesting to note that Iraq, the country with the second-most experience with LO technology—even if it was experience gained at the receiving end of the stick—went to extraordinary efforts to counter the aircraft that demolished its air defense system, its nuclear research facilities, and virtually every important government and communications facility in Baghdad.

Although the 37th accomplished this with no losses, the common perception that the war was a cakewalk is undeserved. "I make a distinction between looking easy and being easy," said Gen. John Loh of the Tactical Air Command (TAC). "The mark of a professional is [that he makes] his work look easy. This was anything but easy. To paralyze Iraq's air force and suppress air defenses in short order as we did was the result of magnificent training, management, and the equipment that went along with it."[21]

In 1993, well over a decade after the first F-117 climbed into the Nevada sky on its top-secret first flight, the Black Jet remained the weapon of choice in missions calling for complete surprise and unwavering accuracy. "You call Team Stealth," said Col. Getchell, "if it absolutely, positively has to be taken out over night."[22]

Chapter 2

The Stealth Fighter

In 1962, Physicist Pyotr Ufimtsev of the Soviet Union published a little-known scientific paper that was to have a huge influence on US engineers attempting to come to grips with the complex problem of how geometric patterns reflect radar waves. Titled "Method of Edge Waves in the Physical Theory of Defraction," Ufimtsev's paper was the first of several—and eventually even a book—that he would produce on this arcane subject. In them, Ufimtsev expanded on the work done by German electromagnetics expert Arnold Johannes at the turn of the century, which had, in turn, been based on the earlier mathematical formulas developed by Scottish physicist James Clerk Maxwell. The defraction theories of these pioneers were, essentially, calculations that allowed one to predict, with some degree of certainty, how electromagnetic radiation would bounce off and be scattered by geometric configurations.

Conventional aircraft have a large number of elements, such as stabilizers, wings, engine intakes, and rudders, that reflect radar echoes back to a transmitting source. This situation is magnified tremendously when aircraft have large amounts of bombs, missiles, and auxiliary fuel tanks—"junk"—hanging from external pylons. The equations of Johannes and Maxwell pointed tantalizingly to the possibility that highly reflective angles and surfaces could be designed away or minimized, but these equations were too cumbersome to be useful in aircraft engineering. The Soviet scientific community considered Ufimtsev's refinements a breakthrough in this area, and he was awarded the prestigious State Prize of the Soviet Union for his efforts. After that, however, his work was essentially shelved. Nearly two decades later, when speaking with Alan Brown, Lockheed's director of engineering, Ufimtsev explained that "senior Soviet scientists and designers were uninterested in applying my theories," and offered the analysis that this "was in accordance with the rule 'there is no prophet in his own country.'"[1]

Ufimtsev's theory would have remained just another forgotten exercise in mathematics but for a sharp-eyed USAF researcher combing unclassified Soviet literature for material relating to the state of the Soviets' scientific thought on radar technology. In 1971, the original Russian-language texts were translated by the USAF Intelligence Agency's linguists at Bowling AFB, Washington, DC, and later, they were made available to six aerospace firms participating in a 1974–75 Defense Advanced Research Projects Agency (DARPA) project to study ways and means of reducing an aircraft's radar, acoustic, and optical signatures. By late 1975, the field of six was reduced to two firms with the most promising designs—Northrop and Lockheed—and Ufimtsev's work played a critical role in each company's effort. "We began to refer to Ufimtsev's theory as the 'industrial strength' theory," said Dr. Kenneth Mitzner of Northrop, because it was "the one that could be applied to a broad range of problems and give us real numbers to put into our calculations."[2]

The same thought was echoed by Alan Brown at Lockheed, who stated that the physical theory of defraction proved to be much more workable than prior ones, and "made a 30–40% contribution" to the ECHO 1 computer program used in the design of the F-117A.[3] As for Northrop's B-2 bomber, Dr.

The F-117A and its diminutive XST predecessor.

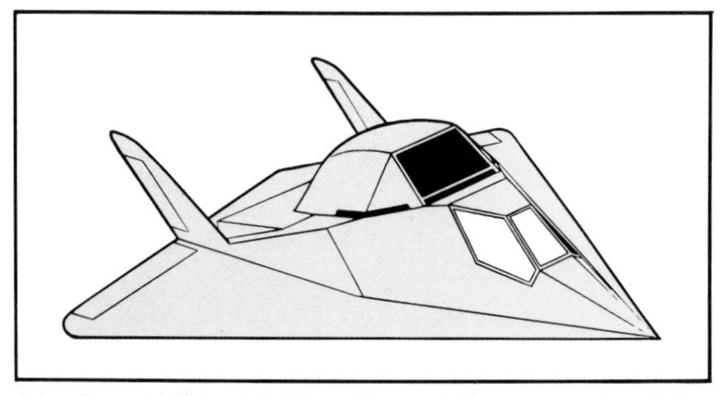

Northrop XST. A full-scale model was produced for RCS tests, but Northrop failed to win the DARPA contract and no flying versions were built. Northrop

Mitzner stated flatly, "I cannot imagine it being designed without the influence of [Ufimtsev's] work. Let me put it this way: Without Ufimtsev, today's Stealth aircraft would probably have looked the way the speculative artists portrayed them before their real shapes were publicly disclosed."[4] The Russian physicist's own suspicions that his work had been used in the development of the F-117 were not fully confirmed until he came to the University of California at Los Angeles as a visiting professor in 1991, when the Soviet Union began to break apart.

The smooth contours on later LO platforms, such as the B-2 and F-22, were a result of advancements in computer technology that allowed engineers to predict accurately how radar waves will scatter from a curved surface. Such technology was not available to the original design teams competing for the chance to produce an experimental survivable test bed (XST). The full-scale radar cross-section (RCS) models that Northrop and Lockheed produced for DARPA in April 1976 both featured the unusual faceted design later used in the F-117A. "You build what you can calculate," said Ben Rich, who headed up Lockheed's Advanced Development Projects Division at that time. "In those days we had no supercomputers and we had to make do with slide rules and calculators. We knew how to calculate the radar characteristics of two-dimensional flat surfaces, and those are what we used.…The three-dimensional calculations you need to design stealthy curves, the kind you see on Northrop's B-2 or our new F-22, were beyond us."[5]

Both firms' faceted mockups contained inward-canted vertical rudders, a minimum number of lengthy straight lines, and no leading-edge break delineating an integral fuselage from delta wings. This wing configuration—with Lockheed's the more highly swept of the two—is commonly associated with supersonic speeds in high-performance aircraft. In this case, however, it was an element in both firms' efforts at low observability, since it was projected that the shape of the wings, when combined with other airframe characteristics, would effectively reflect microwave transmissions away from, instead of back to, a radar transmitter.

But the Northrop design contained one striking difference. A single, large air intake, rising above and behind the canopy, gave it the appearance of a squat, stepped pyramid. Locating the air intake at the apex of the pyramid with an S-duct channeling air down to the engine would make the model's engines less visible to IR sensors and gave the

Lockheed XST number 1, spring 1978. The man in the cockpit is a Lockheed technician, not a pilot. The stealthy curves of the B-2 were made possible by computer software that did not exist during the Have Blue and Senior Trend projects. USAF

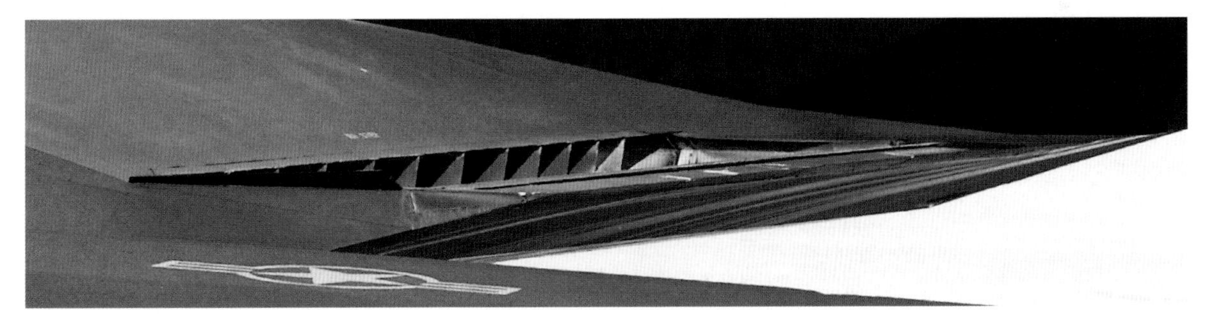

The F-117A's superheated exhaust gases emerge from an elongated, recessed area at the rear of the plane, allowing them to mix more easily with ambient air than do the concentrated streams produced by conventional jets. Channels made of a heat-resistant material, similar to the one used on the space shuttle's tile skin, help keep the unusual exhaust nozzle from warping under the extreme pressure of the jet blast, and funnel air to the outer ends of each platypus to ensure further that the gases will be spread evenly for quicker diffusion, while the aircraft's rear superstructure directs the blast upward. The end result of these efforts is a greatly reduced IR signature. Tony Landis/James Goodall

Northrop XST an advantage over the Lockheed model, which featured intakes that were placed more conventionally along its sides and were less stealthy.

Ultimately, however, this element of the design proved to be the downfall of Northrop's XST entry. The engine was indeed be more stealthy, but in combination with a fine screen for further masking, it was not able to fly the aircraft above Mach 0.65. The heavier grid shielding the engine cavity on the Lockheed XST was marginally less effective, in terms of low observability, but allowed sufficient airflow to the engine to ensure engine efficiency and higher speeds, even though the Lockheed model remained a subsonic aircraft.

DARPA judged that the Lockheed product offered the best blend of LO technologies without serious compromises being imposed on required operating capabilities. Northrop's Irv Waaland, who served as chief engineer of its XST project, admit-

A full-scale mockup, made primarily of wood, was built in 1979 before line assembly commenced. Note the pulley arrangement to allow entry into the cockpit. Lockheed

ted, "It was close but Lockheed was the clear winner where it counted the most."[6]

A contract to build two small prototype aircraft, one to test flight characteristics and another for RCS tests, was awarded to Lockheed by DARPA in January 1977 using funds supplied jointly by the USAF's Flight Dynamics Laboratory and Avionics Laboratory. Work on the demonstrator model was immediately begun at Lockheed's Advanced Development Projects Division, which people within the aerospace industry had named the Skunk Works, after a hidden-away location in the *L'il Abner* comic strip where certain illegal distilled beverages were produced. It was at the Skunk Works' Burbank, California, plant that legendary aircraft such as the U-2 and somewhat stealthy SR-71 Blackbird spy planes were created. Under the direction of "Head Skunk" Ben Rich, the data developed from Bill Schroeder's aerodynamics experiments and Denys Overholser's unique ECHO 1 computer program would be applied to a real plane—the first aircraft to take to the air with no rounded airfoils to assist in its lift. The USAF code name for the project was Have Blue.

Almost immediately, a blanket of security was wrapped around the previously unclassified project. DARPA had done its job well and shepherded the project as far along as it could. However, its largely civilian staff and modest security setup would not be able to shield future project developments from view. Have Blue was pulled from DARPA and transferred to the USAF Special Projects Office, where tight security was the rule. News of the project, which had appeared from time to time in aviation and defense publications, all but dried up and became as LO as the test aircraft Lockheed was building.

Even though Skunk Works engineers were dealing with a completely new type of aircraft, the first plane was finished in December 1976 and flown by Test Pilot Bill Park of Lockheed from the remote government test facility at Groom Lake, Nevada. It has been reported that a last-minute labor dispute forced management personnel to take a more hands-on role than was normal in its final production, and its initial flight was delayed until after Christmas.

The single-seat Have Blue technology demonstrators, generally referred to as XSTs, were considerably smaller and more slender than the later F-117A because they did not contain its large internal bomb bay. At only 38ft long, with a wingspan of 22ft and a gross weight of 12,000lb, the XSTs were essentially half-size prototypes of the F-117A.

To save time and money, appropriate off-the-shelf parts such as the F-5 Tiger II's engines and

The final assembly of FSD-1 at Groom Lake. The yellow objects extending from the aircraft—between the stepladder with the hanging plaid shirt and the blue-jeaned legs disappearing into the forward end of the starboard bomb bay—is an early-version trapeze bomb hoist system. The aircraft is also being supported by hydraulic jacks so that the landing gear can be tested. Note the open parachute doors forward of the original lengthy tail fins, the detachable wings, and how deeply recessed the engines are. Lockheed

landing gear, as well as the F-16 Falcon's fly-by-wire flight control system, were incorporated into the XSTs whenever possible. "You have to design around the things you put inside an airplane," said Rich. With no internal bays, the two General Electric J85 turbojet engines, plus their unique (and necessarily lengthy) Astech/MCI narrow-slot "platypus" exhaust systems, were the primary elements that Lockheed's designers had to contend with. "They partially dictate shape," continued Rich, but "you work around it as best you can."[7]

The purpose of the XST-1, flown by Park and Lt. Col. Ken Dyson a test pilot for the USAF, was not to check the aircraft's ability to evade radar but to learn its flight characteristics. However, limited RCS tests were run against the USAF's extensive array of Soviet radar defense systems on the adjacent Nellis AFB Test Range. The results of electromagnetic tests on a miniature pole model nicknamed Hopeless Diamond had encouraged Lockheed engineers to believe that the XST might be able to achieve an 85 percent reduction in RCS. Once the XST-1 was airborne, it was found that even with a conventional, unstealthy pitot tube and few LO enhancements other than its basic, faceted shape, it appeared to display a markedly lower RCS than any aircraft in the USAF inventory, including the SR-71. The only problem of any consequence was a persistent tendency to sink at an unnervingly fast rate whenever its air speed dropped as it did during the landing approach. To complicate matters, the prototype would hit the runway at speeds in excess of 180mph.

On May 4, 1978, this problem finally caught up with the XST-1 on its 36th test flight when a hard landing jammed the starboard landing gear into a semi-retracted position. The extremely high sweep of the wings and fast approach speed meant that either a single-wheel belly landing or a semicontrolled landing on the nose and uneven main wheels would have the same disastrous climax: the plane would tumble sideways down the field, breaking apart, and the pilot would be killed. After several unsuccessful tries had been made at either bringing the gear up or forcing it down, the XST-1 went the way of most prototype aircraft: Park was ordered to take it to 10,000ft and then bail out. Unfortunately, he banged his head during the ejection

FSD-1 sitting in a Groom Lake hangar surrounded by technicians and strategically placed fire extinguishers before an engine test. The men at right are wearing fire-retardant suits. The outward flare of the Astech/MCI platypus exhaust systems can be partially seen where they extend out and downward from the engines. Lockheed

and drifted to the ground unconscious. He sustained a severe back injury during the hard, uncontrolled parachute landing. For the 51–year–old test pilot, this was one crash too many; after his recovery, Park switched to a desk job at Lockheed, where he retired 11 years later as the company's director of flight operations.

The recently completed XST-2 had not yet been flown at the time of Park's accident, and Dyson did not take it up until June. During the next 13 months, he flew 52 times, most of them against domestic and foreign radars as well as the simulated and captured threat radars at the Nellis AFB range, which accurately mimicked a Soviet integrated air defense system (IADS). His aircraft ran through the normal teething troubles for a prototype, and some that were peculiar only to an XST, such as a section of radar-absorbent material (RAM) lining the inside of an air intake being sucked into an engine, causing it immediately to lose power. Eventually, in July 1979, it was Dyson's turn to take an unscheduled parachute jump. He safely ejected near Tonopah, Nevada, when an onboard fire burned through the XST's hydraulic lines, causing the prototype to go out of control and crash. The twisted remains of both planes are buried, along with other wrecked aircraft, at a site on the Groom Lake facility. Before its demise, the XST-2 convinced even the hardest skeptics that its combination of LO technologies could indeed make an aircraft invisible until it was too late for defensive systems to respond.

Unlike XST-1, XST-2 mounted a retractable pitot tube for RCS tests, and virtually all its surface area was covered with lightweight, flexible RAM made from a carbon-plastic mix, or multiple layers of RAM paint containing fine particles of carbonyl iron material. Different types and thicknesses of RAM coating are less effective than others at absorbing microwaves transmitted in certain frequency bands, but any amount of RAM was judged to be better than none. With it, not only would the facets reflect microwaves away from a transmitting source, but the waves themselves would be weaker after contact with the RAM. Since small protrusions or breaks in a surface can reflect radar waves

FSD-1, aircraft number 780, with a hastily applied camouflage paint scheme similar to that used on the XSTs. Lockheed

in a manner way out of proportion to their size, every effort was also made to ensure that such things as screw heads were perfectly flush with the body. Even barely perceptible gaps around access doors and the canopy were sealed over by a special metallic tape, which was then covered by RAM paint. Whether it's 1978 or 1993, the standing joke repeated by both Lockheed and USAF personnel relates that the last thing you do before a stealth aircraft goes up is wait for the epoxy holding the RAM skin, or the "iron ball" paint, to dry.

XST-2 had proved that an LO aircraft of its design could operate relatively unseen against all ground-based and fighter-interceptor radars. Airborne radars, such as those employed on the E-3 Sentry Airborne Warning and Control System (AWACS), were more problematical. If you divided the XST into lower and upper hemispheres for purposes of examining its stealth characteristics, you would find that Lockheed had designed a platform that would be least observable to ground-based radars looking up at its bottom hemisphere, with those located directly forward of the oncoming aircraft having the most trouble. The upper hemisphere was configured in such a way that it was considerably less stealthy, resulting in a hot-top, cold-bottom design unlike the cold-top, cold-bottom design later developed for the B-2, with the help of advanced computer technology.

Pursuit of a colder top on this faceted aircraft would not necessarily have produced a platform that was more militarily useful yet would have certainly stretched out the design phase of the XST while greatly adding to its development costs and, perhaps, degrading its combat performance. With the overwhelming bulk of threats coming from

Reunited for a 1990 photo are Test Pilots Hal Farley, center, and Dave Ferguson, right, of Lockheed, who, along with Test Pilot Skip Anderson of the Air Force, formed the Senior Trend's first flight test team. Lockheed's Morgenfeld, left, came on the project after the others, as Senior Trend's fourth test pilot. Within months after this photo was taken, the plane in the background and its pilot, George Kelman, were sent with the first element of F-117s to Saudi Arabia. Lockheed

below the aircraft, a more perfectly stealthy aircraft was a luxury that could not be afforded. Proper planning, innovative tactics, and operating so as to make the best use of other USAF assets would negate the advantages that an enemy AWACS-type system might have over this type of plane. The XST-2 had not been invisible, in the common sense of the word, but it was clear that the conceptual mission objectives worked out by the TAC and Systems Command (SC) in the fall of 1975 for "an aircraft with dramatically reduced signatures which can avoid detection, penetrate heavily defended airspace, and attack critical targets with extreme accuracy" could be fully met.

"Prior to the go-ahead," said Ben Rich, "five dedicated air staff officers reporting to Gen. Al Slay, clearly defined a set of top level requirements for the F-117 weapons system. Then a system program office with a minimum number of people was established at the Aeronautical Systems Division, under the direction of the late Gen. Dave Englund, who was then a colonel. A small Lockheed team was also established under the leadership of [Gen. Manager] Norm Nelson [of the Skunk Works]."[8] Dozens of Lockheed workers had been privy to the production of the XSTs in a cordoned-off area of their Palmdale, California, facility, but at this point, according to Rich, only about 20 people, including five USAF generals, were cleared on the upcoming project. On November 16, 1978, the firm was awarded a contract for five full-scale development (FSD) test aircraft under the code name Senior Trend, and the assembly line production in Burbank would eventually be known to hundreds of closed-lipped employees in spite of stringent efforts at compartmentalization. The USAF Office of Special Investigations estimated that throughout the US government, Lockheed Aeronautical Systems Division, and several dozen subcontractors, over 8,000 men and women had direct knowledge of the highly classified "black" project. Beginning in 1981, the British prime minister was also kept apprised on developments in Senior Trend, as were key officials in Britain's Ministry of Defence and RAF.

Although extensive differences separated the XST prototypes and the stealth fighter production models fielded by the USAF, no additional prototypes were manufactured. Instead, when Lockheed's FSD aircraft were flight-tested, the evaluations of their performance were translated directly into changes in them and in all subsequent aircraft. For example, stability and control problems on the FSD-1, which did not show up during wind tunnel tests, were rectified by enlarging and lengthening its tail fins. FSD-2 was retrofitted with the new fins while still in the production jigs, and each aircraft leaving the Burbank plant had this change incorporated into its airframe. Likewise, although the honeycomb structure of the FSD's exhaust system successfully handled a 400deg F. temperature differential between its outer and inner skins, the superheated air consistently caused warping at the four-inch-deep opening at the rear of the platypus. Once the precisely faceted panels lost their shape, the aircraft's RCS increased markedly from certain aspects—a potentially disastrous occurrence for a relatively slow combatant that was also limited in the types of evasive maneuvers it could take. When it was found that an expandable, shingled structure would take care of the problem, that, too, was incorporated into the design.

Although refinements such as these were of great importance to the people who would go to war in the F-117A, the major changes between the XSTs and the production models occurred well before the

FSD-5, aircraft number 784, drops a laser-guided bomb (LGB) during weapons tests. Dave Ferguson is believed to be the pilot on this flight. The bright red projectile is being tracked on its long descent by time-space position indicator cameras mounted in pods flanking the bomb bay. Even with the tail fins only a third of the way to their fully extended position, it is clear that they are considerably shorter than those in the original Paveway III kit, which is combined with a low-drag 2,000lb Mk-84 bomb to make a GBU-24B. The bomb being dropped is a deep-penetrating 2,000lb BLU-109B bomb combined with an F-117–specific Paveway III kit to make a GBU-27A/B. Lockheed and Texas Instruments

FSDs began their test flights. The USAF requirement that the plane be able to carry up to 5,000lb of ordnance or auxiliary fuel or both, coupled with the need to stow these items internally if the aircraft was to retain its LO characteristics, necessitated a large internal bay. Further, airframe and size limitations restricted engine placement to the fuselage. The result: a remarkably wide structure with engines and wheelwells placed outboard of the bay, and the sharp, 72.5deg sweep of the XST's wings broadened to a slightly more modest 67.3deg. This increase in wing area provided better lift for the proportionately heavier FSD while still retaining the ability of its leading edge to reflect radar waves away from threat radar systems.

The dartlike appearance of the original XSTs also gave way when the IR acquisition and designation system (IRADS) was added. Made up of a downward-looking sensor under the fuselage and a forward-looking system ahead of the cockpit, the IRADS's need to retain good downward visibility in the latter sensor resulted in the nose of the aircraft having to take on a steep, blunt shape. This feature added to the FSD's observability but not to a degree that would threaten a lock-on by radars.

The XST's inward-canted tail fins, rising from the outer ends of the platypus system, also had to go. It was originally believed that their arrangement would help shield the upward-facing exhaust surface from aerial IR detection. In practice, however, shielding from above was marginal and the inward-canted structures actually increased observability from below by reining in the exhaust instead of allowing it to dissipate quickly. The split tail was, moreover, structurally inefficient in that each fin was mounted on its own boom. Although this was acceptable on the diminutive XSTs, it clearly should not be pursued on the development and production models because of the exaggerated distance that the two 5ft 5in long platypus exhausts forced the fins apart. The configuration offered no clear and indisputable advantages to the aircraft's ability

FSD-1 in flight, bereft of RAM skin. The pitot configuration was unique to this airplane, and numerous details in the area of the air intakes and FLIR sensor were modified before the photo was originally released to a very select audience in the early 1980s. Lockheed

to accomplish its mission, and the split tail was abandoned in favor of the now-familiar V-tail. The new arrangement was placed at the end of a lengthened center spine to increase its distance from the exhausts. Still more refinements were needed before Lockheed engineers were satisfied with the tail.

Small twin doors immediately forward of the tail encased a parachute breaking system, since, even though the new jets did not have the high sink rate of the prototypes, they did retain its breathtaking, 180mph–plus landing speed. Eventually, improved landing techniques lowered landing speed by 10mph.

All of these changes and more were incorporated into a variety of different models for engineering studies and wind tunnel tests after the initial stealthy airframe was produced by computer. The sophisticated USAF radar range at Holloman AFB, New Mexico, was used for all RCS tests, since proper security could not be guaranteed at Lockheed's Antelope Valley range near Palmdale. As the remaining Have Blue XST continued to gather data from its tests against the "Soviet" radar network at Nellis, Senior Trend moved along briskly, under the watchful eye of the USAF Special Projects Agency. When news of XST-2's crash reached Lockheed officials in Burbank, work on a full-scale wooden mockup of the future stealth aircraft was already underway. Once completed, it was used to refine the shape of each airframe component, including the critically important faceting.

Other unusual elements incorporated into the FSD's design included a tail hook, to be used in combination with a portable arresting cable system, and two hoists that retracted weapons up into the

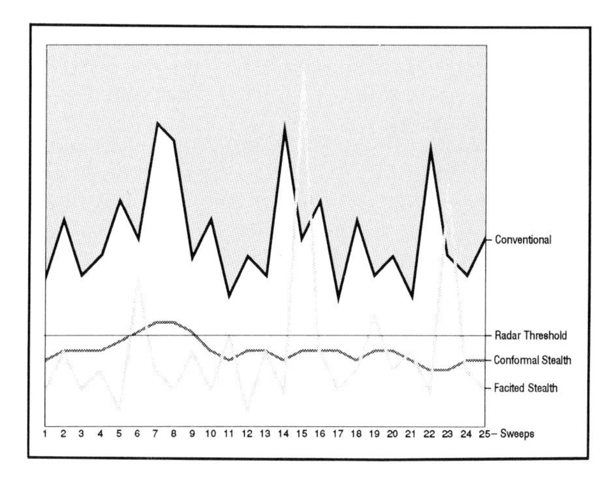

bay. Conventional internal bomb racks similar to those on the B-52 and its predecessors could be made to work, but with design constraints forcing the bay to be sandwiched tightly between the engines, use of the hoists offered the most efficient way to arm the jets and allowed the FSD to carry "a full range of tactical munitions."[9] The hoist system is usually referred to as the trapeze because it swings the heavy-duty weapons pylons in and out of the aircraft in much the same way that the landing gear system lowers and retracts the wheels. But whereas the FSD's tricycle landing gear retracts forward, each hoist retracts rearward on sturdy twin frames that fold neatly into the limited space above the weapons compartment. When extended downward below the aircraft for weapons delivery, these frames allow the operation of rail-launched missiles such as the AIM-9 Sidewinder air-to-air missile and most versions of the AGM-65 Maverick air-to-ground missile.

Production of FSD-1, serial number 79-01780, was begun at the Burbank assembly line in early October 1979. Like the first XST, it was designed to test the flight characteristics and performance of the new aircraft, and differed from later models in a number of areas. The lead FSD was completed in the spring of 1981. The precious cargo was then loaded into the cavernous bay of a waiting Military Airlift Command (MAC) C-5 Galaxy in the dead of night and shipped to the remote Groom Lake test site where the XSTs had flown. Engine tests were quickly followed by low-, then high-speed ground runs, and finally, as dawn broke on Thursday, June 18, 1981, FSD-1 rolled out of the hangar for its first flight.

As a select group of Lockheed and military personnel watched nervously, Test Pilot Hal Farley turned the jet's nose north and started up the runway. The ungainly looking aircraft gathered momentum, and its wheels left the ground, then retracted forward as the jet slowly climbed to the chase planes that had approached from behind. It was the best birthday present Head Skunk Ben Rich, who turned 56 that day, could have hoped for. "It's not often that one has the opportunity to develop and field an aircraft that represents a true technological breakthrough."[10]

Just 31 months and two days after winning the FSD contract, the project was literally airborne. A quick succession of thumbs-up test flights led to a government order for 20 production aircraft, and, one by one, FSDs 2 through 5 arrived at Groom Lake by the end of 1981, with all up and flying early in 1982. These aircraft were completed so quickly—in spite of the time-consuming production of their unique, LO characteristics—in large part because Lockheed had made the wise choice to use off-the-shelf components whenever possible. For example, the F-16's Lear Astronics fly-by-wire control system, used in the original XSTs, was acquired, as was the B-52's Honeywell inertial navigation system (INS). "Using proven components from other aircraft allowed us to reduce risk," noted Rich. "This gave us confidence to proceed concurrently with full-scale development and low-rate production."[11]

Without skipping a beat, Lockheed continued producing the Senior Trend aircraft, with a new airframe entering production about every 45 days. The firm's second production model, delivered to Groom Lake in early June of 1982, became a sort of de facto FSD. It was used along with the other jets to generate performance and handling data and to test the many small improvements that Lockheed's engineers, still very much on the learning curve, had worked into the aircraft. The first production model would have also been used in this manner but crashed immediately after takeoff on its initial flight. A major design change in the flight control system had caught Lockheed workers off-guard: the input points on the flight control computer were placed in a different sequence than they had been on the previous version. When cables were connected the original way, the computer ended up reading pitch as yaw and yaw as pitch, with disastrous consequences. Test Pilot Bob Redenauer was severely injured and forced to retire from flying.

Another problem that developed was a direct

result of the tight security procedures Lockheed and the other contractors operated under. The weapons bay in the new jet was designed to accommodate two 2,000lb low-drag Mk-84 bombs, each fitted with a Paveway II laser guidance system developed by Texas Instruments. The add-on kit consisted of a laser detector; a computer control section and small, stationary fins connected to the nose of the Mk-84 by an adapter ring; and an airfoil assembly that attached to the tail and whose four, folded wings popped up immediately after the weapon was released. The addition of this system to a "dumb" Mk-84 bomb made it a "smart" GBU-10 bomb, a greatly improved version of the precision weapons that had been used to destroy key targets late in the Vietnam War. Unbeknownst to Lockheed, however, Texas Instruments was developing a third-generation system, known as the low-level LGB, under its own veil of secrecy. This new Paveway III was able to be released at both very low altitudes *and* significant stand-off ranges through its use of high-lift, pop-up wings and a state-of-the-art scanning seeker. It was also too long for the GBU-10–sized weapons bay on the Senior Trend aircraft rolling out the back doors of the Burbank plant.

The GBU-24B represented the marriage of the Paveway III to a MK-84 bomb, and the GBU-27A/B combined the Paveway III with the newly developed BLU-109B, a slender, thick-cased 2,000lb bomb designed specifically to penetrate many feet of concrete or earth. The lengthy wings of the Paveway III extended well beyond the rear of the airfoil assembly when retracted, and the forward seeker head was also slightly longer, thus making both GBU-24s too large for the jet. Although this problem certainly fell within the "whoops" category of design, it was easily remedied by shortening the wings so that they would not extend beyond the rear of the weapon when retracted. The new wing dimension was similar to that used on the smaller GBU-12 airfoil assembly from the Paveway II variant designed for the 500lb Mk-82 bomb. These smaller wings significantly changed the flight characteristics of the bomb's glide but presented no challenge that a good tactician couldn't work with—and besides, the stealthy jet was never intended to loft bombs from extremely low levels in the manner of the F-111. The modified Paveway III was immediately sent to Groom Lake for testing. Adapted especially for the Senior Trend program, it created a GBU-27B when affixed to the general-purpose 2,000lb bomb and a GBU-27A/B when used with the 2,000lb "penetrator."

The steady stream of aircraft and experimental munitions being delivered to Groom Lake was matched by an influx of about 20 USAF and Lockheed test pilots who evaluated the aircraft in all flight regimes and engaged in weapons testing. During their early test flights, the flyers discovered a tendency for the jet's nose to "hunt," or oscillate, but modifications to the flight control system quickly rectified this problem. Before the weapons tests, there was some question as to whether the GBU-27 variants would separate cleanly from inside the weapons bay. These somewhat lengthy hybrids were nearly as long as the bay itself, and if the trapeze holding the bomb had to be lowered to ensure a hazard-free release, several seconds would be added to the time that the aircraft bloomed on enemy radars owing to the decidedly unstealthy character of the open bay. In the right set of circumstances, an astute radar operator might be able to get an idea of the heading used by an attacker as it made its final approach to the target and would, perhaps, have enough time to direct triple-A along likely exit routes. Although all of this might sound a bit hypothetical, the key question remained: Why give those extra seconds away to someone who's trying to kill you? Thankfully, the tests demonstrated that the bomb could safely be dropped from within the bay.

During this period, the jets also received their trademark black color. FSD-1's original camouflage paint scheme was retained throughout the summer but was eventually abandoned in favor of the standard gray used on subsequent flight test aircraft. Head Skunk Ben Rich personally preferred gray and would have delivered the entire production run in that color, but the chief of the TAC, Gen. Bill Creech, wanted black, since it would better mask details of the faceting, even in daylight, by making shadows less distinct. "You don't ask the commander of TAC why he wants to do something. He pays the bills," said Rich.[12] "The Skunk Works plays by the Golden Rule: he who has the gold sets the rules! If the General had wanted pink, we'd have painted them pink."[13]

Chapter 3

In the Black—the 4450th Tactical Group's Early Operations

At the same time that Lockheed received its FSD contract, the USAF kicked into high gear with the activation of the 4450th Tactical Group (TG) under Col. Robert A. Jackson on October 15, 1979, and the initiation of a three-phase construction program to improve a small desert airstrip located 26mi southeast of Tonopah in west central Nevada. The USAF wanted pilots who were more than just experienced flyers; they wanted mature officers who had at least 1,000 hours' flight time and were experienced in air-to-ground missions. Consequently, senior captains and majors with a background in F-4s and A-10s originally predominated in the program. Standards were just as high for maintenance personnel, and 1,000 hours' maintenance time on high-performance aircraft was a prerequisite for entering the Senior Trend program. The background and flying history of airmen who were thought to be likely candidates were examined in minute detail; then, Col. Jackson personally interviewed each pilot, all officers, and all senior noncommissioned officers.

One of the first airmen to be called in was Lt. Col. Alton C. ("Al") Whitley, a highly decorated combat veteran who had become a Fighter Weapons School instructor at Nellis AFB after the Vietnam War. He had gone on to command the tough, Soviet-styled aggressor force that US pilots had to engage as part of their training, and now found himself reporting to a nondescript office on the base. "I walked up to the interview room and a man opened the door an inch, peered out and asked me if I was Whitley. I said 'yes' and he asked for my ID card. He closed the door, then opened it a minute later and said 'Yeah, you're Whitley.' They offered me a chance to fly with a new unit, said it would be top secret, that it would require constant separation from my family—and they couldn't tell me much more. I was given five minutes to make up my mind. They said when I walked out the door my decision stood.

"Bob Jackson had done his homework. He had put all the ingredients into the computer as to the guys he wanted to have. Then he met them individually. I wasn't going to pass up the opportunity to keep flying airplanes. I didn't hesitate. Immediately I said 'Sign me up. I'll do it.' I knew very little about what airplanes we would fly, what we would do."[1]

Whitley soon found out that the 4450th TG would guide a revolutionary new aircraft to full operational capability. Initially, the group's flying squadrons, like all other organizations under its command, would go by ambiguous alphabetical designations instead of the customary unit numbers. For example, the 1880th Communications Squadron (CS) was known as C-Unit, Detachment 8 from the 25th Air Weather Squadron (AWS) was D-Unit, the 4450th Combat Support Group (CSG) was E-Unit, and so on. The 4450th TG, itself, was A-Unit. Operating under what an official unit history referred to as "the guise of an avionics test mission"[2] based at Nellis AFB, the 4450th Test Squadron (TS), or I-Unit, was activated on June 11, 1981, under a senior major, William C. Helper. For the time being, the tactical group would remain at Nellis while its Detachment 1, commanded by Whitley, opened up shop at Tonopah as Q-Unit. Lt. Col. Gerry Flemming's P-Unit also came into being in June 1981 but was not actually cut to the tactical group until it was activated as the 4451st TS in January 1983.

Giant C-5 Galaxy transports, flying in and out of Burbank Airport, California, under cover of night delivered both FSD and production aircraft to the Air Force for flight testing. The wooden crate in the Galaxy's cavernous bay contains a set of wings. Lockheed

At first, the 4450th TG's aviators flew only A-7D Corsair IIs to keep their flying hours up while going through an initial ground school at Lockheed's Burbank facility. One pilot recalled that "they taught you wiring diagrams—all that crap we didn't care about."[3] Eventually, as more and more aircraft arrived from the Burbank factory in the winter of 1981–82, 4450th TG pilots and maintainers began to be rotated through Groom Lake, where they could see and feel the jet, get into the cockpit, and talk to the test pilots. They could not yet operate the aircraft, since they were development vehicles, and had to continue to use the trusty A-7s well after the USAF started taking delivery of the first stealth production models. The A-7s were considerably more expensive to fly and maintain than the standard T-38 Talon training aircraft, but provided a much more credible prop for the tactical group's cover as a test unit. A certain affection was soon gained for the old birds, and the pilots even wore a shoulder patch with a Corsair bearing down on a fleeing goat and their unit's nickname, Goat Suckers, emblazoned across the top.

Whitley's first sight of the aircraft that he and his men were waiting for brought mixed emotions: "When I first looked at it, it reminded me of some kind of 'Star Wars' type of aircraft. I thought 'Boy, is this the 21st century!' But at the same time your senses grabbed hold of you and dozens of questions went racing through your mind, as they would with any fighter pilot."[4] Whitley's biggest question, understandably, was, "My God, will that really fly?"[5]

Unlike the other pilots, though, Lt. Col. Whitley was one of the select few officers in Senior Trend actually to follow the development of the top-secret plane at the Skunk Works, and was present when the aircraft were loaded aboard C-5 transports and flown to Groom Lake. "For many

A 4450th TG A-7D serves as a chase plane as Senior Trend FSDs conduct a refueling exercise with a 9th SRW KC-135A. The aircraft in the foreground is FSD-1, displaying its lack of an apex light, its retractable antennas, and its large, experimental blow-in doors over the platypus exhaust system, which were used at one point to test if they would help cool the engines' superheated gases. Lockheed

months," said Whitley, "several of the guys didn't see the aircraft they were going to fly."[6]

At the remote test site, the Lockheed–USAF team adopted the Baja Scorpion as its symbol, after finding a particularly large representative of the species in its office area. Consequently, the original FSDs were designated Scorpion 1 through Scorpion 5. However, when some of Col. Jackson's personnel finally visited Groom Lake during the familiarization process, they took one look at the bizarre creatures and started referring to them by the decidedly less reverent term *cockroach*. Meanwhile, less than 50mi to the northwest, the massive building project to turn a desolate desert airstrip into a fully operational air base was nearing completion.

Immediately upon the October 1979 activation of the 4450th TG and simultaneous order for five FSDs from Lockheed, work was begun to lengthen the 6,000ft asphalt runway, built by Sandia National Laboratories in the 1950s to support nuclear weapons testing at TTR. A taxiway, a concrete apron, a large maintenance hangar, a propane tank, and several permanent buildings were also constructed, and sixteen large, winterized mobile homes were hauled in. These last items had been purchased from Chevron after one of the 4450th's officers, while on a flight from the East Coast to Las Vegas, read in the *New York Times* business section that the company was selling off buildings from an oil-drilling site, at a relatively low price. Col. Jackson "jumped on it," said Whitley. The USAF purchased the buildings for $1.5 million, and Jackson "moved in the old oil field camp for us to live in while the permanent facilities were being constructed."[7]

This opening work, although extensive, was actually little more than a preparation for the huge Phase II and Phase III construction, which was designed to help the base make the transition from a bare-bones facility to a standard USAF base. Begun one year after the 4450th's activation, Phase II expanded the apron and added another taxiway, a 42,000sq-ft hangar, fuel tanks, a dining hall, a water storage tank, a warehouse, a control tower, and support utilities. In the midst of this project, Phase III got underway with the addition of 2,000ft of runway, which topped off the airstrip's total length at 12,000ft; more apron space and taxiways; runway arresting gear; navigation aids; liquid oxygen storage; fuel tanks; fire stations; a 40,000sq-ft warehouse; miscellaneous support facilities; dormitories; and the first individual hangars for the initial production order of 20 aircraft. Both construction projects were completed by early July 1982.

Life for the Goat Suckers at TTR, after initiation of regular flight operations in June 1981, was not too bad even though the base was a frenzy of activity. When not undergoing A-7 training with the 162d Tactical Fighter Group (TFG) at Tucson, Arizona, or specialized training at Burbank and Groom Lake, the men spent only four or five days at the austere location before returning to their family in the Las Vegas–Nellis area for the weekend. "If some guy forgot his deodorant, his shampoo, or that sort of thing, your buddies would take care of you, just like we did in Southeast Asia," recalled Whitley. "Everybody took care of everybody else."[8] Moreover, flight schedules were not yet at the point where pilots and maintainers would be required to work throughout the night, then hastily retire to specially darkened rooms for the day's sleep.

The test range, which abutted the northwest corner of the Switzerland-sized Nellis AFB training area, continued to be used for appropriate purposes, other than simply a proving ground for the 4450th TG, as long as the projects did not compromise its new function. Since the Goat Suckers were, in many ways, underutilized until the tactical group received its Senior Trend aircraft, they were sometimes incorporated into the tests, which they used

A test pilot looks over one of the Senior Trend aircraft. USAF

as an extension of their training mission. For example, during the Joint Cruise Missiles Project, individual A-7s would acquire, then escort at low altitude, Tomahawk cruise missiles over a complex route—an interesting precursor to the unit's operations against Iraq a decade later when its missions were tightly coordinated with Tomahawk strikes against Baghdad. The missiles were launched from the torpedo tubes of a submarine 300mi from a pair of "goal posts" erected on the TTR.

Finally, on Monday, August 23, 1982, Col. James S. Allen, who had assumed command of the 4450th TG from Jackson in May, accepted delivery of the group's first Senior Trend aircraft after it passed its initial set of trials at Groom Lake. Like all aircraft of its type, stealth fighter 80-10787 carried only the last three serial number digits on its tail. It was the third and most recent production model to roll off the Burbank assembly line, and arrived first at the unit because 785 had crashed in April and 786 was tied up in various flight and weapons tests until September. Also in September, Q-Unit at Tonopah was uprated from a detachment of the tactical group to 4452d TS. Whitley remained in command of Q-Unit, and on the night of Friday, October 15, the chief Goat Sucker became the first operational TAC pilot to fly the new jet.

Whitley had seen the FSD models take off, be put through their paces, and land, plus had been able to talk at length with the test pilots, but none of this was the same as taking the odd-looking plane up himself. "The test people had pretty well set the parameters of what our employment envelope should be and would be...[but] the fact that we didn't have a real operational simulator to fly left many questions. In those early days, we simply had an engineering simulator that really didn't have a realistic cockpit configuration." A nighttime, preflight, high-speed ground run helped familiarize him with the locations of the controls, and after a "pleasant" flight, he exclaimed, "Gee, this is an airplane that flies like an airplane!"[9] Shortly after the landing, Whitley was presented with a simple wood-and-brass plaque bearing the inscription In Recognition of a Significant Event, Oct. 15, 1982. It would be six years before he could tell his wife, Ann, that he was the secret unit's first Bandit, a term derived from the aircraft's flight test call sign and adopted by each new pilot upon qualifying in the jet. "I was surprised at how it handled, Whitley recalled, "but you've got to remember, it was using a quadruple redundant flight control system just like the F-16's in the late seventies and early eighties. The F-16 was getting a lot of credit for its high-tech approach to taking a platform that was unstable at pitch and making it able to perform. We took an airplane that was unstable in pitch, yaw, and roll, and made it perform. From a pilot's perspective, when the computer is doing its thing, you had no sensation or feedback through the stick or performance of the airplane that it was anything but just your normal stick-and-rudder airplane. You had control by cables and wires, and [the aircraft] flew like it was supposed to."[10]

Other pilots in the program described flying the aircraft in similar terms. Capt. Scott Stimpert lauded its use of the F-16's fly-by-wire systems and explained that "your flight characteristics become a function of your flight control computer. You can do anything with good flight control computer software these days. The airplane is very conventional stick and rudder...it goes where you point it. In terms of straight handling characteristics, how you take off, how you land, how you fly, how it responds, what you feel in the stick...is pretty much the same. Some airplanes accelerate faster, some slower; some are more maneuverable, some are less...so it falls somewhere in the middle. It's a very honest airplane."[11] Capt. Matt Byrd agreed, saying that "it's similar to most fighters," and adding that "if you fly it within its operating envelope, there are no problems."[12] The only down side of the fly-by-wire system, said Capt. Tim Veeder, is that, as on the F-16, "the flight control computers don't like slow air speed." Capt. Tim Veeder related that this is "a spot where you have to be very careful at what you're doing....The computers have a difficult time dealing with extremely low regimes of flight." The former F-4G Wild Weasel pilot was quick to point out, however, that "we don't typically fly the 117 in that kind of regime."[13]

Many pilots have remarked that they were surprised to find that the aircraft handled very smoothly and was actually easier to land than the F-16. Aviation writer Bill Sweetman believed that delta-winged aircraft like the stealth fighter "have a classic set of advantages and disadvantages" that contribute to its performance. He explained, "Deltas offer plenty of internal volume, low drag at high speed, benign handling at high angles of attack and structural simplicity. On the negative side, low speed in deltas is associated with high angles of attack and high drag; even a sophisticated delta loses speed quickly in a hard turn. On the F-117A, where maneuvering capability was of secondary importance, the designers could live with the negatives.

"The F-117A may also benefit from a favorable phenomenon associated with highly swept wings: at high angles of attack, strong and stable vortices form above the leading edge, and have the effect of keeping the airflow over the rest of the wing attached and stable. This may explain why the F-117A's low-speed behavior and its landing performance appear better than one might expect of a heavy aircraft with a sharply swept wing. Nevertheless, the aircraft lifts off and lands at a relatively high speed: lift-off occurs around 180 knots (207mph) and the final approach is flown at 150 knots (172.5mph)."[14] At least a few pilots, in the early days of the program, first practiced no-flap landings on A-7s before flying the Senior Trend aircraft, if they were unused to high-speed landings.

A 4450th Goat Sucker A-7 flies low as he chases a submarine-launched cruise missile through a target on the Tonopah Test Range (TTR), Friday, July 10, 1981. The missile was launched from the torpedo tube of the USS Guitarro *approximately 300mi from the goal posts at Tonopah.* US Navy

The 4450th TG now began to receive aircraft at a steady rate, with a total of seven on hand by the end of 1982. Three aircraft—numbers 790, 791, and 792—were flown up from Groom Lake in the two weeks before Christmas. One each would arrive in February and April, after which Q-Unit would receive no new aircraft for over three and a half months. From that point on, deliveries would occur on an irregular basis until the 59th production aircraft was presented with much fanfare on July 12, 1990, after the program had taken its first steps into the "white world."

This, however, was still a long way off, and the tactical group had a more immediate goal in mind:

Al Whitley when he came back to the stealth unit to serve as its commander. Lockheed

preparing itself for its first operational readiness inspection, scheduled in October 1983, to determine if the unit was ready to go to war. The Groom Lake facility, where all initial flight tests had been carried out, was hidden away in an unpopulated stretch of the Nevada wastelands: a wide valley southeast of Wheelbarrow Peak, separated from the Nevada Nuclear Test Site by the low Papoose Mountains. TTR was like Grand Central Station. Although few people lived in the desolate area, it was crisscrossed by numerous state and federal highways, in addition to a sparse net of county roads, all serving a handful of small towns eking a living from Nye and Esmeralda counties' scattered ranches and declining mining industry. As a result, Q-Unit was strictly limited to night flying, and the training pattern that would govern all base activities was established.

"We treat [the pilots] like bats," said Ben Rich. "They come in here Monday afternoon and they don't see daylight until next Friday. They won't sleep if they see that sun. It's like a vampire convention. At 4 or 5 in the morning they all run for their housing and get in their beds before they see light. Otherwise, the body won't rest. It's equivalent to living in Korea and working in the United States every week. The guy lives like a normal person, with a normal lifestyle in Las Vegas on the weekend with his kids. Then on Monday he flies up to Tonopah and becomes an F-117A pilot. He never sees the light again until noon the next Friday."[15]

Whitley, who was stationed at Tonopah from January 1981 to June 1985, before tours were shortened to three years, and again from August 1990 to July 1992, after the unit was reorganized as the 37th TFW, explained, "In one of the single-wide trailers, we basically set up a recreation area, kind of tore out a wall in one of the rooms. That's where everybody congregated on Thursday evenings or Friday morning after flying was over, to reminisce for the week and to talk about what we're going to do the next week. It just so happens that located right there were a washer and dryer. While people were sitting around shooting the breeze about last week and tonight's activities and where we were headed, they'd also be washing and drying their clothes, so eventually it became the TOCACL (pronounced *tow-kakel*)—for the Tonopah Officer's Club and Chinese Laundry. Eventually it became a first-rate officers club, if you will. Not great for dining facilities, but in terms of recreation, we had a pool table and shuffleboard table and big-screen TV. It was a good place to let your hair down a bit. The Wild Horse Cafe, which was the first dining facility to open there in the early eighties, was still going strong when I departed there."[16] Work on the base continued unabated during this period, in an effort to flesh out the three-phase project that had gotten TTR ready for the arrival of its highly classified aircraft. "Construction was usually scheduled inconsistent with our sleep periods," said Whitley, "but people were smart about where building was going on versus where we were living. The flying activities and where we slept and messed were about seven miles apart. That's the reason why flying noise and construction didn't really conflict."[17] A round-the-clock shuttle bus system connected the main base with the satellite living area to the south. Periodic yellow caution signs reminded drivers that they were passing through open rangeland, admonishing them to watch for wild horses. Mobile homes making up the original Chevron compound were located on the north side of the living area; after the building of hotel-style brick dormitories, they were used for storage and eventually, in 1985, all of them were removed—all, that is, except the beloved TOCACL.

"After they built the nice, dorm-looking buildings," said Maj. Jerry Leatherman, "they actually redid the TOCACL and took out the laundry machine because all that pounding in the back of the bar was a real hassle."[18]

Recreation facilities also expanded along with the rest of the base. "We made do with what we had

The ninth Senior Trend production model, aircraft 793, prepares for a nocturnal flight at Tonopah. Lockheed

to start off with, which wasn't very much," Whitley recalled. "It was enough to keep the troops interested and competitive in terms of softball fields and that sort of thing. But very early on in the program, a decision was made to construct a fairly modern facility to include swimming, basketball, bowling, racketball, Nautilus, aerobics, and free-weight equipment. It came on-line during the '82 or '83 time frame....The USAF likes to take care of its people. Keep the troops happy, and they'll stay out of trouble."[19]

The efforts to make the remote base livable were greatly appreciated by the pilots and the maintainers, but at the other end of the long, straight, two-lane road, they had plenty to remind them that they were involved in a serious business. Security was always of paramount importance, and the design of photo identification badges was changed on a frequent and irregular basis. Leatherman related that all pilots had at least the second-highest clearance: "We all had these line badges that you had to wear, and ours had a little black square in them. That meant that's how far we were cleared into the program. White basically meant that they could see the airplane, but they couldn't touch it. Green was usually worn by crew chiefs and people like that. They could touch [the airplane] and mess around with it. They knew how all the systems worked, but they didn't know the capabilities of the airplane. Black meant you were briefed on the 'no-kidding' RCS of the airplane. You knew its capabilities and vulnerabilities to all the different radars and things like that. There was even [a clearance] a little further along the line that was even more classified. Being a weapons officer, I got that. It involved things that really didn't affect the pilots per se, but was related to one of the other jobs I did, which was represent the wing in working groups at Lockheed. When the engineers at Lockheed were trying to change software and things like that, I'd have to be there."[20]

The rectangle-shaped heart of the base was surrounded by a double row of barbed wire–topped security fences, which were lighted 24 hours a day and monitored by proximity detection devices. This central compound was flanked on the east by the runway-taxiway system, and on the west by fuel storage tanks and a wide variety of support facilities. Both of these areas were protected by their own security systems. The central compound contained the main operations facilities, control tower, maintenance buildings, and aircraft hangars, with access guarded on the runway side by four double sets of retractable gates, to allow aircraft to pass to and from the hangars. On the other side, heavily armed personnel eyed walking traffic that moved through turnstiles after checking in by placing their right hand down on one of the security building's electronic palm print scanners. Like fingerprints, no two palm prints are exactly alike, and the computer file of palm signatures allowed quick access to the flight line by appropriate personnel who might otherwise get stacked up during individual eyeball checks of identification tags and documents.

One curious trend that developed early on at Tonopah and Nellis was the tendency for airmen working in different aspects of the secret program to give the Senior Trend aircraft different monikers. All the classified paperwork, such as maintenance records, used the code 117 in place of an aircraft designation, but this was not generally referred to until it ended up being adopted as the actual designation. Likewise, any mention of the word *stealth* was strictly taboo. "Nobody, *nobody* would *ever* use the word *stealth*," said Leatherman, "on the flight line, the mess, or anywhere, because if someone got into the bad habit of saying it on base, he or she could more easily slip and blurt it out in a less secure setting."[21] Administrative and maintenance personnel frequently called the aircraft the Nighthawk, and although it was, and still is, completely unauthorized, the use of this bird of prey on numerous official unit crests and patches gave the epithet a certain air of authority. The jet jockeys, however, were never fond of this nickname. Instead, they referred to the aircraft as the Black Jet when they didn't simply call it the 117, and

Personnel at Tonopah boarding a Key Airlines Boeing 727 for a flight to their home in the Nellis AFB–Las Vegas area. Lockheed

after the USAF went public with the program, Stealth Jet saw some use.

The 4450th TG achieved Initial Operational Capability with the 4450th TS on October 28, 1983, the same day it, coincidentally, received delivery of its 14th aircraft, number 799. The 28 months it had taken between the F-117A's first flight and approval for the unit to engage in minimum combat operations if called upon, compared favorably with the time required for other aircraft to become operational in that general period: the F-15A in 25 months, the F-15E in 33 months, and the F-16A in 27 months. Although still four planes shy of a complete squadron, and still incorporating performance information gained at the ongoing Groom Lake flight tests, the unit was judged to be capable of going to war. Its low number of aircraft was not a hindrance to the unit's being declared mission ready because, at this time, few strategic commanders believed that the Black Jets would be employed in groups any larger than six, eight, or perhaps in rare circumstances, ten aircraft.

In five years—half the time it normally takes to move an idea from the drafting boards to combat ready status—the Black Jets were ready for war, with one pair of aircraft ready for takeoff on as little as two hours' notice. But what was the USAF to do with them? The technology behind the stealthy attack aircraft was so valuable that the Black Jets

Technicians rotate a one-quarter-sized pole model of the F-117A during RCS evaluations of improved RAM skins at Lockheed's Helendale, California, test range. Lockheed measures signature data in carefully designed and conducted experiments, and compares results with pretest predictions. The pole model in this August 1992 photo bears the name Al Whitley—the first TAC pilot to fly the F-117A—on its mock cockpit. Lockheed

An F-117A undergoes cold weather testing at the McKinley Climate Lab located at Eglin AFB, Florida. The aircraft is not an FSD but one of the regular production models. USAF

could not even take part in ongoing exercises without compromising its secret. Not even the USAF commanders in chief in Europe, Central America, and the Pacific, who would be responsible for fielding, supporting, or, at minimum, coordinating other efforts with the weapon's employment, had been given more than a cursory briefing on the aircraft, which was kept as a strategic asset. Without a clear idea of what the aircraft was capable of, commanders could not incorporate it into wider war plans, and its most likely mission was envisioned to be one where surgical precision—and perhaps deniability—were required, such as a strike at extreme range against a terrorist leader, or a multiplane assault on the command-and-control network of an outlaw nation during a hostage rescue attempt. "We always thought that that's what would happen," said Leatherman. "We'd make a covert strike somewhere like Libya."[22]

Far-sighted commanders in TAC had bigger ideas. The original goal of fielding "an aircraft with dramatically reduced signatures which can avoid detection, penetrate heavily defended airspace, and attack critical targets with extreme accuracy" had been achieved, and as the plane's capabilities became more fully understood, a one-line addition of far-reaching importance was added to its mission statement: "To serve as a force multiplier, increasing the survivability and effectiveness of conventional forces."[23] Congress approved further purchases of the Senior Trend aircraft that would bring the operational fleet up to 58 planes, enough for a three-squadron wing with adequate spares, and it was up to the 4450th TG to prove that if employed effectively, the Black Jet could shut down even the most sophisticated air defense system. As the number of aircraft grew to 25 and the number of operational pilots climbed past 30, the tactical group's third commander, Col. Howell Estes, led the unit through its first Operational Readiness Inspection with a rating of Excellent in March 1985.

During the summer of 1985, the four-year pilots tapped by Col. Jackson in 1979 and 1980 began a series of scheduled rotations to other units. As "the flying club" began to break up, men who had more recently joined the 4450th TG began to take over the squadrons and flights. For example, when Whitley left Q-Unit to command the 4440th Tactical Fighter Training Group at Nellis AFB on June 1, another old hand, Maj. Dennis R. ("Denny") Larson, headed up the squadron for a couple of months until he, too, transferred out and Maj. Robert D. Williams took over on July 25. These officers were

An AT-38B taxis past security fences separating the runway from the hangars, the flight line, and other critical components of the base such as the control tower—where this picture was taken—and the operations area. Lockheed

the first, fifth, and thirteenth operational pilots respectively to qualify on the Black Jet, with Williams entering the program in 1981. Changes in the other squadrons also took place on June 1. Lt. Col. John F. Miller took over command of I-Unit from Lt. Col. Ervin C. ("Sandy") Sharpe, and at P-Unit, which flew the A-7s out of Nellis, Lt. Col. Medford C. ("Med") Bowman became the first stealth-qualified pilot to command the squadron. Bowman was the 24th operational pilot to qualify on the Black Jet; Miller, being the 35th operational pilot to qualify on the Black Jet, was definitely the new-kid-on-the-block when he took over from Sharpe, the second man to follow Whitley to the flight line during the early days of Senior Trend.

With Lockheed delivering eight aircraft a year, and the four-year pilots moving on, new faces abounded at TTR. The 4450th TG needed to grow to a three-squadron outfit if it was to handle the expansion properly, so the 4453d Test and Evaluation Squadron (TES) was added to the line-up on October 1, 1985, as Z-Unit. That it was commanded by the 56th Bandit, Lt. Col. Roger C. Locher, gives one an idea of the turnover experienced that year. Continuity was maintained, however, by the appointment of Col. Michael W. Harris, who had been with the program since 1983, as group commander when Estes left in December. The tactical group was also operating R-Unit, a small flight test detachment, two of whose commanders that year, Lt. Cols. David W. Jenny and Glen W. ("Wally") Moorhead III, held the twin distinction of being both Bandits and test pilots.

Chapter 4

Stealth Pilots

Entering Team Stealth was, itself, quite an adventure, and remained an invitation-only affair. "I was already stationed at Nellis flying A-10s and working as a weapons officer for the 422d TES," recalled Jerry Leatherman, "and I kind of got asked if I wanted a job. They needed a weapons officer, and since all of the old A-10 guys I'd flown with were already in this unit, they recommended me to the deputy commander of operations. He flew down one day, called me on the phone, and asked me to come to Building 878—the secure building that they flew the A-7s out of."

The young major entered an outer room where a set of heavy, locked doors barred passage into the headquarters. He picked up the wall phone, stated his business to the security man on the other end, and waited for his escort to arrive. "As soon as you walk in, you hear 'Unauthorized personnel in the building!' over the PA system. You don't know what's going on. Then they just hustled me into a little briefing room where they shut the door. Col. [Tom] Pickering, who was the deputy commander of operations then, said, 'Hey, listen, we need a weapons officer, and everybody I've talked to says you're a good guy, so we'd like to offer you a job.' And he goes, 'I can't tell you what the job is other than you'll be flying A-7s and doing a lot of night work.' Yeah, that was an understatement! I knew what kind of lifestyle they had from living at Nellis already for two years. Gone every Monday, then back every Friday, always working nights and things like that. But the reason I took the job was because there were a lot of good guys in the unit that I knew personally. So, I figured, the same way I do now, is if you've got a good bunch of people, you could be digging ditches in the hot summer sun, and it'll still be fun."[1]

Aviators joining the 4450th TG were first sent to Tucson International Airport where the 162d TGF, an Air National Guard unit, trained A-7 pilots. "Then, you came back to Nellis and got a little local-area check-out by the A-7 IPs [instructor pilots] they had working there," according to Leatherman. Then, "sometime either just before or just after you finished checking out, they'd have the Briefing." Unlike the early days when a pilot might not for many months know—much less see—what would be flown, aviators were now given an early peek at the top-secret aircraft. "First off, they'd pull you all into the room, and you'd sit there with a sergeant who was the security manager. It started out with a group of not only pilots but maintenance people and whoever else was coming on. They did it twice a month, I think. The first thing that the guy did was put on this color 16mm film with no sound; it was just the airplane taxiing out of the hangar, then it took off. The guy would tell the maintainers, 'That's what you guys are going to be working on.' He'd say [to] the pilots, 'That's what you guys are going to be flying.' The program had different levels of classification, so the people with other duties, like supply and things like that, would be peeled off, and that's all they'd get to see. For us, they'd take us and give us a more in-depth film with sound."[2]

"You know, when I saw that first film, I thought it was another part of the cover, that they were just showing these guys this little thing. I looked at the plane taxiing around, and said, 'There's no way that thing is going to take off.' A

F-117As parked off the taxiway running between the individual aircraft hangars and the jumbo maintenance hangars at TTR. USAF

friend of mine, Jerry Howait, was sitting there next to me. He and I had been the two 4450th guys down in A-7 training together with a bunch of Guard guys. I turned to him and said, 'Yeah, this is just part of the cover. They're going to hustle these guys out, and they're going to show us what really happens.' But when the next film showed it taking off, I went, 'Oh, shit. I can't believe that.' But surprisingly enough, it does really fly nice. The plane looks ungainly. It looks like it would never take off. You hear the same thing about the other plane I used to fly—the A-10—it just doesn't look like a jet. So you get a little prejudice because it ain't pretty."[3]

"Ain't pretty?" said another pilot. "Jerry's way too kindhearted. Either that or he'd been around Warthogs [A-10s] so long that almost anything looks better. Hog drivers can get that way, but let's face it, the 117's the most hideous-looking beast in the air. You'd just never guess it flies so beautifully."[4] Capt. Don Chapman agreed: when "they showed the film of the F-117 coming out of a hangar nose first, we looked at each other and said, 'Whoa! Ugly!'"[5] As for Col. Tony Tolin, he'd heard it all before. The former stealth wing commander smiled and said he was reminded of a little story novelist Tom Clancy once told him: "The Scottish wolfhound is considered the ugliest dog in all of Scotland. But the owners of the Scottish wolfhounds are always quick to point out that there are no wolves in Scotland."[6]

The briefing film continued to be shown to select, disbelieving audiences even well after the USAF confirmed the aircraft's existence. Eventually, however, it was no longer necessary, and Capt. Tim Veeder simply walked up to a hangar and looked at one of the F-117s on his first day at Tonopah. "Wow," he thought, "I'm going to get to fly this thing," and was surprised by its size. At 65ft 11in from pitot to tail, "it was bigger than I expected it to be," said Veeder. "It really was."[7] But it was Capt. Wesley Cockman's first impression that you hear echoed most by pilots: "Does this actually fly; does it get off the ground?" Like the rest, though, he, "found it to be very responsive," and added, "I felt very comfortable with it very quickly."[8]

Capt. Matt Byrd, like Veeder, entered the program after it had moved from black to, if not white, at least a shade of dark gray. "I walked up to this flow-through hangar which is the same color as the surrounding area—sand color," said Byrd. "The doors open up, and I'm immediately impressed by how clean everything is: the floors are painted white, the lines are painted exceedingly well, and above the canopy is draped an American flag. And then you see this incredible black object. I had seen that one photo that they'd released in 1989, and that's the only thing I had seen. It doesn't do the

The "incredible black object." A brand-new number 836 served as the wing commander's aircraft before it became known as a "bad actor" and "problem child." The area beyond the open hangar door was expertly airbrushed out for security reasons. USAF

aircraft justice. When I saw it for the first time, it kind of gave me goose bumps."[9]

It took three months of intense training before a new pilot could check out on the Black Jet. His time with the unit began with several weeks of textbook and chalkboard work in the "schoolhouse" squadron, which preceded the first session on the flight simulator—an exact duplicate of what the aviator would actually fly in. The real simulator, along with its academic training program, came online in about 1985, and to say that the 4450th TG was happy to get it would be an understatement. In Senior Trend's early days, training was greatly complicated by the lack of a simulator that accurately reflected the internal arrangement of avionics and weapons systems controls in the cockpit—an arrangement that was quite different from what pilots were used to. "The operational simulator doesn't have any hydraulics, probably because it was too expensive," said British exchange pilot Squadron Leader Chris Topham, "but the visuals do a great job of portraying motion. The audio's pretty good too."[10]

The Black Jet's cockpit is focused to support the plane's attack role. Forward of the pilot is a large IRADS video screen tied to the downward- and forward-looking radars used in targeting. The IRADS is flanked by two multifunction indicator screens that can present a wide variety of imagery, mission data, and diagnostic information. Between the head-up display, mounted atop the glareshield, and the bank of display screens is also a unit incorporating a large number of small warning lights that switch on to indicate what, if any, part of the plane has "gone dirty" and is now more visible to threat sensors. Because all of this hardware took up a considerable amount of space, a number of control panel components had been radically displaced, and Leatherman remarked that "at first, you're trying to figure out where all the switches are."[11] It did not take long for an experienced pilot to get used to the placement, however, and the men received at least six to eight flight simulations, each lasting for about an hour and a half—approximately the same length of time as a normal training flight.

Before taking a Black Jet up, Squadron Leader Topham was surprised to find that "we did two final things that I wouldn't expect to see in any other aircraft."[12] Since the simulator staff was not cleared to know various things about the weapons system, another instructor would brief the pilots on this information. The pilots would sit in the cockpit while the instructor ran through "on-the-squadron" techniques. Next came Topham's "first sortie," a two-hour check list procedure in the cockpit. The "second sortie" came three days later in the form of a nighttime high-speed ground run that usually topped 115mph. Although this further familiarized a pilot with the aircraft, its main purpose was to make sure he understood how to operate the jet's unusual drag chute system during landings. "The chute is actually in front of the fins," said Leatherman. "Part of the run was to make sure you could pop and jettison it without dinging up the airplane....If you did it right, you did it just once."[13] Still, even with the most careful handling, a sudden tail wind could wrap the shroud lines around one or more fins, causing damage that although easily repairable, was still time-consuming and bothersome.

Finally, a pilot was ready to fly the Black Jet. As with the A-10, no two-seat F-117s existed, so a first flight was also a first solo. "The only difference was that we briefed it up to be just a local instrument-type mission," said Leatherman of his initial flight. "And the instructor chased me around [in his A-7]. Part of the reason why they had guys with 1,000 hours of fighter time flying the airplane was because you knew what you were supposed to do. You'd been through those check-outs before. So you'd go up and down the list of events that you were going to do, and if you had any questions, you'd just ask [the instructor] on the radio."[14]

A Black Jet prepares to start engines. Note two of the aircraft's many unique features: the apex light at the peak behind the cockpit, and the closed tail hook door. Although the hangars in this and previous photos may look different, they are essentially the same, the visual variation coming from the air conditioning ducts. USAF

Topham found that "the first sortie (proper), you do a lot of things you probably do only once every six months: aileron rolls and manoeuvres that show you the aircraft can do the stuff—it can pull a surprising amount of *g*[s], for example—but which you don't do on a day-to-day basis." He went on to say that "surprisingly enough, it handles just like a Jaguar. It's a very big aircraft and the wings don't look like they'll produce lift in the same way as a normal aerofoil—but they do. Speed, rates of roll, rates of pitch: just like a Jag. It'll turn very tightly. Remember, Tonopah is up at 5500 ft. At sea-level, it's a different aircraft."[15]

Getting checked out on the Black Jet was only the beginning. "Once you come out of training," said Capt. Scott Stimpert, "you are qualified to fly the airplane. You can take off, land and you're comfortable flying it. But that doesn't mean you know how to use the airplane, how to employ it. So you come down to the tactical squadrons and they teach you how to use the airplane, how to employ it tactically."[16] Night refueling and target acquisition, in particular, are two areas in which the new stealth pilots would excel.

Flying the aircraft "is like riding the tip of a spear," said Capt. Philip ("Phil") McDaniel.[17] Tim Veeder remarked that "for me, it's just like an F-4 because there's not a whole lot you can see from the front cockpit. It's kind of interesting because you're sitting way out there on the front of the airplane; if you think about it, the majority of the airplane is sitting *way* behind you."[18] Every aircraft has its own unique flight characteristics, and Chris Topham related that "when you're flying around in turbulence, most aircraft will kick and buffet; this one skids around the center of pressure, which is five feet behind the cockpit."[19] Another pilot added, "You're, of course, informed of that in training, but it still feels really odd the first time you actually experience it."[20]Often, what a pilot perceives seems to be determined by what the pilot is used to flying, and noise inside the cockpit is an example of just how different those perceptions can be. Before coming to TTR from his Jaguar unit in Great Britain, Squadron Leader Topham had flown the F/A-18 Hornet, AV-8B Harrier II, and Mirage 2000. After piloting the Black Jet, he offered this observation: "With most aircraft you get the feeling of speed and acceleration, but with this one there is very little sensation of speed. You can't really hear the wind [as you can] in most other aircraft."[21] On the other hand, Capt. Byrd, a former A-10 jockey, found that "it's not a quiet cockpit. I think that with those sawteeth edges around the canopy, that it disrupts the airflow. They may do wonders for hampering radar detection, but they don't do wonders for laminar airflow. Yeah, it's noisy."[22] As for Capt. Veeder, he felt that the interior sound level was neither very low nor particularly loud: "It's very similar to the F-4s I flew; as noisy as the cockpit of any other Air Force fighter."[23] Maj. Leatherman, though, perhaps summed it up best when he described streaking through a night sky with little or no moon above, and no lights on the desert floor below: "When you're all stealthy up there—no radios or anything—it really seems eerily quiet."[24]

Pilots, like other people engaged in dangerous, stressful activities, occasionally delve into black humor as a way of relieving tension. At the September 1988 Air Force Association convention held in Washington, DC, one or more F-117 pilots apparently joked about the aircraft's tendency to slip briefly during turbulence, just before corrections from one of the four fly-by-wire computers kicks in, and referred to the aircraft as a "wobbly goblin." A *Time* magazine reporter who was not present at the event ended up being passed the term by an unnamed source, and an article duly appeared in the following week's edition under the title "How Wobbly the Goblin?"

As is now painfully well-known, the supposed nickname was gleefully repeated throughout the mass media, and stealth pilots had to spend a remarkable amount of their time denying that they ever called the F-117 that—even after the aircraft's stellar performance in the Persian Gulf War. Personnel involved in the classified project often had to bite into their tongue and fight back the urge to say, "Look, this is the way it *really* is...," as when one trade publication repeatedly ran reports in the late 1980s that the still-secret Black Jet gave off a high-pitched sound during flight. During an interview in the early 1990s, Leatherman grimaced at being reminded about this and some of the other strange things he'd read in the press. "The plane's engines did not change from the time it was made," he said wearily. "We used to have fun laughing at the articles in *Aviation Week* when they were doing all the speculation on what was going on at Tonopah."[25] "You know, depending on the nature of the comment or accusation," said his former boss, Al Whitley, "you would either find it extremely humorous or it would piss you off. I think it's just the price you have to pay."[26]

Part of that price can be very high in human terms, as the high stress levels and fatigue that resulted from the effort to avoid media attention played a part in two fatal accidents. Security needs dictated that hangar doors not be opened until 30 minutes after sunset, and that all aircraft be back down and behind closed doors 30 minutes before sunrise, in spite of an increasingly jammed flight schedule. By the late spring of 1986, the number of Black Jets in the 4450th TG had grown to 34—six more than the previous summer—and about four dozen stealth pilots were working in various phases of the group's training regime, yet the number of hours available for their nocturnal flights was simultaneously being shrunk by the lengthening summer days. Depending on the previous night's schedule, a pilot would awaken anywhere between 10:00am and 2:00pm, but most would be awake by noon with at least six to eight hours of sleep. Around 4:00pm, the day's designated mission planner would arrive at the operations building, followed sometimes by a squadron commander or deputy commander and perhaps a few other airmen. After lunch, the balance of those going up that night would trickle in, between about 6:00pm and 7:30pm.

Capt. Matthew ("Matt," "Birdman") Byrd.

The evening routine would include a mission brief, plus checks of the weather and the flight routes, followed by a short walk or ride to the hangar. Pilots were usually in the cockpit performing systems checks for an hour before pulling out of the hangar, and, if everything was moving along well, the lead aircraft of the early go would taxi to the end of the runway before 9:00pm. It would be back on the ground by about 10:30pm, and the other dozen or so Black Jets would come in over the next two hours. As they landed, ground crews would immediately "turn them around" for the pilots scheduled on the late go. The first of the refueled and rechecked aircraft would take off around midnight, while as many as three planes from the first set were still finishing up their mission. "Everybody was supposed to be down by 3:00am," said one pilot, "because if you made it in any later, it was really hard to get things wrapped up before daylight. In the winter, the clock started moving a lot earlier on both gos, so you'd sometimes have the last guy coming in around 0230."[27]

"We found that the daylight/darkness cycles accentuated the body-clock shift. If a pilot was up all

Unearthly black objects skimming over the clouds. The F-117A visual profile changes radically with the viewing angle. USAF

night and saw the sun come up," said Ben Rich, "his mind would interpret daylight as time for the body to be active, and it was nearly impossible after that to enter a deep, restful sleep. You would have thought you were at a vampire convention as daybreak approached, watching all the night workers scurrying for their blacked-out rooms before they were caught by the sun."[28]

During the first few years, the training schedules were arranged in such a way that a pilot was unlikely to "get caught." But as more men and machines were added to the program, the number of aircraft in each set crept steadily upward and the 3:00am target became a thing of the past on short summer nights. "What that translated to," said Capt. Scott Stimpert, "was some late flying hours and I sat at the end of the runway more than once at 2:00 o'clock in the morning waiting to take off."[29] This type of routine would soon become exhausting even for the most mature pilots. As one pilot explained, "The bad part was that you come home on Friday, and have normal days over the weekend. You had to change your body clock eight to nine hours every week. You get used to it, but you get a little more tired as the week goes on. Monday wasn't too bad, but by Thursday morning you were a wreck."[30]

"For a lot of guys on Thursday night, after the last landings, you'd finish your debriefing and normal squadron duties, and it would be five o'clock," said Maj. Leatherman. "You'd go down to the TOCACL to have a drink and wait. You'd watch the sun come up, then wait a while longer and catch the bus [back to the base]." Airmen returning to their family in the Nellis–Las Vegas area would commute home on civilian Boeing 727 jetliners operated by Key Airlines—and flown by specially cleared pilots—so, once they got back to base, they'd "catch the Key home, then go to bed."[31]

This setup turned out to be especially hard on the wives and children of the stealth pilots, who knew nothing about what the aviators did during the week. In theory, at least, the pilots were to do nothing that would tip their family off to the odd hours they were keeping at Tonopah. Any efforts along these lines quickly became moot, however, as it was hard for a wife not to notice her husband either collapsing into bed as soon as he walked through the door or making a bleary-eyed attempt to stay awake and in good humor. This type of existence actually proved harder on some families than the lengthy separations that military life sometimes entails, since children knew dad was home all weekend, but couldn't really see him very much until perhaps Sunday. As early as 1986, the USAF brought in a psychologist to counsel the families of pilots on the Senior Trend project both in group sessions and individually.

Col. Al Whitley noted that when he was at Tonopah, the divorce rate for 4450th TG personnel was not "significantly different from that at Nellis

To help ensure that the brake chute's shroud lines don't become tangled in the tail fins, the lines are designed to flare from a point beyond the tail. Wrapped lines can damage the fins by getting caught in the rudders' Z-shaped hinge lines and can also harm the RAM coating. USAF

AFB." By the summer of that year, however, the strain was evident and a topic of much discussion. One pilot later stated that a posting with the unit then "was almost a guaranteed divorce."[32] Although this was certainly an exaggeration, several officers referred to how hard it was to suffer from chronic jet lag and still deal effectively with being a husband and a father.

It has been reported that "the [USAF] brought extra flight surgeons into the program to investigate fatigue among the pilots, concerned that the problem was being underreported. Their studies intensified in the summer of 1986, as the increasing pace of operations coincided with shorter summer flying hours."[33] One of the pilots at Tonopah that year didn't recall this level of official interest before a fatal accident in July 1986. "If there was an influx of doctors to take a look at what was going on, they sure must have kept themselves well hidden. I mean, the training schedules were arranged about as well as they could be under the circumstances. But where there could have been some good done—say, extra leave every few weeks or so to let the body catch up—there certainly weren't any kind of changes like that."[34]

Although at least this one aviator apparently thought extra rest would have been desirable, a memo from Lt. Col. John Miller seemed to say that the pilots themselves were pushing the pace. Miller, who by now had commanded I-Unit for over a year, voiced concerns to officers in TAC and to the new 4450th TG commander, Col. Michael Harris, about the rising level of fatigue among the men. The July 10 memo warned that "if we liken our usual late-go to a time-bomb waiting to go off, then our extended summer hours are accelerating the countdown to zero. I believe we are on a collision course with a mishap." He recommended that the USAF "force extra time off every two or three weeks." Ben Rich later noted that "the typical, macho fighter-pilot attitude is that 'it's not manly to say you're too tired to fly.'"[35]

The same night Miller wrote his memo, Maj. Ross E. Mulhare prepared for a single-ship mission that would take him over south central California and back into Nevada. Mulhare, who had cut his teeth on the F-4 Phantom and was known for his skill in tactics development, had been an F-15 instructor pilot before being accepted into the Senior Trend program, becoming the 49th operational pilot to qualify on the Black Jet. He was an experienced and aggressive flyer, but that night, as he suited up, he complained to a buddy that he had grown increasingly tired, "and just couldn't shake it."[36] He lifted off in aircraft 81-0792 at 1:13am on one of the last scheduled sorties of a tough workweek.

Jack Shaw in the F-117A's cockpit simulator. The IR sensor display, flanked by smaller MFDs, is the main focus of a stealth pilot's attention during the final attack run. The unusual array of horizontally placed controls includes such things as, right, the IRADS, INS, retractable antennas, and oxygen regulation, and, left, controls for engine tests, the laser, inflight refueling, and the apex light. The master arm switch and the bomb bay door controls are forward of Shaw's left knee. Shaw is wearing leg boards to display additional flight and mission data. Pilots quickly adapted to the unusual cockpit arrangement, but they generally remained less happy with the position of the radio, forward of the central pedestal, because they had to lean forward, look down, and turn up the lights to see the numbers on the system. After this photo was taken, the F-117's monochrome displays were replaced by color displays and moving maps. Lockheed

Mulhare, who used the call sign ARIEL 31, proceeded to the eastern portion of California's San Joaquin Valley. The sky was clear, and moon illumination was at 14 percent. Flying under standard instrument flight rules (IFR) conditions through a moderately trafficked area, Mulhare's plane was not operating in stealth mode. His navigation lights were switched on, and radar enhancers made his aircraft appear to be just another Tonopah A-7 on a training flight. All radio transmissions were routine, and after a turn to the southeast toward the weapons range at Edwards AFB, California, Mulhare called Los Angeles (LA) Center and requested and received permission to descend to 17,000ft. At 1:44am, he canceled IFR with LA Center. His subsequent acknowledgment of receiving the message was the last transmission from ARIEL 31; the aircraft promptly vanished from a score of civilian and military radar screens. At approximately 1:45am Pacific Daylight Time, Mulhare's jet slammed into a hillside at 2,280ft above sea level.

The plane and its flight data recorder disintegrated on impact. According to the crash report of the investigating officer from TAC Headquarters at Langley AFB, analysis of the fire pattern, crater, and scatter pattern of parts indicated that ARIEL 31 was in a "high velocity" dive of "no less than 20 degrees and probably in the neighborhood of 60 degrees" and was not tumbling. A USAF security team was helicoptered to the crash site, 15mi northeast of Bakersfield, California, in the Sequoia National Forest, and immediately declared it a national security area. For several weeks, USAF personnel combed the area for even the most minute pieces of radar-absorbent skin, and the firefighters at the crash sight signed agreements swearing them to secrecy.

Interviews with nearby campers ascertained that the F-117's engines were still running at the time of impact, and an examination of what remained of the ejection system indicated that Maj. Mulhare had not attempted to bail out of the plane. It is believed that he had become spatially disoriented during the southeast turn and descent, and flew his plane into the ground.

After Mulhare's death, no apparent changes or restrictions were incorporated into the training schedule, and flight operations were not curtailed. Instead, pilots were more closely monitored for signs of fatigue and were given increased training in how best to maintain their situational awareness while in a high-performance aircraft like the Black Jet. Most of all, however, senior officers in the 4450th TG worked hard to instill in pilots a safety-first attitude and a realization that admitting you are not ready to fly a mission is not a sign of weakness but a sign of strength.

The men needed little encouragement. Very few of the unit's pilots had seen combat during the Vietnam War, and almost none of the nonveterans had personally known someone who had died, or even been injured, in a flight mishap. The violent death of a trusted colleague, who only the week before had celebrated his Fourth of July birthday, served as a wake-up call for the whole unit.

The 4450th TG worked its way through the

Armed security personnel ensure that if you get too close to Matt Byrd's Habu II, *you'll regret it. Before public disclosure in 1988, the base resembled a ghost town until late in the afternoon and came fully alive only at night. Aircraft would emerge from their hangars no sooner than an hour after sunset, and late-starting sorties tried to be back inside an hour before sunrise. All TTR flights were conducted at night, whereas operations at the more desolate Groom Lake site were allowed more flexibility.* Lockheed

Stealth Pilot Marcel Kerdavid with one of his young daughters. Lockheed

rest of the summer with no serious problems as more of the four-year pilots moved on to other jobs in the USAF and the influx of new faces continued. Winter hours brought some relief to the night-flying airmen, even though five more Black Jets were delivered between June and December and, as always, base construction continued at its regular frenzied pace. A medical trauma center, a maintenance training facility, and a new double row of aircraft shelters were being either built or funded for the main base; ground was broken for 500 more dormitory-styled rooms in the living area; and a much-needed renovation was begun on the control tower.

Four more aircraft were added to the inventory in the first half of 1987, to bring the number of Black Jets at TTR to 42, with the number of operational pilots at roughly 55, counting those in training. Lt. Col. Med Bowman, who had been the first operational stealth-qualified pilot to run P-Unit, the A-7 squadron at Nellis, had moved over to Q-Unit the previous August, and his place at Nellis had been taken by Lt. Col. Robert E. Bruce, Jr., an officer who was not qualified to fly the Black Jet. Bowman's time with Q-Unit was limited, and Lt. Col. Arthur P. ("Art") Weyermuller was tapped to take over command on January 7, 1987, with Lt. Col. David T. Holmes assuming command of I-Unit on January 16. Weyermuller's stay with Q-Unit was also short-lived, however, and he was moved over to Z-Unit, where he would command for two years. The top spot at Q-Unit was filled by Lt. Col. James G. Ferguson, who moved into the commander's office on August 14. As for A-Unit, the group itself, Col. Michael T. Short assumed command from Col. Harris on April 3. Stealth Bandits Short, Holmes, Weyermuller, and Ferguson were respectively the 50th, 70th, 83rd, and 92nd operational pilots to qualify on the Black Jet.

Chapter 5

From Black to Gray

By the spring of 1987, the previous summer's accident seemed like ancient history, especially to the many pilots who were filling out the tactical group's ever-expanding squadrons and replacing the last of the four-year members. The advent of short summer hours soon brought with them the same problems that had undoubtedly contributed to Maj. Ross Mulhare's accident. In spite of increased command emphasis on the aviators' knowing their limitations and acting responsibly, the tendency was still strong for pilots not to pull themselves out of the line-up when fatigue threatened their performance, and some were noticeably less sharp by the end of the workweek. Still, the problem was perceived to be not as bad as it had been the year before.

The simple-but-effective Black Jet–specific techniques to help ward off spatial disorientation appeared to be promising—if they were actually followed—and, most important, everybody looked out for everybody else. If a pilot seemed to be getting "wound up a little too tight," a buddy would discreetly step in to engage in a bit of "private counseling." Professional and personal relationships between the aviators were firm enough that advice was not generally seen as meddling and was nearly always followed. "We were not hotshots in the Tom Cruise (*Top Gun*) sense, but neither were we the kind who'd play it overly safe," said one officer. "The 117 was, and is, a strategic asset, and [the USAF] wanted mature pilots who knew themselves, knew their job, and would not go stupid and crack up their bird."[1]

One such airman was Maj. Michael C. Stewart, "Mike" to his friends. Like all the 4450th TG's pilots, he was qualified for both the group's classified Black Jets and their A-7s. Over the years, he had racked up 2,166 hours in a host of high-performance fighters that also included the F-4C/D Phantom, the F-5E Tiger II, and the F-15C Eagle, of which 449 hours were instructor time. Stewart had flown a total of 76-6/10 hours in the Black Jet and was highly regarded as a solid airman who had spoken on several occasions about the importance of not taking unnecessary risks. Spatial disorientation, however, is a stealthy killer that patiently waits for a momentary lack of attention from even the most experienced pilot. At 8:33pm on Wednesday, October 14, 1987, Stewart's aircraft dropped off the radar screens at TTR control tower.

Stewart was just 40 minutes into a routine, single-ship sortie when his plane, number 83-0815, crashed into the gently sloping, high desert terrain 53nm east of Alamo, Nevada. According to the crash report, BURNR (pronounced *burner*) 54's "procedures after take-off and radio calls...were normal," the weather that night was "clear with unlimited visibility, [and] there was no moon illumination at the time of the mishap." The crash report also found that BURNR 54 departed on "the planned heading of 273," but "the last radar plot of the aircraft shows...deviation from the planned track." The aircraft struck the earth "at a steep angle, digging a hole approximately six or seven feet" deep, and investigators came to the conclusion that Stewart "was commanding slightly nose up with a moderate left bank" at the time of impact.

Like Mulhare the year before, Stewart made no attempt to eject, and neither crash offered any evidence that an aircraft or subsystems malfunction

Brig. Gen. Joel T. Hall of the 57th Fighter Weapons Wing answers reporters' questions in the aftermath of a crash of a 4450th TG A-7 in Indianapolis that killed nine people. The stealth pilot was not injured in the incident and was judged to be blameless in the tragedy. Spc. Joseph B. Garrison, US Army

had occurred. The culprit, again, was almost certainly spatial disorientation.

Yet another crash occurred less than a week later with another stealth pilot, this one flying an A-7. On Tuesday morning, October 20, Maj. Bruce L. Teagarden's plane lost power and he attempted to make an emergency landing at Indianapolis Airport, Indiana. Limitations imposed on him by weather and the lack of power prevented him from bringing the stricken plane down on his first approach, and he came around again for a second try. The weather conditions included a low, 800ft overcast and, below that, about a 4–5mi visibility in fog. Having only limited control of the airplane as he plummeted to the ground, he ejected and landed safely. Now pilotless, the A-7 continued and smashed into the main lobby of a Ramada Inn, killing nine people. Although Maj. Teagarden's affiliation with the 4450th TG was released to the press, the USAF succeeded in keeping the group out of the media's eye by, among other things, not sending the group's commander, Col. Michael Short, to a hastily called press conference in Indianapolis. Instead, the commander of the 57th Fighter Weapons Wing at Nellis AFB, Brig. Gen. Joel T. Hall, was sent to field reporters' questions, thus implying that Maj. Teagarden was not engaged in other-than-routine activities.

Although tragic, this accident had nothing to do with the chronic problem of fatigue felt to some degree by most of the group's aviators. This was not immediately apparent back at Tonopah, however, and coming right on the heels of Maj. Stewart's death, it caused many pilots to reexamine their own situation. But little could actually be done until the flight schedule could be shifted to earlier gos, and that could not be accomplished while the program was still secret. For the indefinite future, late-night flights and the abrupt change every weekend would be the rule, and pilots would have to live with the knowledge that their "circadian rhythm is just going to be screwed up."[2]

Spatial disorientation almost always occurs

During night refuelings, aircraft were directed into position by a series of lights underneath the tanker. USAF

A "boomer's" view of a thirsty F-117A using night vision goggles. The Black Jet's apex light has not yet been switched on. USAF

when pilots are flying solo either in adverse visual conditions or at night. Then, the normal visual cues that tell a person up from down cannot come into play, or are tricked, as when lights on the ground become confused with stars in the sky during a turn. "The fluid in your inner ear and the little hair particles in there stabilize in a certain position," Capt. Wesley Cockman explained. "It tells your brain you're in level flight, when actually you're in a turn. When you come out of that turn and need to go in a different direction, you think you're in level flight and therefore you turn even more. You get yourself in a big turn, maybe descending or climbing, and it really messes you up."[3]

Focusing intently on certain tasks other than flying can also be disastrous. An example of this dangerous channelization of attention is the true story of a bombing demonstration in which, after the first pilot missed his target, his wingman became so fixed on scoring a hit that he forgot to pull up his aircraft and drove it straight into the ground. "The tasking can get real high-paced," said Capt. Tim Veeder, "and we concentrate on reminding everyone that 'hey, guys, not only are you trying to bomb a target, you're also flying an airplane. Don't forget the basics of flying.' You have to think about everything you're doing, but your number one priority is flying the airplane....If you do something stupid with it, it's going to treat you badly."[4]

During a turn, even simple distractions like moving one's head to the side to look for a switch in an unfamiliar position, or leaning down to see the numbers on the radio (which on the Black Jet is behind the control stick), can instantly give a pilot "the powerful and urgent impression that the plane has rolled and climbed."[5] The pilot's instinctive reaction to get the wings back into the correct angle of bank and to reverse the climb by getting the nose down can be fatal if the aircraft is not high enough to recover. At night, a pilot might not ever even realize she or he is in trouble. This can also be compounded by the pilot's momentary distraction from the control panel and the instrument crosscheck that could save the aviator's life. Col. Tony Tolin, who commanded the 4450th TG after Col. Short, later remarked, "That desert is really dark. It's little wonder that there were two, and not more crashes of production aircraft."[6]

Maj. Jerry Leatherman related that "the thing that probably affected most guys right off the bat was just the location of some of the instruments, because of what they were used to coming from—mostly fighter airplanes—where the instruments are dead-straight right in front of you. But this one has the sensor display in front because that was the most important thing to look at, and that necessitated moving some of the other instruments around. It took awhile getting used to. What we used to call the instrument crosscheck was not the same as you would have in a normal airplane." Leatherman then straightened up in his chair and faced his head directly forward. "In a normal airplane, you could just sit with your head like this, so when you're flying instruments, you don't have to move your head around—you'd just induce vertigo by doing that. You could just sit with your head like this and see all the instruments you needed to see." Still facing forward, Leatherman now began to move his eyes from side to side and explained: "With this one, you have to kind of move your eyes back and forth because the instruments are spaced out so much. Most instances of spatial disorientation are because of moving your head around while the plane is on instrument conditions."[7]

Stealth pilots found that you could often count on at least some disorientation in certain situations. Capt. Cockman, for instance, related that "you'll get that on a tanker in the weather—in a turn, in particular."[8] Possibly because night refueling from aerial tankers offered the potential for spatial disorientation to develop, this facet of the weekly training regime was regularly scheduled on Monday night, and occasionally Tuesday night as well, before reaction times and attention became less sharp. "If you flew Monday, you had a tanker mission," said Maj. Leatherman. "Most fighter squadrons now only have two [training days with tankers] every six months. [Tankers are] a scarce asset because they're needed for all deployments. For routine training, we probably had more tankers than anybody, and every week, we had tanker missions. You see, unlike most fighter squadrons, the way we were going to be employed meant that we were going to have to go with tankers. They wouldn't let us land at a normal base, then turn and take off and do what we needed to do. We planned missions that were going to be 18 hours long just because we were going to have to fly there and back."[9]

While the Black Jets remained classified, they were refueled only by specific crews flying KC-10As out of March AFB and KC-135As operating out of Beale AFB, both in California. The Beale tankers became known as the Beale Bandits. This changed somewhat after the aircraft emerged from the black and other tanker units began to train with them in

Hasty repairs on RAM skins. Top, strips of RAM have been applied over portions of the rudder on the port tail fin on Dark Angel, *aircraft 810. Bottom, a hairline crack in the skin runs horizontally through the bottom portion of the US roundel, then down vertically beside an access door, where it splits into a series of lesser cracks. Form-fitted edges around the door and recessed screws are covered with a RAM putty. If more time had been available to the airmen maintaining this aircraft, the putty would have been made level with the surrounding RAM skin; the chipped-off skin below the door would have been cut square to match the size and shape of an impromptu patch, as on the tail; and the entire area would have been sprayed over with radar-absorbent paint.* Tony Landis/ James Goodall

order to broaden the knowledge base within the refueling community. Oddly enough, though, in spite of the great number of hours these tanker units worked with the 4450th TG, some crews were still a little leery about the Black Jets. Fuel boom operators observed that fly-by-wire aircraft, including the F-117A, were more stable during aerial refuelings than other aircraft, but had the impression that whereas the stealth pilots could see the underside of the tankers and the directional lights on the wings fairly well, they would have difficulty seeing the boom operator's station from the center pane of the three small windows at the front of the cockpit. One Beale Bandit pilot remarked that "crews take the F-117's visibility into account" and that they

A close-up of the RAM skin and stealthy design features. Guy Aceto, *Air Force Magazine*

"are prepared to break away if the boom operator says the aircraft is approaching dangerously."[10]

This bit of information about a visibility problem never failed to flabbergast stealth pilots. "Jesus!" said one man, shaking his head while burying his face in his hands. He looked up and, in a slightly exasperated voice, remarked, "You know, we do this stuff more than anybody, *anybody*!"[11] An incredulous Matt Byrd explained that "if you move your head, you can see the [boom operator's] window fine." Byrd continued, "One guy asked me—and maybe I should have caught on quicker—he asked me, 'Well, how do you see out of the front of that thing?' And I go, 'Through the window, of course.'...I never realized that [a question about visibility] was occurring in the refueling community."[12]

"I've seen it from both ends because I've been in the tanker when the guys refueled," said Jerry Leatherman. "I think the problem is it's a black airplane at night, okay? Once you turn off the [detachable red] rotating beacon, and roll over the refueling door, the apex light is the only thing that [the boom operator] sees. If you've ever been in pitch-black trying to judge distance on something that's just a light, that's what he sees. You could dim the light, but then you wouldn't see the light at all; you had to have something to light the slipway door. Anyway, once they get used to that, it's not too bad." Apparently, whoever briefed the boom operators prior to their first missions with the Black Jet had impressed upon them the importance of the radar-absorbent skin to keeping the aircraft stealthy, since Leatherman added that "a lot of the boomers, the new ones especially, were terrified about dinging up the RAM."[13]

On Lockheed's new F-22 fighter, exotic RAM skins and radar-absorbent structure (RAS) were only used in the selected areas of the aircraft that present the greatest danger of detection, such as edges and engine cavities, but Alan Brown, the company's director of engineering, exaggerated only slightly when he remarked that on the F-117, "we were going for broke and coated everything."[14] It's not so much that RAM is significantly more fragile than a standard aluminum skin as that "it's a real time-consuming puppy to repair."[15] In a study on the viability of using LO aircraft in the US Navy, Cdr. Mark P. Grissom, an F-14 Tomcat pilot and squadron commander, discussed "the difficulty of repairing composite and RAM-coated surfaces vis-a-vis aluminum."

Although Cdr. Grissom believed that the problem was not insurmountable, it had to be realistically addressed because "the inescapable fact remains that aircraft maintenance and movement in the close confines of an aircraft carrier still routinely result in dents and scrapes. Now with stealth, however, these imperfections would increase an airframe's radar reflectivity with respect to high frequency air intercept radars, undermining the very purpose of its low-observable design."[16] Although this is, of course, considerably less of a problem for the USAF, special care must still be given to ensure that maintainers don't create extra work for themselves and excessive downtime for the aircraft. Simple solutions, like having ground crew wear protective boot socks when walking across the top of the aircraft and placing leading-edge protectors along the wings during routine maintenance, are highly effective but of little good if a hailstorm catches up with an aircraft before it can get under shelter. When a sudden, unannounced storm front begins to roll in on exposed aircraft on the flight line, the nervous look on the faces of pilots and maintainers alike is a thing to behold.

"We remove the [RAM] coating for access, then we reinstall it as needed," said SM/Sgt. Gary Martin. "And, yes, that takes some maintenance, and that takes some time. You just can't rush it. You can only progress. You have different cure times that you're waiting for sealants to set."[17] A special epoxy-mix sealant, or "glue," is used to bond the flexible, linoleumlike sheets of RAM to the aircraft, but quick repairs can sometimes be made by simply spraying several layers of RAM paint over a damaged area. The repair is then checked with a handheld device developed by Engineer Paul Jost of Lockheed. Appropriately named a Jost gun, it looks much like a police radar detector. A RAM putty also exists that can be used for such things as filling imperfect joins between facets. Still, though, "you always have to wait for that glue to harden before you can progress to the next step," said Martin. "You just can't accelerate that. You can't work any faster than what the materials allow you to work with."[18]

Critics of the F-117 have maintained that the aircraft needs far more attention than is worthwhile, but the plane's maintenance history does not give any weight to this charge. "The TAC standard is a goal that establishes that, all things being equal, your aircraft will be [flyable] at X percent," said Sergeant Martin. "It varies from aircraft to aircraft. You may have one or two airplanes that may be 'a bad actor,' or you may have a problem you can't troubleshoot, or keeps coming back, but we've exceeded the TAC standard consistently."[19]

The sergeant added, "People think it's the high technology that makes things difficult, but it's not really. It's just that the way the airplane was designed and the way they had to go about building the plane generated some unique problems that just take time to fix because there's no easy way to do it."[20] Certain parts of the aircraft—some found only on the F-117A, like the grilles at the forward air intakes and the extendible trapeze weapons racks—sometimes present challenges to those trying to keep the aircraft flying. Lockheed's Paul Martin explained, for example, that "the exhaust system handles very hot, very fast-moving air. In contrast to other aircraft, the F-117 blows hot air through the airframe structure itself. The exhaust system was designed ten years ago, and it has become one of the more burdensome areas of the airplane."[21]

None of these problems ever presented stealth pilots with even the possibility that they wouldn't have enough aircraft available to go to war and accomplish their mission. The unit's readiness rating even went up during combat operations in southwest Asia, although the Black Jets were flying vastly more sorties than anyone had anticipated. "As far as maintaining [the] ability of the airplane to do its job," said Sergeant Martin, "had somebody told me that we were going to do what we did in Desert Storm, six months before we went there, I would have said, 'No, you're crazy with the heat.'"[22]

Aircraft 802 glides serenely over a lake in the western United States. USAF

At the time of Maj. Mike Stewart's accident, however, the unit's deployment to Saudi Arabia was still over two years away, and the men concentrated on perfecting their craft as controversy began to swirl around them. From the mid 1970s through the late 1980s, an increasing amount of speculation appeared in the press, on the development of stealth technology and a top-secret unit tasked with operating what was believed to be a rounded, futuristic-looking aircraft. The earliest articles were brief, fairly accurate pieces in trade publications like *Aviation Week & Aerospace Technol-*

Stealth Pilot Tom Bell performs one of a long series of preflight checks. Lockheed

ogy. As interest grew, so did the number, size, and inaccuracy of the articles, even in publications that were not commonly known for rushing to print with questionable material. The USAF could do nothing to stop the speculation, but tight security procedures set up early in the Senior Trend program kept dangerous leaks to a minimum. Interestingly enough, the sheer quantity of material, based on the ruminations of one "knowledgeable expert" or another, actually helped drown leaks of accurate information in a sea of questionable data, and this persisted even after confirmation of the existence of the F-117 was publicly released by the government in November 1988.

The aviators at Tonopah were amused to read that they were flying a supersonic fighter called the F-19 with sloping features similar to those of the SR-71 Blackbird, and Lockheed employees who had worked on the Have Blue project found that the prestigious *Jane's All the World's Aircraft* had learned that the original technology demonstrators were called XSTs but assumed incorrectly that the acronym stood for experimental stealth technology. A teardrop-shaped model kit of the mythical F-19 "with full cockpit detail" was even released. A less amusing development was the unauthorized removal of a large quantity of stealth-related documents, films, and photographs from Lockheed's files. In another instance, one of the firm's employees was arrested for having removed blueprints of the Senior Trend aircraft. He had rolled them up in a newspaper, secreted them from the office, and showed them to his girlfriend and his former wife. Congressional hearings, chaired by Representative John Dingell in June 1986, looked into the question of the lost documents, and government payments to Lockheed were subsequently cut off. They did not resume until document security was tightened.

By 1988, enough press had been generated on the Black Jet that people in the southern California area, with its large population of aerospace workers, couldn't help but notice that something "different" was cruising over their head, even though flights out of Tonopah were conducted exclusively at night. The sheer number of aircraft involved in the nocturnal training missions had long before forced them beyond the confines of the huge complex of test ranges in Nevada, and 4450th TG planners found they had little choice but to increase the number of sorties over populated areas within roughly 300mi of the base. The group's aviators also paid visits to a number of prospective overseas bases in their A-7s, to gain some familiarity with extended overseas flights and different weather conditions.

The United States and the United Kingdom had agreed that Senior Trend aircraft could operate from British soil in case of an emergency, and RAF pilots began rotating through the program in 1987 quid pro quo. Although consideration had originally been given to flying surreptitiously pairs of stealthy jets to secret locations in the belly of C-5 Galaxy transports, this idea was discarded very early on as being unnecessarily cumbersome and time-consuming. Even if a few aircraft were stored with their wings disassembled, a crisis situation would probably already be over and done with by the time the jets were loaded, transported, and reassembled with their RAM painstakingly put back into place. It was far simpler just to fly an appropriate number

Final Verdict, *aircraft 814, with John Savage at the controls. The FLIR (facing forward) gives way to the DLIR (the dark area starboard of the nose wheel) during the final seconds of an attack. The open blow-in doors supply additional air to the recessed engines at low speeds.* Tony Landis/James Goodall

of aircraft to some remote base, like Machrihanish near the tip of the Kintyre Peninsula in western Scotland, where they would have some degree of security from prying eyes. Eventually, one operational stealth squadron would be tasked with operations across the Atlantic, and another would prepare for Pacific deployments.

Freed from the confines of the Nevada test ranges, aviators were now able to hone their combat skills against a much larger range of "targets." Approximately six to ten aircraft might fly solo missions at specific intervals along a route. A night's flight operations began with a briefing that covered weather along the routes and at the target; flight information on takeoff times, turn points on the route, and "deconfliction" if another route was involved; and sometimes, mock intelligence information on threatening radar and missile sites. After additional, personal study of the target and route, a stealth pilot entered this information into a thick computer cartridge called an electronic data transfer module (EDTM) at either the primary mission planning computer or a separate work station. The EDTM was then loaded into the cockpit's data transfer unit to program the Black Jet's onboard mission planning computers, and, if necessary, last-minute changes could be made in the cockpit itself with the aid of a small keypad.

The alignment of the aircraft's INS began with the fixing of its exact location at that moment. Although a full INS ground alignment could easily take over 40 minutes and included a drift of as much as 0.12nm in an hour, Squadron Leader Chris Topham described its accuracy as "unbelievable."

Following takeoff, the mission program, integrated with the plane's autothrottle and autopilot, would fly the pilot through an intricate set of turn points, altitude adjustments, and air speed changes that allowed the aviator to strike the target in perfect harmony with other stealth pilots. In training and in war, bombs were often dropped within seconds of the planned times. "Apart from the attack runs," declared Topham, "there's no need to touch the control column—it's a hands-off operation."[23] Maj. Clarence ("Doc") Whitescarver explained that "this airplane, with its unique capabilities of stealth, allows us to concentrate on what we're going to do because most of the planning has been done on the ground before we get in the air. There's very little the pilot has to think about except doing the mission. He doesn't have to think about how

On target. A 2,000lb LGB seconds before impact during weapons testing. Texas Instruments

he'll have to react to a threat if it comes up. It makes the plane very comfortable to fly in combat because you're not worrying about all these things that might happen. With lots of airplanes, you're heavily dependent on how you react to defenses to keep yourself alive."[24]

Topham fully agreed and added: "If you compare it to the Jaguar, the Jaguar is much more of a flying aircraft. By that I mean you're actually flying it every second. It's a high-intensity job because there is no auto pilot. The F-117A is actually a very easy aircraft to fly," said Topham, "and it's so capable that between target runs it's much less intense and busy than the Jaguar. Most other airplanes have the pilot monitoring everything—even air threats. But because of the stealthiness, we can concentrate on weapons delivery to the exclusion of everything else."[25] Punctuating this last statement was a comment Col. Whitley made to Lockheed's Ben Rich after the Persian Gulf War. Whitley stated flatly that: "When I was in Vietnam, the pucker factor over Hanoi was very high. But when I went over Baghdad I was perfectly relaxed."[26]

Once the stealth pilot was within sensor range of the designated target—which, depending on altitude and atmospherics, could be anywhere from 10–15mi out—the pilot resumed control of the aircraft and guided it to the bomb's release point. The pilot observed the target area rushing toward the aircraft as an IR video image on the display screen directly in front of the aviator. The thermal image seen by the pilot was exactly what was being picked up by the Black Jet's DLIR and FLIR target and acquisition systems, which were also integrated into the plane's weapons delivery and INS systems. At first, the aviator used the wide-view FLIR to pick out the target while still some distance to the target. Closer in, the image of the target or target area was automatically handed off to the narrow-view DLIR.

During the run-in to the target, the stealth pilot slued the cross hairs of the laser target designator onto a point predetermined to inflict the most damage to the target. At the precise second that the onboard system computed as the optimum moment, the LGB, which had already had a predicted trajectory fed into its internal guidance system, fell from the Black Jet's open weapons bay. The gimballed laser designator of the autotracker kept the cross hairs fixed on the target even as the pilot maneuvered away, and an invisible laser beam guided the bomb during its last seconds to the impact point. Under optimum conditions, the 2,000lb bomb struck within one, or perhaps two, feet of the laser spot. If the target was a "hardened" structure, a second and even a third bomb, usually from additional aircraft, may have been dropped directly into the hole blasted by the first.

Sounds simple, doesn't it? It's not.

A critical part of the pilots' training involved learning how to adjust the display screen's level (brightness) and gain (contrast) during the final run on the quarry. The thermal image the pilot saw on the display screen was determined by the differences in temperature of elements in the IR imager's viewing area. Targets that varied somewhat from their surroundings might require only slight modifications to the screen's image. On the other hand, Topham noted, "if you were going, for example, for a 'dirt-on-dirt' target where there isn't going to be much thermal contrast, then you wind the gain a long way up."[27] "The hardest stuff was cold things," said one pilot. "Buildings where people lived and there was heat, you could find. Bridges were fairly easy. The hardest things were manmade structures, like a fire warden's shack on a mountain in the trees. There wasn't much heat coming out of that thing, and it might be covered with snow, and it might not be exactly on top of the mountain although the map shows a little symbol sitting on top of a hill. You might get within a mile of it; now you have to search that area, trying to find the cold object in the middle of the woods."[28]

Sometimes, though, the targets assigned to the stealth pilots just could not be found no matter how hard the pilots tried. "Some of them were real minuscule, piss-ant targets such as an intersection of a couple of dirt roads in the middle of nowhere. One of the hardest was a dock on the Marina at Lake Tahoe. That was a bitch and I don't know if anyone did find that. The water is so cold that it didn't show up at all."[29] In a case like this, the aviators could sometimes try another tactic to come to grips with a target. "If you've got something that just won't generate a decent picture, like say a com[munications] tower, you use a structure at a known distance from the selected aim point as an offset track point. You pick that up on your FLIR, and if you're lucky, by the time you're on the DLIR, you can make [the actual target] out. If you still can't find it, you can still use the track point to guesstimate the aim point."[30]

Although some of these targets may seem a trifle unusual, this training is more realistic than is readily apparent, especially when one considers that in Iraq, stealth pilots were in some instances aiming at underground bunkers in the middle of a wheat field or a specific spot in a blank rooftop—targets much trickier than the ventilator shaft drops made famous on Cable News Network (CNN). And besides, as potential opponents became more adept at thermal screening, through use of simple tools such as paints that change the way heat is radiated from a surface, targets were likely to become, if anything, more difficult to detect in the future. "We picked hard things," said one aviator, "because the normal targets were easy."[31]

Training missions included one target for each of the Black Jet's two LGBs and at least two turn

Neil McAskill pulls from his hangar and is surprised to find that the Nevada skies have begun to shed some water. USAF

The original, indistinct photo of FSD-1 released by the Air Force, and a hilarious artist's conception.

points, but "turkey shoots," with a dozen or more targets to be found within a specific amount of time, were sometimes scheduled as often as once a month. After the event, strike videos of all the pilots were examined, and the "winner" declared.

Virtually all flights out of TTR were still being conducted at night, but this was destined soon to change. Key officials in the Pentagon argued that strategic planners needed to know much more about the aircraft if it was to be treated as an available asset in general war planning, and the TAC commander, Gen. Robert D. Russ, was anxious to start getting the Black Jet integrated into ongoing exercises like Red Flag at Nellis AFB. Even a slight modification of its classified status would allow these things to happen—and happen quickly. The USAF proposed that it release various details to the press, such as the aircraft's actual designation, the number of planes in service and on order, as well as a very brief history of the program. Basic information on the performance, weapons system, measurements, and even cost of the Senior Trend aircraft were to be withheld. Its attack mission, similar in many ways to that of the A-6 Intruder, would likewise be masked by calling the plane a fighter. Agreement was reached to allow the stealthy jet to edge out of the black world, but the Senate Armed Services Committee requested that any public announcement be held until after the November 1988 presidential and congressional elections.

Much to the shock of the aviation-military press and aircraft enthusiasts, the F-117A they got was nothing like the F-19 they were certain they already knew about. In a highly successful bid to keep details of the design out of unfriendly hands, the USAF announcement was accompanied by a single high-contrast, grainy photograph that revealed little of the aircraft's true dimensions and faceting. Lockheed joined in on the fun, too, by providing a full-color artist's conception of the plane from the same angle but with the alignment of the facets distorted and a laughably small man in the cockpit, which implied that the F-117 was nearly 50 percent larger than its actual size. Amateur photographers hanging out on public land were also able to snap some indistinct shots.

The end result was that when *Jane's All the World's Aircraft* fashioned conjectural frontal and sideview drawings, it ended up with a squat, pregnant-looking airframe that in some ways resembled a faceted, "bow-legged version of the Messerschmitt-163 Komet," a World War II–vintage German rocket plane. Stealth pilots passing through Nellis were handed Xerox copies of the *Jane's* renderings, which ended up on the TOCACL wall and various bulletin boards. "Some guys laughed so hard they started to cry," said one pilot.[32] As a practical matter, though, the USAF had succeeded in opening up the F-117A to the people and organizations that would benefit from its integration into their plans and exercises, while hiding its true nature from countries that would desire to produce countermeasures to stealth or to develop their own LO platforms. In theory, it was possible for almost any nation with a well-developed aircraft industry to mimic some aspects of the older, faceted approach to stealth, embodied in the F-117A—and easier than it would be to duplicate the approach used in the conformal airframes of the B-2 and the F-22. A copycat stealth would present almost no tracking problems for the US armed forces but could be highly destabilizing if introduced into some Asian or South American regions where boundary disputes still abounded. The longer the design of the aircraft could be kept ambiguous, the better.

Edging out of the black had some immediate benefits for the stealth pilots. Flight schedules were immediately shifted two hours forward and the prohibition against opening the hangar doors until 30 minutes after sundown was lifted, which meant that flight operations would not creep later and later as the summer wore on. Capt. Scott Stimpert found that whereas all of his flying had been at night before the change, it was now running about 70 percent at night, with even more daylight flying in the training squadron. That was still "some serious deep night flying," said Stimpert, "but it's not as late now as before. We're probably always on the ground by 1:00am."[33]

Maj. Jerry Leatherman related that "in the old days," the irregular late starts "and the fact that you had to be down by three o'clock in the morning" meant that "you were always trying to cram in a lot of stuff. Being able to fly in the day meant you had a more continuous schedule of flights, so you just didn't have to worry about running out of nighttime."[34] Being able to take off at sunset was particularly useful for the newest pilots in the unit; Col. Tony Tolin commented that "it is a lot easier, especially on your first ride in a single-seat airplane, if you can see outside."[35] The advent of daylight flights was also easier on the aviators' families because, said one pilot, "it didn't shift your weekends so radically from what you had during the week."[36]

The lifting of the "black veil" also put the 4450th TG firmly on the road to inactivation, since a group-level organization was no longer needed. The F-117A would soon enter the mainstream of USAF operations as part of an air wing. The trusty old A-7 Corsairs were also no longer needed to provide the 4450th TG with a cover for its activities. In January 1989, they were replaced by T-38 Talons, which were easier to maintain and noticeably streamlined the 4453d TES's training operations. The 4453d was referred to less often by its stealthy moniker, Z-Unit, and the same was true for the 4450th (I-Unit) and 4451st (P-Unit) test squadrons, except by the old hands who continued to use the code names. The 4452d TS (Q-Unit), the original Goat Suckers, was inactivated on May 30 along with the old A-7 unit at Nellis AFB, 4450th TG Detachment 2 (R-Unit), during the group's reorganization and run-up to wing status. R-Unit's local area training function was picked up by the 4453d. The last commanders of these two organizations were respectively Lt. Cols. Keat Griggers and Richard C. Groesch.

During this period, and indeed all through the 1980s, the F-117A still was a prime example of a system being procured and developed simultaneously. "We learned as we went along," said T/Sgt. Randy Charland, a Black Jet crew chief. "The more we learned, the better we got, and the easier it became."[37] The USAF Aeronautical Systems Division was responsible for new development modifications, and, since no depot maintenance program existed, the Sacramento Air Logistics Center oversaw all upgrades performed at Lockheed's facility at Air Force Plant 42 in Palmdale.

One by one, unforeseen engineering or software problems would develop and be dealt with as quickly and efficiently as possible. The nature of the beast, however, meant that new surprises always seemed to crop up. The intake grilles that helped mask the engine cavity, for example, originally suffered from ice build-up that would starve the General Electric engines of air with potentially disastrous results. Missions had to be planned to avoid areas where ice build-up was likely, until a base coat of electrically resistive paint could be applied to act as a heating element beneath the regular layer of radar-absorbent paint. Later, in 1987, a tail fin "fluttered off" of FSD-1 when it experienced a severe side slip during a daylight weapons test at Groom Lake. As the black tail with its large white 780 fell to earth, the pilot was unaware that anything had happened until the chase plane told him. The aircraft was brought in safely, but restrictions were placed on certain regimes of flight and the all-moving metal fins were eventually replaced by thermoplastic ones. As late as April 1990—barely four months before a squadron of Black Jets was deployed to war in the Persian Gulf—the unit's outgoing commander, Tony Tolin, would state proudly, "We are now *close to* [author's emphasis] maturity with the aircraft,"[38] and the pilot who received the last production F-117A in July 1990 would find that it had "a lot of gremlins."[39]

After Maj. Mike Stewart's crash in October 1987, the 4450th TG was operating 41 aircraft, and the number had risen to 49 by the time the USAF went public on the plane's existence. As the number of fielded aircraft climbed into the fifties, more of the plane's training activities came under the scrutiny of land-bound air enthusiasts who gleefully observed them 2,000–8,000ft above their head.

Dan Decamp's Black Jet lifts into the sky after the ban on daylight training has been lifted. Lockheed

The colors and locations of navigation lights, the times of flybys, and even the positions of access doors—partially exposed because RAM skin was removed for easier access to internal components—were duly recorded in the aviation press, along with widespread reports by "aerospace employees...accustomed to high performance aircraft" that the Black Jet's engines or, perhaps, its unusual grille air inlets let out a high-pitched sound in flight; "it even set the dogs off before we could hear it," claimed the workers.[40] This observation left stealth pilots scratching their head, but surfaced over and over again. A mustachioed Tom Morgenfeld, who had been test flying the aircraft for Lockheed since the early 1980s, said, "We were amazed about the reports of the strange sounds heard when the F-117 was spotted during its flight activities. I never heard anything more than the standard GE [General Electric] F404 engine noise."[41]

Stealth pilots had little time for the oddball press speculations, as the reorganization and training program remained at the forefront of their attention throughout 1989. Finally, on October 5, 1989, TAC inactivated the 4450th TG and concurrently moved the 37thTFW from nearby George AFB, California, to Tonopah, where it assumed the group's mission and assets. The individual squadrons were, likewise, renumbered, redesignated, and, in some cases, renamed, with the 4450th ("Nightstalkers") and 4451st test squadrons becoming respectively the 415th ("Nightstalkers") and 416th ("Ghost Riders") TFSs—the new wing's combat elements. The 417th Tactical Fighter Training Squadron (TFTS) ("Bandits") assumed the training roles of the 4453d TES ("Grim Reaper") as well as the death specter from the 4453d's emblem. Although some attached units "went away" as their functions were amalgamated into similar organizations, for many, the process of inactivation followed the same pattern as that in the flying squadrons, where the reassignment of assets and personnel amounted to little more than a name change. For example, Col. Raymond J. Bartholomew's 4450th CSG, the old E-Unit, simply became the 37th CSG.

The "new" stealth wing remained under the command of Col. Tony Tolin. Its 415th TFS retained Lt. Col. William J. Lake in the top spot, and Lt. Col. Gerald C. Carpenter, from the 4453d, did a "TAC swap" to move into the 416th TFS's command slot instead of staying with the 417th TFTS. Command of the 417th TFTS went to Lt. Col. Keat Griggers, who had run the 4452d TS, inactivated earlier that year, and assisted the reorganization until the group was elevated to wing status. Tony Tolin, Bill

Robotic arms at the Sacramento Air Logistics Center carefully maneuver x-ray devices along George Kelman's Lone Wolf, *aircraft number 816, to scan for hairline cracks and other structural problems in the airframe. Aircraft are checked periodically or if an unknown condition develops such as a vibration at certain speeds.* SM/Sgt. Robert Wickley, USAF

Lake, Jerry Carpenter, and Keat Griggers were respectively the 102d, 103d, 136th, and 94th operational pilots to become Stealth Bandits. Under these men, the training regime that would take the unit to the Persian Gulf War and beyond was firmly established.

Col. Tolin said each pilot flew about 15–20 hours a month in the Black Jet, with pilots qualified in the T-38 flying as many as ten extra hours, and that the wing's standard staffing ratio was five pilots for every four aircraft. One might assume that having roughly 65 to 70 pilots a month trying to maintain this much flight time would be difficult in an organization owning aircraft with a reputation for being somewhat maintenance heavy and a mission-capable rate hovering around 81 percent. However, better adhesives and a growing body of experience in maintaining the plane had paid off handsomely when combined with a close working relationship between aviators and their ground crew. SM/Sgt. Gary Martin was the noncommissioned officer in charge of the 416th Aircraft Maintenance Unit (AMU) during the transition period, the Gulf War, and the return to "normal" operations. He remembered that "the pilots *always* paid a great deal of attention to the needs of the maintainers, and that had a tremendous positive effect all the way down the line."

Aside from more flexible work hours and increased visibility to both the public and the USAF at large, another big, though less apparent, change accompanying the unveiling of the F-117 came in how airmen joined the stealth unit. "The leadership wants to mainstream the F-117 into the regular

Crowds at an air show are kept far enough back from Wing Commander Tony Tolin's F-117A to ensure that any object thrown by an onlooker would likely fall short of the aircraft, while a few people at a time are allowed forward to take pictures. After the Gulf War, spectators were routinely allowed as close as the photographers in this picture, without restrictions. Lockheed

USAF community without everything being so supersecret," said Capt. Tim Veeder. "They still have the same requirements as when the program was completely black: 1,000 hours of fighter time, good background, and a history of doing a variety of things in your last assignment." But instead of recruits being hand-picked for the unit after an ol' boy network referral and subsequent background checks, personnel openings are publicly announced. "There was a message that came out from people who work assignments that said if you would desire to fly this airplane, put together several pieces of paper—military resume, past records of [your] flying history, OPRs [office of primary responsibility reports], and a couple of letters of recommendation—and submit it to the wing," said Veeder. "The wing had a [selection] board with several people sitting on it. They're the ones who decided. I actually applied for this assignment in March 1990, and then found out that I was selected for it around August of '90. Then, I was coming to the assignment in March 1991, so it was basically a year process from when I sent in my paperwork to when I actually walked into the wing and said, 'Here I am.'" After the Gulf War, the recruitment procedure changed again, and Veeder remarked that "now it's even more in the hands of the people who normally handle assignments—more routine." He then chuckled and added, "But I don't think you'll ever see guys straight out of pilot training coming into the stall."[42]

Within two months of the 37th TFW's activation, the ongoing crisis in Panama came to a head and stealth pilots were tasked with taking part in a coordinated air-ground operation called Operation Just Cause. On the night of Tuesday, December 19, 1989, a flight of six Black Jets from the 415th TFS lifted off from Tonopah into the cold desert night for a destination over 3,000 air miles away. The F-117As needed five aerial refuelings to make the round trip, which included two passes over the Yucatan Channel separating Cuba from Mexico. One pair of aircraft were to take part in a still-classified operation by special operations forces to capture Panamanian strongman Gen. Manuel Noriega while two others struck an army base at Rio Hato, 65mi southwest of Panama City. The third pair were backups in case mechanical difficulties forced any of the primary aircraft to turn back.

The mission to grab the dictator was canceled when intelligence reported he was not at any of the potential target sites, but the other jets continued on to Rio Hato. Their target was a large, open field beside barracks housing two companies of troops belonging to Battalion 2000, an elite unit known to be fiercely loyal to Noriega. It was planned that the aircraft would drop two large, loud bombs close enough to the buildings to stun the sleeping soldiers so that they could not adequately respond to nearby nighttime parachute landings by the 2d Ranger Battalion and elements of the 3d Battalion. The explosion of 2,000lb bombs at a designated point of impact just 50 yards from the barracks would do just that, and fused to detonate after they had penetrated a few feet of earth, they would not cause many casualties. Unfortunately, things did not go exactly as expected.

Lt. Gen. Carl Steiner, commander of the 18th Airborne Corps during the operation, had picked the F-117A for the job because it was the platform most likely to be able to place ordnance into a precise spot at night and "stun them in their barracks long enough to get the Rangers on the ground," yet not "collapse those barracks and kill them all." However, the Panamanian Defense Forces had been tipped off to the US operation three hours before the assault, and at H-hour were already at one of the Ranger's objectives: the 4,389ft runway that bisected the Pan American Highway and had been used to receive arms shipments from Cuba. Moreover, a last-minute change in the attack plan and confused communications resulted in the first pilot, Maj. Gregory A. ("Greg") Feest, dropping his bomb where the second was to strike. His wingman, thinking the attack had reverted to the original plan, dropped his bomb 325 yards wide. The chairman of the House Armed Services Committee, Les Aspin, later stated that problems in targeting also added to the confusion because "the humid, varied, vegetation...lowered the contrast and gave the [IRAD] system problems."[43]

In spite of the targeting being off, Gen. Steiner said he was pleased with the results because even though the Panamanian infantry companies were already deployed and alert, the explosions still produced considerable confusion, with other soldiers seen "running around the area in their underwear" and some troops at the airfield "throwing down their weapons and running off."[44] Several Rangers were killed and more than a dozen wounded in the ensuing fight, but use of the Black Jets had still saved lives on both sides.

Capping off the less-than-auspicious first mission was the Air Forces' uncharacteristic act of passing a message to Secretary of Defense Richard ("Dick") Cheney that the F-117s had scored direct hits, before conducting a battle damage assessment (BDA). Cheney, in turn, triumphantly passed on this information to media representatives massed and circling for word on events in Panama. He was very displeased when he eventually learned of the actual results of the strike, over three months after the fact.

Coming on the heels of the Wobbly Goblin rumors and other negative reports, such as *Aviation Week's* unsubstantiated recounting of a near-midair collision between a Cessna 152 and an F-117A near Palmdale, this bit of news about the Panama strike was most unwelcome. Partly to counter the continuing bad press, the USAF decided to bring the F-117 even more into the open through a series of public unveilings at air shows. Appropriately, the first event was held at Nellis AFB on Saturday, April 21, 1990, so that the families who had been kept in the dark about what their relatives had been doing for the last few years could see the Black Jet up close. More than 100,000 people came out to see two of the bat-shaped creatures swoop in for a landing and taxi to a heavily guarded spot on the tarmac. For months to come, the stealth fighter was the major draw at air shows across the United States.

On Thursday, July 12, 1990, the USAF took delivery of the last F-117A, aircraft number 87-01843, which topped TAC off with an operational fleet of 56 aircraft. Altogether, 64 of the once–top-secret aircraft had been produced at Lockheed's Burbank plant. Five of those aircraft, designated YF-117s, were FSD models (FSD-1 and -2 would soon be retired to museums). Fifty-nine were production models that had been built to fulfill government orders for 58 planes because one aircraft crashed before acceptance by the USAF. Two others had crashed during routine training missions. The 37th TFW thus carried a full complement of 18 Black Jets in each of its two combat squadrons, plus up to 15 more in the training squadron, with the balance used to fill in as needed when aircraft were down for maintenance. The 37th was ready for war.

Chapter 6

Team Stealth Prepares for War

It had been a busy, and in many ways historic, tour for Col. Tony Tolin. In his two years commanding the stealth unit, it had been nudged bit by bit into the white world, been reorganized into the 37th TFW, and conducted its first combat mission. In August 1990, he prepared to leave many good friends behind and head for his new assignment with TAC at Langley AFB, and the wing eagerly awaited the arrival of Al Whitley after an absence of five years.

Now a bird, or full, colonel, Whitley was not personally known to many at Tonopah but did carry the aura of a local legend. Few on base did not know of his 233 combat missions in Vietnam, the initial operational flight of the Black Jet with his hand at the throttle, and his founding of the original, top-secret Goat Suckers. It was planned that Whitley would guide the 37th TFW through a much-needed offensive capabilities improvement program (OCIP), prepare the wing for its move to its future home at Holloman AFB, and maintain the high standards he had helped set for the unit.

Col. Whitley was just winding up his duties as TAC's director of fighter training and tactics at Langley and was in the midst of making final arrangements for his family's move to Nevada when, at 1:00am on Thursday, August 2, Saddam Hussein moved three divisions of Iraq's Republican Guard troops into little Kuwait. (Note: Unless otherwise stated, all times given in this and subsequent chapters are for the time zone in which the event occurred.) The oil-rich kingdom was swallowed whole within hours, and both Arab and Western nations protested vehemently as Hussein cast his envious gaze at the massive Saudi petroleum fields one day's drive down the Persian Gulf coast. "I knew this thing had great potential for blossoming into a full scale contingency," said Whitley.[1] And he immediately began spending time with the TAC battle staff as it monitored events in the Gulf.

That Saturday morning, President George Bush and Secretary of State Dick Cheney met with the commander in chief of CENTCOM, Gen. H. Norman Schwarzkopf, and his air component commander, Lt. Gen. Charles Horner, who presented a relatively standard campaign plan designed to repulse an invasion of Saudi Arabia and eventually drive the Iraqis from Kuwait. Although it was essentially a one-size-fits-all plan, it was reasonably well tailored to the emerging situation in the Gulf, thanks to the recent conclusion of a computer-based command post exercise, code-named Internal Look, based on just such a scenario.

The president immediately dispatched Cheney, Schwarzkopf, and Horner to meet the Saudi monarch, King Fahd ibn Abdul Aziz. It was their job to reaffirm America's commitment to the defense of Saudi Arabia. Plans for Operation Desert Shield were proposed to the king and his advisers, and late in the afternoon of Monday, August 6, agreement was reached to allow US and Coalition troops onto Saudi soil as long as no war was launched against Iraq without King Fahd's permission.

Within 24 hours, a C-141 Starlifter was on its way to Dhahran, Saudi Arabia, with an airlift control element, followed closely by F-15C Eagles from Langley, as well as KC-10 tankers, E-3 AWACS aircraft, and C-5 transports carrying the 82d Airborne Division's "ready brigade." The mission of these

A remarkable line-up of Black Jets assembles at Langley AFB. USAF

varied forces was to protect the highly vulnerable ports and airfields through which nearly all US personnel and materiel would funnel into the Gulf. The F-15Cs were flying combat air patrols (CAPs) along Saudi Arabia's long border with Iraq and occupied Kuwait only 38 hours after orders came to deploy. Over 120 air-superiority and multirole jets arrived within the first five days of Desert Shield. Although these aircraft could certainly be used offensively, they would remain essentially defensive weapons until platforms with a deadly long-range punch entered the theater of operations to allow the gathering force to strike directly at Iraq.

Gen. Schwarzkopf asked the USAF to expand on the plan originally submitted to President Bush by developing a strategic campaign plan aimed at the heart of Iraq's war-making capacity. He wanted it by the end of the week, and the air staff's high-level Checkmate planning group in the Pentagon, under John Warden, duly obliged on Friday, August 10, by presenting the general with a 12-page briefing paper outlining a strategic air campaign. The concept developed for the war against Iraq was the antithesis of the prolonged, disjointed approach to aerial warfare embodied in the Vietnam War's Operation Rolling Thunder, which allowed the North Vietnamese to adapt to—and even anticipate—gradual increases in the bombing campaign. Operation Instant Thunder was the code name used during the initial planning stages of the Desert Storm air campaign. This action would entail a massive application of force designed to paralyze the Iraqi leadership by destroying 84 key targets in just the first week. The 37th TFW was slated to be a key player in the campaign.

The TAC contingency staff tasked the unit to develop a concept for F-117 operations against strategic targets in Iraq, and a contingency planning group was formed around the 37th's weapons officers, Capt. Marcel Kerdavid and Maj. Jerry Leatherman. Kerdavid and Leatherman also found themselves talking often to a former stealth pilot, Capt. Mike Ritchie, on the secure phone to the Pentagon. Ritchie had just been assigned to the rapidly growing joint "Checkmate" planning staff because the full capabilities of the recently declassified plane were still known to very few officers in the USAF. Even at this late date, the strategic planners were in the dark along with everyone else. "They were trying to figure out all the basics," said Leatherman. "You know, asking 'How much gas is it going to take you to get to Baghdad? What kind of profile is that going to be?' to figure how many refuelings we're going to need."[2]

Meanwhile, Col. Tolin had not been told specifically that his "Atlantic" squadron, the 415th TFS, would be ordered to ship out, but with the number of announced deployments growing daily and the humming lines to Washington and Langley, it seemed a sure bet that the Nightstalkers figured

It's a big ocean, and flying solo over that much water was a first for some pilots. S/Sgt. Scott P. Stewart, USAF

Wes Wyrick's Sneak Attack, *aircraft number 821, is towed out to the flight line just before sundown.* USAF

into some of the scenarios being examined and might soon be heading east. Anticipating that if the 415th did deploy, it could well be gone for an extended period of time, "Col. Tolin began looking at things with a long-term perspective," said Col. Whitley, "and the organization began picking all the right airplanes," thus ensuring that no F-117s would have to be sent home prematurely because they were scheduled for depo-level maintenance at the Sacramento Air Logistics Center.[3]

The time finally came when Col. Whitley had to report to his new command at Tonopah, and after a round of good-bys, the Whitley family caravan set out for Nevada. "I can assure you, we watched the news and read the papers with great anticipation, wondering if we were going to get to Nellis in time to be part of the action," Whitley recalled.[4] They arrived at Nellis AFB on Wednesday, August 15, and the wing got a look at its new boss the following day when he flew up to Tonopah for a two-hour tour. At 10:00am on Friday, the change-of-command ceremony was held at Nellis, "and four hours later, the word came in to deploy our first squadron," said the colonel. "Saturday, I said good-by to Mrs. Whitley, the two kids, two parked cars, and a moving van, and said, 'I'll see you when I see you.' I departed from Tonopah, Nevada, less than 24 hours after I assumed command. We were on our way on Sunday morning." Events were indeed moving with breathtaking speed, and Whitley marveled at the situation he found himself in: "I had seen combat as a lieutenant in an F-100, and later in A-7s. Now here I was an old man—45 years of age—going into combat for a third time in a third airplane."[5]

Before dawn on Saturday, August 18, the stealth wing began processing people and cargo for the first of over a dozen MAC C-5 and C-141 transports deploying the 415th TFS to Saudi Arabia. The following day, just ahead of the Black Jets, Col. Whitley flew in the lead C-5 Galaxy with the Nightstalker's commander, Lt. Col. Ralph Getchell, and a wide variety of other personnel who would serve as the squadron's advance contingent. "I had never met Ralph. And here I was inheriting a wing of 2,500 people in Tonopah. I was about to inherit a wing of 1,500 in Saudi, 800 of which were from Tonopah and 700 of which were from 36 other locations throughout the Air Force. Ralph and I sat down and began to formulate how to bring this group from all over the world to form a *team*. That's what prompted us to call it 'Team Stealth.'"[6]

At 6:45am on August 19, tankers of the 9th Strategic Reconnaissance Wing began lifting off from Beale AFB, California, and they were marrying up with F-117s from Tonopah by 8:00am. About a dozen of the tankers escorted 22 Black Jets on the first leg of the Mideast deployment, in a formation made up of three tanker cells and at least one spare tanker. The pair of Black Jets on each tanker would close to within 20–30ft from its wing tips whenever the cells passed through clouds, and would retain visual contact from that position until they were in the clear. Two more refuelings were conducted before the first F-117s reached Langley AFB in the early afternoon, but three KC-135As were forced to land short of their Plattsburgh AFB, New York, destination because stiff head winds at the formation's 22,000–25,000ft cruising altitude had forced up their fuel consumption. A tanker that was discovered to have a faulty fuel system nevertheless continued on to Plattsburgh with the rest of the formation.

Black Jets of the 415th TFS in one of the remarkable King Khalid Air Base hangars. USAF

The stealth pilots' cross-country flight was quite a hop, but nothing compared with what awaited them the next day. Once they were all assembled at Langley, the flyers did their best to relax and tried to get a good night's sleep, because the next leg of their journey entailed a nearly 15-hour, nonstop flight to their secret base in Saudi Arabia.

By the time the F-117 pilots awoke the next morning, the Beale Bandits, which had continued after just a few hours on the ground, were winging their way over the Mediterranean. Tanker support for the F-117s this time around came from KC-10As of the 22d Air Refueling Wing from March AFB, which rendezvoused with the Black Jets once all were airborne around midafternoon on Monday. After ensuring that all the aircraft had taken on fuel, the spare F-117s turned back toward land, leaving 18 stealth pilots to their solo flights.

"It was all kind'a new and adventuresome," said Capt. Rob Donaldson. "You get to feeling pretty puny looking down at an ocean for 12 of those hours with no land in sight. Of course, most of it was under cover of darkness so you couldn't see anyway."[7] Inflatable rubber rafts and a portable radio-rescue beacon were carried aboard each plane to help ensure that if someone had to ditch in the ocean, that person had a reasonable chance for survival until help arrived.

With piddlepacks for kidney relief and air-filled plastic doughnuts to help take the pressure off their tail, the pilots hunkered down for the seemingly endless flight. Under the supervision of the wing's flight surgeon, the amphetamine Dexedrine was also issued to the pilots, for emergency use, but rock'n'roll—the louder the better—was the preferred stimulant to help keep the stealth pilots awake through the long night and eight time zones. Before the pilots had gone out to their planes, cassettes were exchanged in a last-minute flurry. "We passed a lot of the time listening to tapes," said Donaldson. "Nearly everyone had a Sony Walkman hooked up in the cockpit to their helmet." The cells were also kept very loose, and except for minor adjustments and refueling, the men pilots left their aircraft on autopilot. "I had magazines that I read and I could still keep an eye on the tanker....It was boring to tell you the honest truth," said Donaldson.[8]

The Black Jets set down at King Khalid AB around noon local time on Tuesday, August 21, and pilots were helped from their aircraft by anxious ground crew. The C-5 bringing Whitley's advance team, and follow-up MAC transports with additional personnel, had not made prolonged stops before crossing the ocean, and they had arrived the day before in considerably better condition than the stealth pilots. Upon disembarking relatively fresh from the Galaxy, Whitley and Getchell had been met by the base commander, Brig. Gen. Abdulaziz Bin Khalid Al-Sudairi, and the flying wing commander, Col. Faisal Eurwailli, and given a tour of the remarkable facilities. Tucked away in the Asir Mountains outside the small city of Khamis Mushait in the extreme southern tip of the Saudi kingdom, the base offered the most workable combination of assets and liabilities, of the potential operating sites hastily examined in five area countries.

"Rapid and often intense negotiations resulted in international agreements providing access to airfields," said Gen. Horner.[9] Unlike the first A-10 squadron deployed to Saudi Arabia, which was based so far forward that Horner instructed its commander to "be prepared to launch and then recover in the United Arab Emirates because you could be overrun in hours,"[10] the F-117s were simply too valuable to risk being sent within range of Iraqi ground or air elements.

Combat missions to Iraq would require three aerial refuelings from King Khalid AB, but this was a small price to pay for being well beyond the range of Hussein's Scud B medium-range ballistic missiles. Moreover, the hardened aircraft shelters (HASs) in Saudi Arabia, built to US military standards under the direction of the US Army Corps of Engineers, were the finest facilities of their type outside eastern Europe. Throughout the 1970s and 1980s, the corps' Middle East Division managed a program responsible for the construction of $14 billion worth of military facilities for the Saudis. The Saudi Air Force portion of the project consisted of teaming up with the USAF Logistics Command to construct support facilities at four sites for F-5 Tigers and, later, F-15 Eagles, and the base near Khamis Mushait, was completed in 1980. The extra shelters at the far end of the runway, sealed for over a decade, were turned over in mint condition to the stealth unit, in addition to a portion of over $1 billion in US prepositioned supplies in Oman that Gen. Horner referred to as "our term insurance."[11] Even if the Iraqis' modern Su-24 Fencer strike aircraft could somehow fight their way through to the base on a one-way suicide mission, the likelihood that they could cause any significant

Midnight Reaper *parked near its hardened aircraft shelter (HAS). A portion of another HAS can be seen at upper right. The white bus on the road beyond the rock outcrop is part of the shuttle system moving personnel between King Khalid and the McDonnell Douglas compound.* USAF

disruption to flight operations was minimal.

The first impression of the 37th's airmen was uniformly one of awe. Leatherman, who came over on the first C-5 with Whitley and Getchell, spoke with near reverence when describing what he found: "The shelters that we moved into had never had anybody in them. I mean, the paint didn't even have footprints on it. They've got the best facilities that money can buy. Money was no object. All of the pilots slept in the hardened aircraft shelters. The HASs were like alert facilities and were built with bedrooms in them. It would be like four of us to a room; they had bunk beds. On one end of the shelter were these huge diesel generators that had six months of fuel with them, so that if power went out on the base, you could fire one of those babies up. They had gas warning systems, and you could shut the doors and overpressurize. Those were some awesome buildings."[12] According to Sgt. Gary Martin, "These things were *fully* loaded. They had blast doors on both ends of that bay, and you could do anything you needed to do to that airplane. If you had the engine stand, the support equipment that you needed inside, there wasn't *anything* that you couldn't do, and you'd never have to go outside."[13]

Unlike Tonopah, King Khalid AB contained no single-plane hangars. "These shelters would hold a total of eight aircraft," explained Capt. Matt Byrd. "They'd be two to a bay, nose-to-tail, in four sections. The guy in the front airplane can't start his motors with an airplane behind him, so they'd tow that one out and put it at the end of those 'canyons' you saw. He'd start up outside and taxi away, and then the guy inside the canyon, he could stay there, and he could start them up. They'd open the doors and the air [would blow] through, so there's no one behind him to get the jet blast."[14]

The pleasant surprises didn't stop at the operational side of the base. "As the F-15 followed the F-5, and the Tornados followed the F-15," said Whitley, "they had to have a great deal of contractive support. So, commensurate with Northrop and McDonnell Douglas and British Aerospace coming in there, obviously there had to be not only what I call Western housing, but a lot of the messing and shopping and sports facilities. When we arrived, the heydays of all these kinds of things I just mentioned were long gone. But the physical plants, the chow hall for example, was still there. It just wasn't being used....It's great when you can go in and simply clean up a place and dust it off, get the ovens going, set the pool pump going, clean out the pool, remove all the garbage, and make the place functional again. It wasn't easy, and it wasn't free—a great deal of effort and time went into it—but we had something to start with." Whitley also recalled that "we were sitting there in a mile-high city in the mountains, at 6,800 feet, when everyone else was up in the Persian Gulf area sweltering in the hundred-degree heat."[15]

Before the Americans could find time to clean out the swimming pool, though, more important matters were at hand. The term *controlled chaos* probably best describes Team Stealth's determined effort to make the base operational as quickly as possible. By Thursday, August 23, work had pro-

A Saudi Tornado and an F-15 pull up beside Capt. Rob Donaldson's Black Jet during a series of orientation flights. USAF

An F-117A is serviced in one of the broad alleys that run between each eight-plane HAS. A parallel HAS can be seen at upper left. USAF

gressed to the point where the 415th TFS and the host wing were able to launch a series of orientation sorties. The Saudis used four F-5Es, three F-15Cs, and one Tornado IDS to pair up with and chase eight Black Jets around the countryside in an effort to familiarize the Americans with the area. These flights were to be the last daylight takeoffs of F-117s from King Khalid until the air campaign started five months later.

Gen. Al-Sudairi made every effort to assist the US build-up at his base, and a superb Bedouin officer, Lt. Col. Said Al-Khatani, was also attached to Team Stealth. "We were blessed with having a liaison officer who had all the contacts," said Whitley. "I don't care what the issue was—from bottled water to toilet paper, rental vehicles to food to whatever—we had a young man who spoke excellent English and had been in the school here in the US. He knew his business!"[16] Because Khamis Mushait and the larger city of Abha were close by, supplies that were taking forever to reach the base from prepositioned stocks in Oman could be acquired quickly on the open market.

The two biggest problems during the early days of the deployment were generally considered to be a severe lack of drinking water and an overburdened communications setup. "I figured we were headed for a problem," said one officer, "when I got off the plane and noticed that even the Saudis were drinking bottled water. The pipes in the shelters were still sealed and had apparently never been turned on, and the system at the McDonnell Douglas compound had been shut off for Lord knows how long."[17]

The Americans quickly set to work bringing the new base up to full operational capability. The similarities to Tonopah Test Range in terrain, weather, and the facilities themselves were so striking that for a time, it was fashionable to refer to King Khalid AB as Tonopah East. They even had a long drive out to the former McDonnell Douglas compound, that was reminiscent of the similar trip to the satellite living area 7mi off the Nevada base. The most visible differences were that the new base had two 12,000ft runways to Tonopah's one, it was flanked by fewer outlying support structures, and virtually everything of importance was encased in tons of concrete. Flying high over the massive HAS complex occupied by the 415th, one could see its sides sloping gently up from the desert to a broad, low mesa. Across this billiard table–flat plain, it

looked as if some giant hand had swooped from the sky to scratch long straight canyons in a single pass. The nickname Tonopah East soon gave way, as airmen of all ranks began referring to the base by the name of the nearby city, Khamis Mushait, even though only a handful of the Americans would ever be allowed to travel there.

On August 26, one week after the Black Jets lifted off from their home base, the 415th TFS was ready to do battle and F-117s assumed alert duty for the first time. "Although the immediate threat to Saudi Arabia was growing less every day, that wasn't really all that apparent at that time," said one stealth pilot.[18] An intense period of training was begun, and continued into January, when it merged almost seamlessly into the actual bombing campaign. About this time, CENTAF also began issuing an updated air tasking order (ATO) every day. The ATO contained information such as targets, the aircraft that would strike them, the type and number of munitions to be used, tanker and

George Kelman pulls up to the pump in Lone Wolf.
USAF

Team Stealth maintainers troubleshoot a problem with a Black Jet's unique trapeze munitions hoist.
USAF

electronic countermeasures (ECM), and so on. All of this was arranged in time and space so that operations could be effectively implemented without friendly forces getting in each other's way.

Strategic target lists were frequently updated, and Team Stealth's deployed combat mission planning cell, under Maj. Leatherman, struggled to keep up with the ever-changing information and with computing its effect on sorties, munitions, timing, and fuel. Said Donaldson, "We perfected the air refueling procedures we would use with the tankers—and this was on a nightly basis. We practiced going after the targets we thought we might be going for in Iraq [and]...were harder on ourselves than what we actually experienced during the war."[19] Capt. Don Chapman added that "the mission planning was as intense as the mission itself. It got to the point you were anxious to get off the rock and cruise a little bit. The mission planning was so intense, you just wanted to get into the mission itself because of that intensity of the preparation."[20]

"The intent of the training," said Maj. Doc Whitescarver, "was to...reduce the stress level on the pilot by making the evolution to the drop-off point [where the stealth pilots headed into enemy territory individually] as automatic as possible. So we practiced continually the procedures for getting on and off the tanker, the radio calls we made, etc."[21]

Long before Iraq invaded Kuwait, it had been

A large American flag lends a touch of home to a King Khalid HAS as it sways in the high-plateau breeze of the Asir Mountains. Note the thickness of the HAS walls protecting Maj. Jammer Moore's Black Jet. USAF

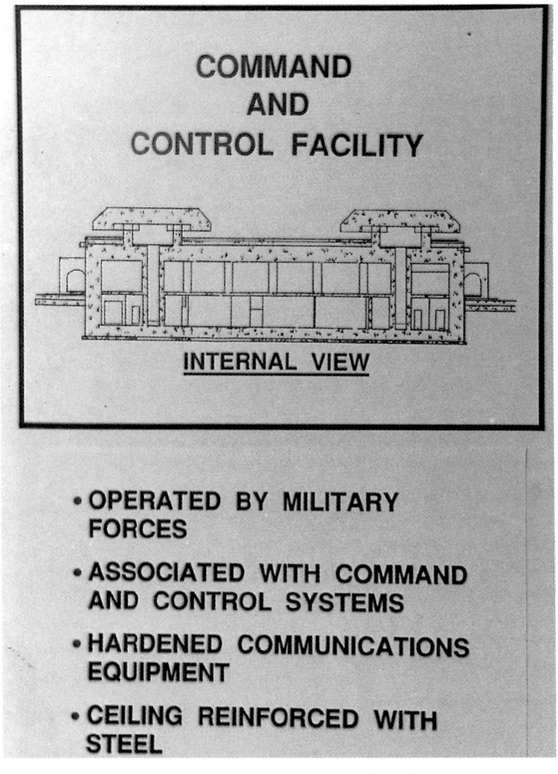

Blueprints of nearly every military bunker and government facility in Iraq were obtained from a variety of sources, greatly assisting the work of CENTAF targeteers. When displayed to the press at news briefings (above), such material also helped deny the Iraqis a propaganda windfall when the United States was able almost immediately to demonstrate that a "shelter for Iraqi civilians" was actually a functioning command-and-control bunker. DOD

Dave Deptula, seated center left, discusses aircraft allocation for the next day's air tasking order (ATO) with Lt. Col. Baptiste in the Black Hole. They are the directors of respectively the Iraq Strategic Target Planning Cell and the Kuwaiti Theater of Operations Planning Cell. The man at left, foreground, is one of the British officers attached to the section. USAF

argued in some USAF circles that deploying F-117s beyond the US borders would be a grave mistake, not just because of security concerns but because the plane's special needs would inevitably send its readiness ratings spiraling downward. A responsive supply system from the United States and Team Stealth's innovative maintenance system, coupled with a judicious bit of cannibalism, all kept more Black Jets on-line than anyone would have dared hope for before the deployment.

During the early stages of Operation Desert Shield, the 415th TFS got caught along with everyone else when the huge volume of supplies being shipped to the Gulf caused back-ups at the major ports and airheads. To rectify the problem, a priority airlift, called Desert Express, was established to fly critically needed assets directly to the theater of operations. "Back at Tonopah," noted Martin, "when an airplane breaks, we wait for the parts direct from the factory, and have a pretty good turn time. The parts would get to us pretty quick; we don't wait long. But I couldn't believe the response we had from the States. We just called straight back to Tonopah and said, 'We need this part.' They'd put it on a Desert Express airplane, and normally, within 72 hours, anywhere from 48 to 72 hours, we'd have the parts in hand in Saudi Arabia."[22]

Before Desert Express was up and running, however, the stealth unit put its own plan into effect to keep the Black Jets flying. The Nightstalkers had deployed with war readiness spares kits and mission support kits, which would, in theory, cover most needs until the wing's avionics maintenance vans arrived 30 days into the deployment. But with the logistic system in such disarray, the unit's maintenance officer, Maj. Guy Fowl, felt it wouldn't be prudent just to pull defective avionics systems from planes and let them sit in an extra shelter. On September 4, Maj. Fowl initiated the Shade Tree Aircraft Repair program to fix broken line-replaceable units, otherwise known as avionics or black boxes. "He had enough foresight," said Col. Whitley, "to see that...we needed to do whatever we could to test, adjust, and fix whatever black boxes for our airplanes."[23]

About 30 days into the deployment, support equipment van sets, Elvira I and Elvira II, arrived right on schedule. Aside from a complete mission data planning system, the vans contained additional maintenance equipment and a complete avionics diagnostic system, which was a great boon to the continuing Shade Tree program.

In spite of everyone's best efforts, though, it became necessary, on occasion, to raid a Black Jet for parts. "You just can't afford to carry every single part that the airplane has in your spares kit," said Sgt. Martin. "So you may not have a particular component [when you need it]. We did a lot of cannibalizing. That's a fact of life for Air Force units."[24]

As for the maintainability of the F-117's RAM skins and specialized exhaust system, Gen. Horner stated, "Frankly, I had some reservations about our ability to generate the sorties we needed every day....In fact, it was not the problem that I personally thought it was going to be....The maintenance of it was better than what we experienced in peacetime."[25]

On Wednesday, September 12, the USAF chief of staff, Gen. Michael J. Dugan, paid a how-goes-it visit to Team Stealth. In less than a week, he would be out of a job for making "inappropriate" statements to the press, implying that Saddam Hussein would, himself, be considered a strategic target. In the course of a lengthy pair of interviews conducted on flights to and from the Gulf, Dugan had said that instead of "nibbling at the edges....the cutting edge" of the air campaign "would be in downtown Baghdad." The general explained, "If I wanted to hurt you, it would be at home. Not in the woods someplace." And although he considered the original strategic target list of such things as nuclear

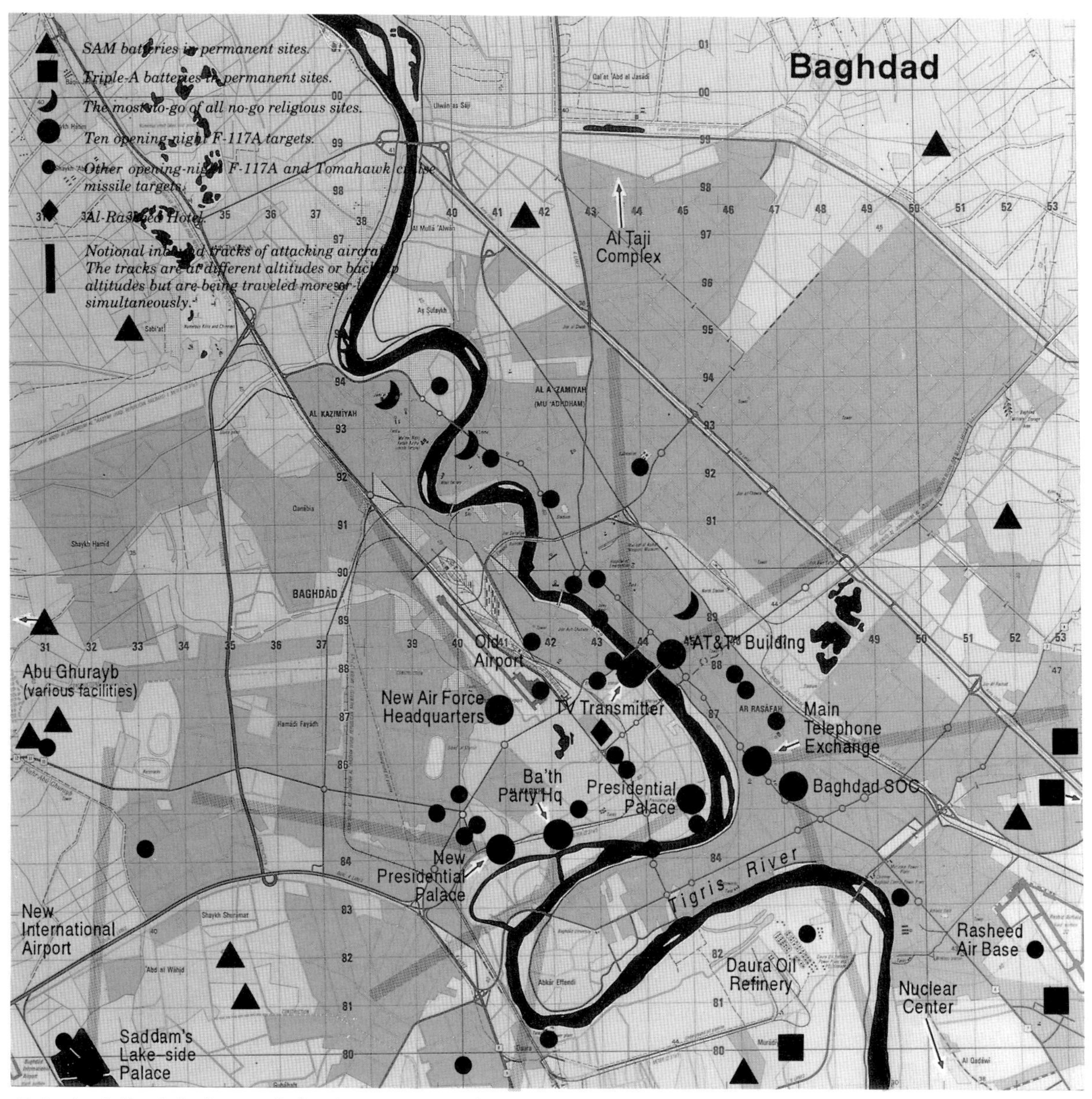

Principal Baghdad-area defensive concentrations and opening-night targets. Defense Mapping Agency

and biological production sites, communications sites, and powerplants "a nice list of targets," they were "not enough."[26]

For all practical purposes, the strategic air campaign, as executed, was carried out in the manner that the dismissed chief of staff intended, but with the broader objective of decapitating Iraq's leadership by attacking its centers of command. Eventually, the stealth pilots would deliver their LGBs into virtually every known command and control bunker. "Now that would not have 'targeted Saddam Hussein,'" Gen. Horner later explained with a straight face, "but it targeted key command-and-control facilities, and he should have been present for duty."[27]

A standing joke used by stealth pilots to describe the extreme accuracy of their weapons systems stated, "You pick precisely which target you want: the men's room or the ladies room." But the ability to target not just buildings, but individual rooms within those buildings, does little good without the intelligence to support the targeting; as Gen. Dugan put it, "If you attack the Ministry of Defense, you need to know where the minister's office is, and not where the computer paper is stored."[28] The Checkmate staff's boss, Col. John Warden, made sure his planners reached beyond the more traditional intelligence sources available to them, and described how their information-gathering system worked: "On one wall, we had a huge

Deployed stealth pilots circa October 1990. Left to right, standing, are Clarence Whitescarver, Phil Mahon, Brian Foley, Joe Bouley, John Savage, Bill Behymer, Dave Francis, Kevin Tarrant, Paul Dolson, Lou McDonald, Bobbie Bledsoe, George Kelman, Joe Salata, and Mike Riehl. Left to right, front, are Greg Feest, Rob Donaldson, Lee Gustin, Jerry Leatherman, Wes Wyrick, Squadron Commander Ralph Getchell, Barry Horne (who would later command the 417th TFS), Blake Bourland, Bob Warren, Mark Lindstrom, Dan Backhus, and Marcel Kerdavid. Most of the airmen are from the 415th TFS, but Savage and Bledsoe from the 416th were attached to the Nightstalkers to round out the squadron, as had been Neil McAskill for the initial deployment. The Black Jet is Rob Sarnoski's from the 417th. "Sarno" was the wing guy responsible for simulator and training operations, and his aircraft beat him out to Saudi Arabia by five months. He finally deployed with other replacement training unit pilots and maintainers in late January 1991. The pilots were required to wear sidearms because of the ongoing terrorist threat. USAF

A trio of Black Jets emerge from their caves to greet the morning sun. The aircraft in the foreground still bears the name of Squadron Leader Graham Wardell, Royal Air Force exchange pilot, in large white letters, which led to early speculation in the British press that one of their own was bombing Baghdad with the stealth unit. USAF

A 416th TFS jet pops its chute during the squadron's arrival at King Khalid AB in December 1990. T/Sgt. Hans Deffner, USAF

satellite picture of Baghdad. Intelligence people and others who had worked in Baghdad, like Ambassador [April] Glaspie, for example, were invited to help us identify targets. Standing in front of the satellite photo, they would say, for example: 'There was a military command center on the second floor of that building. I drove by it on the way to work.' We'd check the information against other sources, and if it checked out, we'd put it on the list of targets."[29]

Checkmate personnel would nominate what they believed to be a worthwhile target and, in marathon sessions around conference tables, would try to come to a consensus of just how important or vulnerable a target actually was. From the standpoint of the airmen performing the actual targeting, and the stealth pilots maneuvering LGBs, it boiled down to a question of "critical nodes," or the elements that are essential to the function of a given target.

"How critical a node is," said Capt. Daniel Thomas, who served as joint combat targeting officer, "depends on its ability to be repaired, its vulnerability, and its repair time. For example, destroying the [electrical] plant's turbines and generator cripples the plant, but the generator building's sturdy construction makes this difficult. Attacking the plant's water supply also could shut the plant down, but since this is easy to fix, the plant could resume operations quickly. On the other hand, the plant's transformers are not only critical but are difficult to repair and relatively easy to hit. Thus, the transformers present the most lucrative aim point. Next, the targeteer compares the enemy's like components and determines which ones are most important. For example, if a single plant produces 75 percent of the enemy's electrical power, it becomes a higher priority target than all the other plants combined."[30]

David A. ("Dave") Deptula and two other lieutenant colonels who had helped develop the air plan submitted by Checkmate, were sent to Riyadh in August to brief Horner's director of campaign plans, Brig. Gen. Buster C. Glosson. After the briefing, Glosson joked, "I hope you guys brought more than three days' supply of underwear,"[31] and for the next six months, they were part of the general's staff, with Deptula acting as the director of the Iraq strategic target planning cell. Glosson's work space was a large, open room next to Gen. Horner's office in the basement of the Royal Saudi Air Force building in Riyadh. Popularly known as the Black Hole because of the tight security protecting it, their subterranean post became the nerve center from which the air campaign would be orchestrated.

As chief of Team Stealth's mission planning cell, Maj. Leatherman had to work closely with Glosson's planners. "I'd go and visit the Black Hole to get some of the initial intelligence information on the targets they gave us in Baghdad," said Leatherman. "I probably made eight trips up there to visit them before the war, to iron out some of the details. Our other wing weapons officer, Maj. Bob Eskridge, was at Riyadh working on Glosson's staff as the F-117 representative. Tony Tolin was brought in there later, but Eskridge was the guy they grabbed first. I mean, he never even got to land at Khamis. They wanted him *so bad*! They had the tankers drop him off at Riyadh because Gen. Glosson wanted an F-117 guy.

"That's kind of the way that staff was formed. They pulled people out of all the wings that were represented in the Gulf, like there was a couple of F-16 and F-4 guys, F-111 guys, a special forces guy, and all these other flyers who were working on his staff. The staff was separated from the TACC [Tactical Air Control Center]; in fact, the TACC didn't know anything about the Desert Storm plan until almost December. That's the same as it was with the pilots. Initially, at Khamis, it was just me and Marcel [Kerdavid] who knew about the thing. We

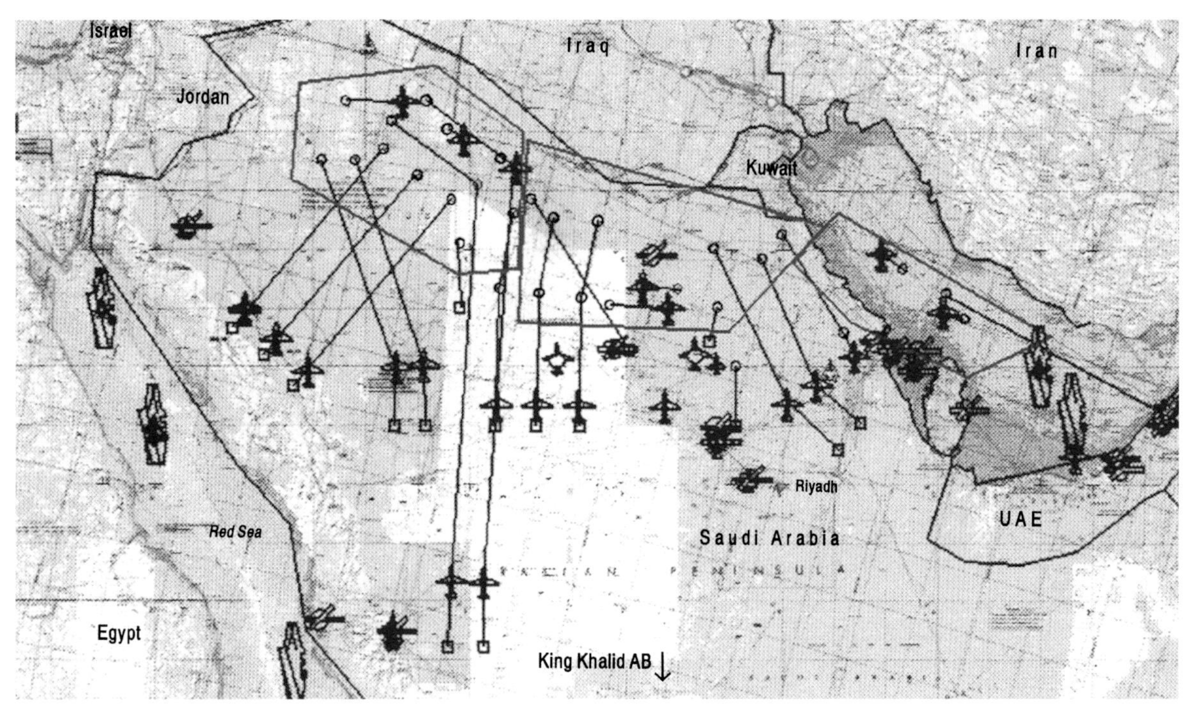

A Black Hole model of air refueling tracks during the opening night of Operation Desert Storm. The small square boxes define the air refueling initial points (IPs), and the small circles represent air refueling control points, intermediate away points, and end–air refueling points for both tankers and customers. The irregular-sized boxed areas were used in an analysis of airspace deconfliction. Analysts computed the number of aircraft moving through each box and plotted it against time to provide a feeling for airspace congestion before and after H-hour. The two tracks running north from the bottom of the chart were used by the F-117As. Unlike the tankers for conventional aircraft, which stay in generally the same area from which they separated from their customers, the 37th's assigned tankers doglegged to the west to make way for the wing's follow-on waves, and to give plenty of flying room for launches and recoveries. This deviation was necessary because the stealthy fighters operate under "radio-out" conditions, which prevent normal coordination procedures. USAF

An F-117A decoy designed to mislead aerial and space-based intelligence assets as well as draw aerial attackers away from real targets. US Marine Corps

had a special room that nobody else was allowed into except Col. Whitley, and Lt. Col. Getchell, me, Marcel, and the guys that ran the intel[ligence] side of the thing. We gradually got more guys as the workload increased."[32]

During this period, subtle modifications were made to the opening phase of the air campaign plan, because of changes to the air defense network in the Baghdad area. The public comments by Gen. Dugan in September had apparently reinforced Iraqi perceptions that Baghdad would bear the brunt of any air offensive, and satellite reconnaissance confirmed that the capital's already formidable air defenses were growing to truly amazing proportions. By the end of the Iran-Iraq War, 14 permanent, revetted battery sites for SA-2 and SA-3 SAMs, complete with command and missile storage bunkers, encircled the city. Other SAM batteries, including SA-6s, SA-8s, and French-made Roland Is and IIs, had brought the number up to about 20, but in just September and October, the number had roughly doubled, with clear indications that even more batteries were displacing to Baghdad. The number of antiaircraft guns—which were actually more of a threat to the Black Jets than were SAMs—had also risen to nearly 1,000, with hundreds more on the way.

Gen. Glosson had originally intended to include a strike by unstealthy F-15Es, F-111Fs, and A-6Es between the first two waves of F-117s, but his suspicion that the Iraqis would shift increasing numbers of antiaircraft weapons to the capital after Dugan's comments was borne out by the emerging intelligence picture. The sky over downtown Baghdad was clearly going to be too hot for conventional aircraft. However, Baghdad's expectations opened up some interesting possibilities for the imaginative fellows toiling in the Black Hole. If the Iraqis were priming for an all-out assault, why not simulate such an event, and when their tactical radars lit up to acquire the incoming aircraft, target them for destruction with high-speed antiradiation missiles (HARMs), which home in on the radar transmitters? The conventional strike aircraft that would have hit leadership and communications sites were dropped in favor of F-4G Wild Weasels, F/A-18 Hornets, and A-7 Corsair IIs carrying over 200 HARMs.

For obvious reasons, operational security (OPSEC) on the revised plan was extremely tight. Majs. Leatherman and Kerdavid believed, however, that the type of split-second night attacks the Nightstalkers were to undertake in Baghdad would be performed more effectively if training specifically for them could begin immediately—especially since the crisis could lead to hostilities with little or no notice. "I think it was after one of the trips that Gen. Glosson made down here [to King Khalid] that we said, 'Hey, sir, listen, we're used to keeping a secret, okay? We want to inbrief all of the other pilots; will you let us do that?' That's what we said; he let us do it. I understand from all of the other wings, though, that this didn't take place until maybe a month before, and sometimes less than that, for them. But our guys, somewhere around October, we were allowed to inbrief everybody, so all of the pilots knew what we were doing."[33]

October also saw the first of several exercises to test Team Stealth's ability to work as a unit. On Wednesday, October 3, Col. Whitley initiated the first Sneaky Sultan, a limited operational readiness exercise, to challenge the unit's response capability. A little over a week earlier, the colonel had signed orders assigning all attached personnel at King Khalid AB to the 37th TFW for the duration of Desert Shield. But although Special Order 1 could dictate that Team Stealth was more than just a name, would the men and women at King Khalid actually perform effectively as a team? Whitley said, "I was confident about our operators and maintainers—they had exercised a great deal at home—but one of the major purposes of the exercises was to bring all the support people together. You see, probably a little less than half or maybe half of them were from Tonopah. We brought the...rest from 36 other locations throughout the world. They all had important roles; they were all important members of the team. We wanted to make sure that they understood our mission, the requirements, and everyone could respond across the board to wartime tasking."[34]

Back at Tonopah, the training course scheduled for November was pushed up two weeks and greatly accelerated. Col. Whitley had not flown the Black Jet since 1985—back five long years that had seen many changes to the aircraft—and took this course along with the other new stealth pilots. "I came home on the 18th of October 1990, for about six weeks, because having been the wing commander for only four hours before we got our deployment order, obviously, I wasn't even checked out on the airplane. So I came home and crammed a three-month course into six weeks. I got to meet the 2,000 people or so that I left behind and, as it turned out, to prepare the second squadron [the 416th TFS "Ghost Riders"] as a much larger increment to go back over for Desert Storm."[35]

Weapons bay art from Magic Hammer, *number 810;* Nachtfalke, *number 826;* Habu II, *number 837; and the dreaded* Christine, *number 836.* USAF

A portion of the training for both the new pilots and those who had been with the wing for a while included sorties against special targets in the Nellis AFB range. During the cold war, various sites at Nellis had been designed to mimic eastern European defense nets and facilities, but as tensions began to escalate in the Gulf, some of these had been rapidly reconfigured to resemble defense lines in Iraq. Mock oil derricks and Scud missile sites were constructed, and even new runways were added to one target airfield.

The personnel trained hard. "As we approached November," said Whitley, "it became obvious, if you go back and look at circumstances back then, that Saddam was stiffening his rhetoric and was not going to back down at all."[36] And neither was the Coalition. On November 8 came a statement from President Bush announcing a huge increase in forces committed to the Gulf region, followed immediately by a similar announcement in Great Britain, and soon by other Coalition members as well. On the president's orders, US ground forces would rapidly surpass the peak deployment during the Vietnam War and include three full corps: the 18th Airborne Corps, the 7th Corps from Germany, and the 1st Marine Expeditionary Force. US air strength in the Gulf would nearly double, eventually peaking at just over 600 Navy and Marine fixed-wing aircraft and nearly 1,400 USAF planes of all types, including the 37th TFW's second tactical squadron.

Some prospective stealth pilots, fearing they might miss the coming war if they went on to training with the 37th, tried to work it out so that they could stay with their deploying unit even if it meant they might miss their shot at flying the F-117. Other flyers, who had recently rotated out of the wing, were upset because of their misfortune at losing a chance to go to war in the Black Jet. Squadron Leader Graham Wardell of Britain's RAF left the unit at about the same time as Col. Tolin and was later described by a friend at Tonopah as being "one unhappy puppy" at having his aircraft—with his name still painted in large white letters under the canopy—"fly off to Khamis without him."[37]

Nachtfalke *in its HAS just after the close of the Christmas-time exercise Sneaky Sultan III. Saudi Arabia's national flag hangs from the ceiling high above the jet.* SRA Chris Putnam, USAF

A Black Jet landing at dawn on January 10, 1991, after a training mission along the Iraqi border. T/Sgt. Rose Reynolds, USAF

Another RAF stealth pilot was in a rather different fix. Wardell's replacement, Squadron Leader Chris Topham, found himself deploying to Thumrayt, Oman, with his Jaguar unit during the initial British deployment in August, and wondered if events in the Gulf would prevent his posting to the 37th. Right on schedule, however, he was pulled back to Great Britain and, after a four-week leave, traveled with his wife in mid-October to set up house outside Nellis AFB in Las Vegas. Unfortunately, when reporting for duty, he was informed that "while [his] clearance had come through from the military, it hadn't come through from the Department of Energy [DoE]; and," added Topham, "the DoE owns the Nellis test area." Topham waited for six frustrating weeks while the paperwork problems were sorted out, and was not able to set foot on TTR until December, just after one accelerated training period had ended and a month before the next was scheduled to begin. The exasperated airman later remarked, "If I'd been on that November course, as soon as I'd finished, I would have been sent out there."[38]

While Topham cooled his heels in Las Vegas and Whitley reacquainted himself with the F-117, the 37th's deputy commander for operations, Col. Klaus J. Klause, "kept the guys in the right direction and ready for combat."[39] Sneaky Sultan II was initiated by Col. Klause on Monday, November 12, to test Team Stealth's ability to generate sorties on short notice in support of planned D-day operations. After a series of evaluations the following day, Team Stealth joined the large, six-day Imminent Thunder exercise, flying 32 sorties against a simulated "mirror image" of Kuwait and southeastern Iraq.

It was also becoming apparent that the Black Jets were going to remain the only manned aircraft to attack Baghdad. Any chance that nonstealthy platforms would be put back into strike plans for the capital were effectively laid to rest when the Studies and Analysis Agency team, which had joined the Black Hole staff late in October, formulated attrition models that projected prohibitively high losses even after Gen. Glosson had assumptions of the actual quality of Iraq's air defenses revised downward. The analysis team also looked into CENTAF's worry that the raw quantity of planes in the air could lead to midair collisions, especially in congested aerial refueling tracks, but possible losses of both F-117s and conventional aircraft were found to be within acceptable limits.

By the end of November, the 416th TFS was ready for its flight to King Khalid AB, and finally, on Sunday, December 2, the Ghost Riders flew to Langley AFB. At 7:03pm the following evening, the squadron commander, Lt. Col. Gregory T. ("Greg") Gonyea, lifted into the sky leading a six-plane element to its tanker cell and a 15-hour journey. Another six- and then two four-plane elements took off behind him at half-hour intervals. The entire group of 20 Black Jets arrived the next day, December 4, including one that developed severe engine problems on the last leg of the journey. Both of the 37th TFW's combat squadrons were now concentrated in Saudi Arabia, and Whitley experienced few problems getting the Ghost Riders squared away. "When the first squadron got there in August," said Whitley, "there was plenty of space available. Fortunately, about the time the second squadron was getting there in December, the Saudis were sending some of their F-5s and F-15s off to forward bases. It worked out great. Maybe somebody in high places knew about that all along. I certainly didn't. But it worked out to everybody's advantage. So, by the time we showed up, they were leaving, and we were ready to put all of our airplanes up in the hardened shelters in just a few days."[40]

"Everybody was really glad to see the rest of the wing come over," said one stealth pilot. "It either meant that we, that the US was finally getting serious and was going to let us kick Saddam's butt, or," he said with a grin, "that the 416th would be our replacements. They'd stay, and we'd get to go home. But it didn't take too long to figure out that if we let this thing drag out, *nobody* was going home soon. There's a grand total of two stealth warfighting squadrons, and *both* of us were at Khamis. There were no more replacements."[41]

The arrival of the Ghost Riders galvanized the Americans at King Khalid. "From about the time that the second squadron got over there to when the war started," said Whitley, "things were on an 'up slope'; the attitude was focused." Team Stealth was also gratified by increasing support from home. "The chocolate chip cookies were coming in by the planeload," Whitley added, "and we were getting thousands of letters, literally. I mean, it was more than we could possibly read and answer. Comments were consistent; everybody understood why we were there, and they were behind us. They wished us the very best."[42] The 37th TFW's commissioned and noncommissioned officers also made it a point to keep their people busy on their time off, and with a little hard work, the amenities at Khamis were getting better all the time.

"Frankly, we were not hurting," said Whitley. "We probably had less to complain about than anyone else in the theater."[43] After the war, at the Army's Command and General Staff College, Schwarzkopf's deputy commander, Lt. Gen. Calvin Waller, recalled that before visiting the new base, he had inspected the Third Armored Cavalry Regiment in its forward area near Kuwait: "They had put up a big German tent for the mess," he told the assembled officers. "Occasionally, they'd show a movie in there if the sand was really blowing, but normally they'd do that under a big camouflage net....Showers were simply big 55gal drums on top and you could turn the water on. They'd play volleyball out in the sand. The commander, Col. Doug Starr, was very proud of what he was doing to take care of his people, and the soldiers were not complaining.

"So, then I go and visit this air wing, the stealth guys flying the F-117. They say, 'Follow me, General.'...When you go to the dining facility, they have hot and cold running everything, Coke machines, steam tables— it's better than Truesdale Hall [at Fort Leavenworth]! At 3d ACR, there are two tin cans filled with cement with a rod between them, and guys are out there pumping. Here, there's the latest Nautilus equipment—Arnold Schwarzenegger stuff—and it's air conditioned. There's a library, a movie theater....They had showers—*regular showers;* and no defecating and urinating in cut-off, 55-gallon drums where you put in a mixture of kerosene and diesel to burn it out—they have a sewage system. And, gentleman," he said, pausing for effect, "they have porcelain toilets."[44] Leatherman, who was attending the staff college at that time, just shrugged his shoulders and smiled. "I always tell the Army guys, 'Hey, you screwed up. You should have joined the Air Force, because we've got to go where there's a base.'"[45]

Morale in the Gulf was not as high as CENTCOM would have liked, but neither was it as bad as the news media frequently reported. It was just part of soldiering, and something commanders had to do their best to keep ahead of. "After the novelty of getting there on the airplane's first worldwide deployment," said Whitley, "everybody settles into place and people start to ask, 'Why are we here?' 'When are we going to do something?' 'If we're not going to do something, why don't we just go home?' But as the war drew nearer, there were a lot of kids who were looking around, saying, 'Hey, let's make the best of this.'"[46]

"Guys might run or work out to keep in shape," said one stealth pilot, "but after a long shift, most people just wanted to unwind. Just let your mind go blank in front of some [movie] tape or maybe just go straight to bed. You'd see some Heinekens or Miller Lites, but alcohol was no-go in Saudi and people played it pretty straight, so there was never a drinking problem."[47]

One of the most critical parts of the campaign plan, aerial refueling, was finalized at this time. "Riyadh dedicated tankers to us," said Leatherman. "We originally had the [KC-135A] guys from Beale that we'd been training with, but when CENTAF found out that they were going to need more of us—our role in the plan increased—then they gave us the [KC-135] R-model reserve guys out of Grissom [AFB, Indiana]. A lot of times when I went to

Left, a munitions crewman examines Mk-84 bombs stored in a thin-walled dummy hangar that has an exterior exactly like that of a normal HAS. The adapter rings for laser seeker heads and special "clipped-wing" tail assemblies are already in place so that the Paveway II or III guidance systems can be speedily mated to the bomb. The final products will be respectively a GBU-10 or a GBU-27B. Right, weapons loaders affix a Paveway II seeker head to a BLU-109B bomb on John Hesterman's Lazy Ace, *number 791. The end product is a GBU-10I (Improved). In nearly all cases, however, the BLU-109B penetrators were used with the newer Paveway III seekers.* T/Sgt. Hans Deffner, USAF

Riyadh, I'd go face-to-face with Lt. Col. Bob McCafferty and his guys and coordinate to the point of taking maps and drawings and giving them accurate coordinates and an understanding of the game plan. We invited them down in December, I think it was, when we had one plan fairly stable, and told them exactly what we expected out of them. We let them know what we were doing, showed them our targets, and explained why we had to be there at certain times; why it was so critical to do that."[48]

On December 20, the enlarged wing was redesignated a provisional unit by CENTAF, to standardize and stabilize its organizational structure. While the 37th TFW—P made ready for the combat ahead, it was sometimes easy to forget that its own base might well be targeted by Saddam Hussein's forces. Although King Khalid AB was well beyond the range of Scud missiles and could not be effectively attacked by Iraq's air assets, its location suffered from one potentially dangerous problem. The base was practically within spitting distance of one of the most radical states in the region: Yemen. At least two of Iraq's intelligence and security services, Estikhbarat (Military Intelligence) and the Da'irat Al-Mukhabarat Al-Ama (General Intelligence Department, or GID) were well established in Yemen, and Iraq's Ba'th party had many close ties with Yemen's business and political elites.

The what-ifs were many, and even an unsuccessful attack would serve Hussein's purposes by encouraging support from the "Arab masses" and raising the specter in the West of "another Vietnam." What if the GID built up a clandestine force that worked its way across the border to attack Khamis, or an Iraqi commando unit, hidden aboard a container ship in Jordan, was sent via the Red Sea to Yemen, where it unloaded its helicopters from sealed containers, secretly attached the rotors at night, then launched its assault? What if Yemen granted the Iraqi Air Force permission to base aircraft or conduct "training exercises" in its territory? The possibilities seemed endless.

The large King Faisal Military Cantonment, housing roughly an Army brigade, was located near King Khalid AB, and the Saudis vigorously patrolled their borders in this area, since relations with Yemen were less than cordial. However, Team Stealth was taking no chances. The 37th Civil Engineering Squadron's Black Knights, who had performed such tasks as building the new control tower at Tonopah when they were known as J-Unit, did much of the initial work to bring the peacetime base up to a war footing, and were soon joined by the 554th Civil Engineering Squadron. Outer defenses were built, various facilities were "hardened," and a bunker was constructed around a 120,000gal fuel bladder that supplemented King Khalid's underground storage capacity. Crash barricades designed to stop a vehicle traveling at 200mph were also erected. Referring to a 1982 truck bombing of Marine barracks, Capt. Harry Arnold of the 554th stated, "We didn't want to be a repeat of Beirut."[49]

The Americans tasked to defend the base with the Saudis were the heavily armed 37th Security Police Squadron, the former K-Unit, who were to be augmented by personnel from Team Stealth's other units in an emergency.

Judging the holiday season as being Hussein's best time to reap the maximum political benefit from a terrorist attack, CENTCOM initiated Threat Condition Charlie on Sunday, December 23. "It's easy, in retrospect, for one to question if perhaps it was an overreaction," said Whitley, "but at the time, I can tell you that if I were the bad guys on the other side looking our way, wouldn't it be interesting to strike the Black Jet at the furthermost point from their homeland. I think it would send just the wrong message throughout the American and Coalition forces. So, you bet, we did beef security up. Myself and my senior advisers—first sergeants and a lot of unit commanders—made every attempt to try to get around to all of the foxholes and outposts on Christmas Eve and Christmas Day, to visit all of the people. Santa Claus would visit along with Mrs. Claus, and give them a little gift and remind them that it was Christmas and that we appreciated everything that they were doing. On the one hand, yes, it was Threat Con Charlie, but on another hand, we tried to make it a somewhat light, but important, moment."[50]

Col. Whitley had also chosen this time to initiate the last of the wing's exercises. The results of Sneaky Sultan III would allow him to evaluate Team Stealth's ability to accomplish taskings outlined in the D-day ATO, but he had another objective in mind as well. "We did it on Christmas Eve just to get people's mind on what they were really there for; not to sit around in their foxhole, if you will, just sulking about their dilemma. To keep them focused on what the heck they were doing."[51]

Team Stealth personnel were also aware that although they could not call home over the holidays, other units were allowing their personnel to do so. For the members of Team Stealth who had been with the unit when it was still black, limitations on the number of calls that could be made, and what could be said, were just part of doing business. For others, things had been different back in the States. "We were able to call [home] every day," said Maj. Joe Salata, who kept in close touch with his wife, Martha. "They just didn't know where we were calling from."[52] Once the team was in Saudi Arabia, however, almost half of the rapidly expanded organization had little experience with the tight security arrangements that were commonplace to the old hands. "Some guys just never seemed to get it that nobody was supposed to know exactly where we were," said one stealth pilot. "You may personally know that so-and-so isn't going to say something stupid, but if you let a few guys make regular calls, people are going to know about it. Then, if you don't let everybody do it, morale goes straight down the toilet."[53] "I put restrictions on people on calling home because that's what our headquarters told me to do," said Whitley. "Our location was classified, and certainly if that was true, we didn't need our people calling home....Another reason why I wanted to artificially limit the number of calls that people could make is that these young enlisted people didn't have the kind of money it was going to take to pay for a $3- or $4-a-minute phone call."[54]

One thing that Wing Commander Whitley did allow—and that turned out to have a much more positive effect than anyone would have imagined—was the addition of personalized art to the Black Jets. The colonel had his people do all the painting on the inside of the bomb bay doors. "Bombing was our business, and we wanted to show our stuff when we were doing our business," said Whitley, "but nose art on the exterior of the airplanes had been disapproved as being inappropriate. In some of these hangars where the aircraft were parked, the maintainers had some art up on the side of the wall, inferring that if they had the chance to put nose art on the airplane, here's what it would look like. What I did, after I came back with the second squadron, was tell them that they could go ahead and put that on their airplanes if they wanted to."[55]

Eventually, every aircraft except number 812, flown by Capt. Brian ("Axel") Foley, would receive a name, and most would have artwork painted somewhere on the white interior panels of the two bomb bay doors. A small amount of name duplication inadvertently occurred within the wing, before more care was taken to make sure such things were avoided. For example, both squadrons had an aircraft named *Black Magic*, but unlike the 415th's number 789, aircraft 802 in the 416th was adorned with a sinister-looking witch. *Christine*, number 836, was reputed to be a bad actor and was named after a possessed car in a Stephen King novel. It flew with the 416th and sported a devil red F-117 designation. The 415th, which had originally owned 836, had *Affectionately Christine*, aircraft 843.

One pilot remarked that "compared to the kind of stuff that appeared on the old B-17s, it was pretty tame. But the maintainers were really proud of their work. I think that a couple of times, maybe more, they'd have their best guy doing it, and near the end, everyone would add a brush stroke so they could all say they had a hand in it."[56] Another stealth pilot recalled that his crew chief had been warned away from using the unclad female figures of World War II fame so as not to offend the wing's Saudi hosts, and, apparently, art was discreetly added to some aircraft before they even left Tonopah. Jerry Leatherman, who flew *Something Wicked*, said, "I think it was only one or two airplanes that had art in there beforehand, but a lot of them already had the name inside the door." Leatherman noted that "the tradition was that the crew chiefs would get to name their airplane."[57]

Black Jets bearing names like *Fatal Attraction*, *The Overachiever*, *Aces and Eights*, *Delta Dawn*, and *It's Hammertime* had been flying training missions up to the Iraqi border since September. At first, these runs occurred only one or two times a week, but the frequency soon increased till they became a nightly affair. The Iraqis were always given plenty to look at. A cell of three, four, or five big tankers escorting the F-117s would move to a point roughly 25–35mi from the border in the vicinity of Rafha, Saudi Arabia, where they would enter a racetrack-shaped holding pattern. Iraqi radar operators would watch this cell, and perhaps a half-dozen other similar formations supporting other units, pull up along their airspace as high-flying CAPs skirted the border flying cover. CENTAF was reasonably confident that the Iraqis did not see the Black Jets peeling off from their station at the wing tips of each tanker to perform practice runs at locations in Saudi Arabia, sometimes within a few miles of the border.

CENTAF's leadership knew how effective the F-117 was supposed to be against the Soviet-made tactical and strategic radar systems in Iraq, but was still suffering from a limited familiarity with the aircraft. Consequently, it decided to run a few tests of its own—not against simulated threats but against the *real* bad guys. On one occasion, Gen. Glosson had the Black Jets "fly dirty" when they left the tanker cell, and make straight for the Iraqi airspace at a low altitude but just high enough to be seen by the specific radar they were teasing. The radar operators viewed the green blips of high-subsonic aircraft barreling down on the border and then saw the objects disappear from their screen just short of Iraq. The Iraqis assumed that the low-flying planes had dipped below radar coverage and continued on to invade their airspace. When Baghdad protested the perceived overflights the next day, CENTAF knew stealth worked. Instead of crossing the border, the Black Jets had simply gone into stealth mode, turned on a dime, and returned to the waiting tankers. It was believed that if the Iraqi radar had seen the aircraft turn away, Baghdad wouldn't have protested.

New Year's Day, 1991, came and went with little fanfare except a few semiprivate get-togethers, and the Christmas trees were taken down in the briefing area of the operations HAS and the McDonnell Douglas compound's mess. The intensity of training over the following weeks was kept high but stable so that the 37th TFW—P's personnel would neither peak nor burn out before combat operations commenced. And, of course, the home-baked cookies continued to flow in from the States.

On Sunday, January 13, the wing started a gradual load-out to prepare for war. "We got our bomb folks in the munitions storage area working with our weapons loaders in the aircraft shelter areas," said Col. Whitley. "Crew chiefs were given a minimal but realistic warning as to how much time they would have to prepare both the airplanes and the munitions and get them mated up in the right order, to fit the schedule," when the go order was received.[58] The same day, the Joint Chiefs of Staff notified units worldwide that hostilities were imminent, by declaring Defense Condition (Defcon) 2 in effect. "Actually, I—and I think a lot of the guys—were actually relieved when we heard we were in Defcon 2," said one stealth pilot, and another remarked that he "didn't really think it surprised anybody." "Let's face it," said Whitley, "everybody knew that the president had drawn a line in the sand and said, 'The 15th of January is the day that if you don't comply, we're going to kick your butt.'"[59]

Chapter 7

Operation Desert Storm

The clock had finally run out. Iraq had allowed the January 15, 1991, UN deadline for its peaceful withdrawal from Kuwait to pass with nothing more than statements of defiance to the world body, and vile condemnations of the United States. Just after midnight, January 16, the Pentagon issued orders to units in Asia, North America, and the Indian Ocean, to execute their D-day taskings against targets in Iraq.

Around 11:00am at King Khalid AB, the stealth pilots awoke to find that they would bomb Iraq before their workday was done. At Barksdale AFB, Louisiana, it was 2:00am of that same Wednesday, and the crews of seven B-52G bombers had already finished breakfast and were on their way out to the flight line. Within three hours, all the B-52s would be airborne and on the first combat mission of Desert Storm, carrying not rack after rack of 500lb bombs, as during the Vietnam War, but 35 AGM-86C air-launched cruise missiles (ALCMs)—weapons that did not yet officially exist and wouldn't for another year. As stealth pilots and night shift maintainers in the Middle East milled about in the crisp mountain air after breakfast, waiting for the buses that would take them back to base, the B-52s had already cleared the Florida coast. The stealth pilots and the bomber crews would meet that night in the skies over Saudi Arabia.

"The day before that first mission," said Capt. Rob Donaldson, "about noon time in Saudi Arabia, they told us to go eat a good meal. We kind'a knew then that something was going on. We reported to the squadron about 3:00 in the afternoon and they said, 'This is it; we're going against Iraq tonight.' The mood there was quiet, somber, very determined. They handed out the targets and the photos to each individual. Everyone took time to study them and get together with their wingman to iron out the small details. For me, personally, it produced a lot of feelings all balled up into one...some apprehension, a little bit of tension...the thrill of the unknown."[1]

Targets, refueling and attack schedules, and information on threats were disseminated to the men well before the night's mission briefing. "You have a private time," said Capt. Matt Byrd, "your own personal time to assimilate the information. What I may do to find a target is different from what some other pilot may do to get his mind on how to locate a target among all the other clutter, the other buildings, the other bunkers out there. You color your photos or do whatever you need to do to make sure that when you're over, when you finally see the target, that you can identify it and be able to hit it."[2]

Col. Al Whitley said, "Fear was one of the many emotions I experienced. It's a little different if you're a bachelor first lieutenant—you park your Corvette and go to war—as opposed to a 45-year-old wing commander, responsible for 1,500 people in Saudi, 2,000 back home, with a wife and two kids. On one hand, you're carefree. You think you're bulletproof and it will never happen to you. On the other hand, you've got 23 years' experience, and you know anything can happen to anybody at any time. You just hope you've done everything you can, not just for yourself but for all the guys who are flying; that you've given them the best airplanes, the best intelligence, and the best mission planning you can."[3]

Col. Whitley knew that the coming mission

Maj. Jerry Leatherman performs cockpit checks prior to takeoff. USAF

would be a pivotal experience in each of these men's life; that he'd see "a lot of 'old' boys become 'young' men" on this first mission. "There were only four guys out of the 65 I had over there, that had ever seen combat," he explained. "One of those had only one combat mission."[4] At the briefing that evening, he did his best to level with them and tell them what to expect; what it would feel like when the whole world seemed to erupt around them and they could do nothing but continue and get the job done. "I told them there would be hormones that would flow that they had never tapped before. I told them they would know what I meant after they got back."[5]

In the shelters, maintainers went about their business of fueling and arming the aircraft, performing hundreds of checks, large and small, while the rock'n'roll that normally predominated on the base public-address system was periodically bumped by multiple playings of Lee Greenwood's "God Bless the USA." Nobody complained about the change. "The maintainers were the only ones who really knew that we were going to go to war," said Maj. Jerry Leatherman, "because they hadn't announced to the rest of the support people that the war is going to start for OPSEC and COMSEC [communications security] reasons, but the maintainers knew because they had to load up the no-shit weapons on the airplanes."[6]

One by one, pilots started showing up at the hangars, around 10:30pm. As they stepped inside from the cool, moonless night, their eyes were stung by the bright lights that bathed the cavernous bays. Brief, informal conferences with their crew chief apprised the stealth pilots of their aircraft's status, and they immediately began their own walk-around to make visual checks of tires, flaps, the RAM skin, and other exterior features. Ducking under the broad delta wings, the men moved to the wheel-wells and bomb bays, where they straightened up to examine the various hydraulic mechanisms for

An F-117A on the 415th's side of the field pulls past Saudi F-5E jets on its way to the flight line. The open-air structure in the background was jokingly referred to as "the car port" by stealth pilots. USAF

Stealth pilots awaiting permission to take off are barely visible in this view through night-vision equipment. The lights below the cockpit allow the pilot to visually check for ice build-up on the engines' intake screens. USAF

leaks, with small pocket flashlights, then bent to look over the ejector unit wiring and bomb fuse settings. Once satisfied that everything was in order, the pilots stepped toward the front of the aircraft and prepared to enter by special angled ladders that skirted the faceted leading edge of the wing, and allowed easy cockpit access without fear of damaging the stealthy structures.

After a pilot climbed in and eased his body into the ejection seat, a maintainer mounted the ladder after him to hand over a small mountain of mission paperwork and gear from a bulging helmet bag. The amount of paper the stealth pilots took with them was impressive, despite the slight reduction afforded by use of the multifunctional display (MFD) screens. Sometimes, it seemed to fill the spacious cockpits. It included three or four maps and perhaps the same number of target photos, a lineup card, and other extraneous pieces of paper running the gamut from a variety of check lists to mission-specific information on the distances from points on the pilot's projected route to the nearest emergency landing site, with estimates of how much fuel it would take to get there. The pilots even wore leg boards attached to their thighs. These curious items displayed mission data for instant viewing and also provided a flat surface across which yet more items could be easily laid.

The likelihood that the Iraqis would resort to the use of poison gas necessitated that stealth pilots bring along protective suits and masks in case they were forced down in a contaminated battlefield or had to land at an airstrip struck by gas-laden Scud missiles. Lightweight Motorola radio-transponder beacons would aid rescue aircraft searching for a downed stealth pilot, and each aviator carried a "blood chit," written in both Arabic and English, offering a substantial reward to anyone helping the pilot to reach Coalition forces. Standard survival gear also included a 9mm Berreta model 92F automatic pistol for personal protection. The search and rescue personnel were the best, and the pilots knew they would do everything they could to extricate a downed flyer from Iraq. As for any Black Jet crashing within reach of Iraqi forces, it would be targeted for a friendly air strike to keep as many of the plane's secrets as possible out of Iraqi hands.

The pilots put on their helmet and plugged in the cables to the radio, the intercom, and the Walkman before beginning the hour-long series of checks that preceded each flight. Avionics and weapons systems were tested, and engines switched on.

Much to Capt. Marcel Kerdavid's horror, his port engine wouldn't start. He couldn't believe it; he had trained hard for over a decade for the moment he would enter combat, and now something as innocuous as a loose wire was keeping him glued to the earth. Quickly grabbing up numerous key papers and the thick EDTM cartridge containing all his mission data, he scrambled out of the cockpit and into a waiting truck. At another HAS a quarter mile away, an extra aircraft was being readied for just such an eventuality. Kerdavid was rushed to the site and performed the walk-around and cockpit checks in record time. He wasn't about to miss the most important mission of his life!

Just before midnight, the pilots finished run-

A Black Jet sticks close during the long ride with its tanker. T/Sgt. Hans Deffner, USAF

ning their cockpit checks and the INSs were set. The maintainers had run every imaginable test, and the last bomb bay door had been sealed. Senior Airman Paula O'Connor looked up at the stealth pilot perched above her. Through the radar-reflective glass, she could see the eyes, businesslike and impassive, above the rim of his oxygen mask. "Bring it back safe," she said into the crew chief's headset. The captain raised his gloved hand in a thumbs-up and replied, "You bet. See you tomorrow."[7] Aircraft in the forward sections of the two-plane bays had already been carefully towed out into the long canyonlike taxiways between the hardened shelters, and eased into position beyond the entrance before engine start-up. In hangars where the second aircraft were scheduled on the opening strike, the chocks were pulled from the wheels and the pilots gently increased the thrust on the twin engines. Under their own power, the planes moved slowly at first, then picked up speed as they rolled through the bays and turned up the canyons, gliding past the ground crews to the darkened flight line.

"The day shift guys had just got off and the night shift launched the first strike," recalled Sgt. Gary Martin. "Some of the day shift guys were actually in tears because they couldn't launch their own aircraft."[8] The airmen shared a strong feeling that they were present for one of those rare moments in history upon which the fate of nations turn. "I remember pulling out of the hangar," said Leatherman, "swinging to the right, and turning on my taxi light to head out, and the whole taxiway was lined with all of the maintenance guys. They all saluted me. I still think about that."[9]

Since Col. Ralph Getchell's 415th TFW had been in Saudi Arabia the longest, Col. Whitley selected it to strike the first blows in Baghdad. "My job as wing commander," said Whitley, "was to make sure all the ducks were in line, that all the airplanes were properly configured, that all the intelligence was properly disseminated, and that everything was going to go without a hitch. To make sure the first wave got off as planned, I put myself in the second wave....I took the young kids who had been over there since the 21st of August and had made the sacrifices, who had been over there all that time, and gave them the honor of being the first guys across."[10]

The first aircraft launched shortly after midnight. One by one, the ugly birds rose into the clear desert night as its pilot concentrated on the dim instrument panel and heard the cockpit sounds unique to the jet's takeoff: the dull hiss of the bleed air increasing when the landing gear was fully retracted; the loud *thonk* of the blow-in doors closing. By 12:22am, all were airborne and the airmen on the ground saw their navigation lights begin to blink off. The Black Jets were invisible.

In complete radio silence, they glided in pairs to the tankers that would escort them to and from the border in parallel tracks. It was going to be a long night. As the crow flies, downtown Baghdad is roughly 1,060mi north from King Khalid AB, and 260mi from the realigned Saudi-Iraqi border of 1982. Some aircraft would log over 2,500mi before they set down six hours later, with the second and third waves of F-117s landing in daylight.

East of Taif, Saudi Arabia, or approximately 180mi from King Khalid AB, the Nightstalkers made the night's first aerial refueling. Another would be finished up about 35mi from Iraqi airspace, and the thirsty aircraft would drink up again after returning to Saudi Arabian airspace. "It was just like every training flight we'd flown the previous five months," said Capt. Donaldson; "all the procedures were the same. Nothing changed. We took off in pairs, went to the tankers, followed them to the borders, then we peeled off and the tankers went into orbit until we returned. Up to that point it was all like before, except that we were now crossing into Iraqi airspace."[11]

"Basically it was just a flash of Stealth airplanes headed north," said Col. Whitley.[12] Unseen by the stealth pilots, hundreds of other US and Coalition combat aircraft were forming up with a huge armada of nimble tankers just beyond the range of the Jordanian and Iraqi radar nets that reached well south into Saudi airspace. "We had 160 tankers airborne on several tracks at one time," said Lt. Col. David Deptula. Deptula, who headed the Black Hole's strategic targets planning cell, stated that "tankers were stacked three deep, with only 500 feet separation between them. The weather was marginal to bad. Hundreds of fighters rendezvoused with their tankers, sometimes in clouds."[13]

Following an hour behind the first wave of Black Jets, Col. Whitley, eight Ghost Riders, and three Nightstalkers hugged the wing tips of their tankers as they followed their assigned route through the mass of aircraft. "All that night as we proceeded north on a tanker," said Whitley, "there was nobody to talk to because we did all our rendezvous and refueling 'com out' [no radio]. Nobody talked to the Stealth airplanes. We were plugged in and could talk to the boomer or the pilot of the tanker, if we had to. They all had the code words they could relay to us, indicating that this was all just a dream, or just an exercise, and was now canceled. I kept waiting from the time I took off until the time I left the tanker, for somebody to blurt out some kind of code word that would indicate that Saddam had come to his senses, and really wasn't as out of it as he turned out to be. But it never happened."[14]

Oddly enough, the takeoff of the stealth wing's own tanker support for the first wave, the 350th Refueling Squadron, was a rather public affair that quickly reached Iraqi ears. These Beale Bandits, based at Riyadh's old international airport, usually launched only a few late-night sorties in support of the 37th's nightly training. Tonight, though, all the KC-135As lifted off, thundering low over the Hyatt Hotel across the street from the Saudi Ministry of Defense. "It was a real window rattler," said the 350th's Kelly Godbey, a staff sergeant. Godbey and a Naval Reserve officer were handling the night shift at CENTCOM's Joint Information Bureau in the Hyatt when, he said, it seemed as if "every one of the 600 reporters in the building were beating down our door....It's tough to have that many tankers take off unnoticed." The reporters were used to hearing aircraft operating at all hours, and in spite of increased international tensions, had not seen any indications of imminent action at the evening press briefing. But now it was obvious that "something different" was going on, and they demanded to know what it was.[15]

Godbey knew nothing more than they did, however, and the flood of reporters quickly dissipated as they rushed back to their room to place calls to their home office. Soon, television and newspaper editors from New York to Bombay were phoning their representatives in Baghdad as the GID undoubtedly listened in with great interest on the tapped phone lines. "We had known by midnight that the war was about to begin," said the British Broadcasting Corporation's (BBC's) John Simpson. "Messages were coming through from London, Washington, Paris. By 2:00am we were planning in earnest. My crew and I decided it was best to leave the Al-Rasheed: Once the bombing commenced, armed guards were to make sure we remained in the hotel's massive underground shelters."[16]

When Gen. Dugan had said that "the cutting edge" of the air campaign "would be in downtown Baghdad," and the USAF said that the stealth fighter was designed to strike "heavily-defended, high-value targets," the Iraqi military took them at their word. The Iraqis added two plus two and came to the perfectly logical conclusion that the war was likely to start with a surprise attack on the capital by F-117s, which, because of the relatively small number of LO aircraft available, would be followed by large-scale conventional assaults. This prospect did not unduly disturb the people charged with defending Baghdad.

Following long-held Soviet counterair doctrine, the Iraqis were confident that "their success [would] be measured not by the aircraft destroyed, but rather in the number of bombs or missiles that [would] miss their targets because a pilot had to evade SAMs or AAA (antiaircraft artillery)."[17] In the end, the Iraqis believed that whether or not an infidel jet could be seen by radar was largely irrelevant; it would still have to fly through the dense fires thrown up from a defensive network rivaling that of the Vladivostok and Moscow areas—one that was certainly more concentrated than anything an American flyer would have had to face over the Soviet bloc countries of eastern Europe. This idea of achieving victory through the suppression, rather than the attrition, of an enemy force was well understood by the Iraqis and was the guiding principle behind a wide variety of tactical

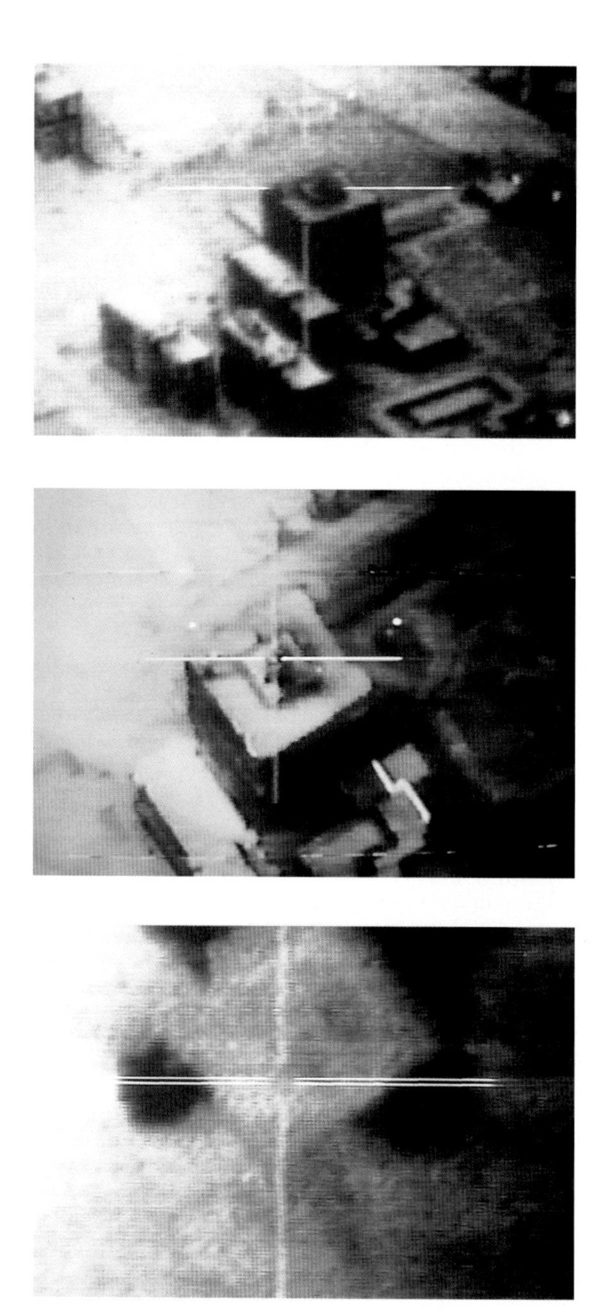

The view on Mark Lindstrom's display screen as his infrared acquisition transitions from its forward-looking to its downward-looking system. As his Black Jet pulls past the new Iraqi Air Force Headquarters building, its four walls are seen exploding outward. DOD

innovations used by some west-Asian and European armies as far back as those in the eastern Roman Empire. The armies of Byzantium, for example, would have their archers send showers of arrows down on an adversary, knowing that few of their enemy would be killed but that the well-timed, concentrated barrage would tend to disorganize an opponent and divert the foe's attention at critical times during a battle. Events would later prove that the stealth pilots were not easily distracted.

Prudence dictated that at the first sign that the long-awaited Mother of All Battles was upon them, virtually all the nearly 1,300 triple-A pieces in the Baghdad area would begin shooting into the air even if they had no visible targets. The city on the Tigris would become one massive "pillar of fire that the Yankee lackeys of Zionist imperialism would not dare enter."[18] Prudence also dictated that complete faith would not be placed in the capital's defenses, and Western reporters in Baghdad noted that "the Iraqis evacuated key personnel and documents in the days before the bombing." According to the London *Times'* correspondent, Marie Colvin, "the Foreign Ministry, the day before [the attack] started, suddenly had a new phone number and an unknown location."[19] From the Iraqi perspective, it was a good thing that some agencies took such precautions, since the air campaign did not unfold as expected.

At 1:30am on Thursday, January 17, US Navy ships in the Red Sea and the Persian Gulf initiated the long-awaited air campaign with multiple launches of Tomahawk land attack missiles (TLAMs) at "soft" Baghdad area targets like communications relay stations and municipal powerplants, which did not require a pilot's eyes on them for instant BDA. The passage of the TLAMs across Iraqi territory was detected by the Iraqis' IADS or ground observers at roughly 2:30am, and confirmed within moments. Baghdad's triple-A came on line at roughly 2:35am. CNN's international editor in Atlanta, Georgia, Eason Jordan, received a frantic call from correspondent Bernard Shaw pleading, "It's happening, it's happening! Get me on, get me on!" at 6:35pm Eastern Standard Time.[20]

All along Iraq's southern border, the screen of forward-deployed radar sites was virtually whited out by the jamming of EF-111A Ravens, but several minutes later, at 2:39am, more evidence surfaced that a full-scale assault was underway when a pair of surveillance radar sites roughly 200mi southwest of Baghdad went off-line. The sites, near the Saudi town of Ar'ar, had been struck by a US helicopter force made up of Army AH-64 Apache shooters and USAF MH-53J Pave Low III pathfinders. This attack was soon followed by a similar raid far to the east near Iraq's sole naval base, Umm Qasr, by Marine AH-1W SuperCobras. These radars were obliterated with great speed and violence, and adjacent units were immediately aware that they had been attacked, although the extent of the damage was unknown at that time. The triple-A in Baghdad, meanwhile, continued to thunder and rattle.

At the intercept operations center (IOC) near Nukhayb, Iraq, which was the reception point for information from the now-destroyed radars near Ar'ar, the path of two noisy Ravens was monitored as they escorted formations of F-15E Eagles and GR Mk. 1 Tornados to the fixed Scud sites near the Jordanian border. Located 160mi southwest of the capital, this IOC coordinated all air defense efforts in the region. As the center's personnel passed information through IADS communications links to the Iraqi Air Force Headquarters in Baghdad, the southeast sector operations center (SOC) at Tallil AB near Nasiriyah, Iraq, and the four southern airfields where fighter interceptors were based, they had no inkling that a laser-guided 2,000lb bomb was already plummeting toward their ziggurat-shaped bunker.

Time-lapse shot of dense antiaircraft fires slicing into the Middle Eastern sky. The Iraqis were confident that the advantages of stealth technology would prove to be irrelevant in the face of such concentrations. The fire was even more dense than it looks, since only one out of five or eight rounds—the tracer—is seen here. Inset: destroyed and abandoned ZSU-23-4s at an Iraqi airfield overrun by US ground forces. Pilots often described its unfocused fire as looking like a pinwheel from above. US Army

Maj. Greg Feest's Black Jet was actually positioned behind the stealth force closing on Baghdad, but, as in Panama, he was again striking the first blow. Pulling away from his target, he kept his eyes riveted on the autotracker cross hairs displayed on the cockpit's IR screen. "I saw the bomb go in. I saw it penetrate," said Feest. "Then the explosion came out the hole the bomb had made and the doors blew off the bunker. I turned to my next target. I looked back and that was the first time I had ever seen anyone shooting at me. They started shooting as soon as my bomb went off. I thought, 'Boy, I'm glad I'm through there and don't have to fly through that.'" The major's next target was the section operations center (SOC) at an air base named H2 near Ar-Rutba in western Iraq, almost 20 minutes away. He turned forward and was surprised at what he saw: "It was the same as downtown Baghdad. Tracers, flashes, flack all over the place....The whole country came alive....Looking out and seeing what was in the target area was scary. I had to go into that stuff."[21]

Iraq's National Air Defense Operations Center–SOC in Baghdad saw the Nukhayb IOC go offline at 2:51am, and lost communications with the SOC at Tallil AB about a minute later when the center was struck by Capt. Blake Bourland. The Iraqis at the center knew that air bases H2 and H3 in the west would soon be under attack, and that lumbering cruise missiles from the Gulf were moving up the river valleys toward the capital; the cruise missiles from the Red Sea had probably not been detected. It is also probable that, in spite of the intense US jamming effort, Iraq's IADS was able to perceive that two large formations of strike aircraft were beginning to move in from the southeast and southwest. Although expected, the F-117 attack on the capital had not yet materialized; the triple-A continued to boom, with only occasional lulls when batteries shut down to allow overheated gun barrels to cool.

"They were shooting up in the sky because they felt we were coming, but they didn't have a clue to where we were coming from," said Getchell.[22] It soon became apparent that whether or not the stealth aircraft were going to make an appearance, two immense strikes were going to converge on Baghdad sometime after the TLAMs' impacts. It had been a long 20 minutes since the capital's air defenses had been activated, and the eruption of triple-A still tore at the night sky. If a halt was not called soon to let the overworked guns cool, many would become permanently damaged and be virtually useless when the conventional aircraft—which the Iraqi's *knew* were coming—reached the city. At roughly 2:56am, the order to cease fire was given and a deafening stillness descended over the still brightly lighted city.

The approaching stealth pilots had viewed the fireworks over Baghdad with some apprehension, but were far too focused on their IR sensor displays and the smaller MFDs flanking them to give much of a look. The relief was genuine, however, when the triple-A seemed just to blink off—almost as if someone had simply pulled a plug. Converging on the capital from all points of the compass, the pilots had already changed their onboard computer from Nav mode to Attack, and turned to new headings at the initial points (IPs). All eyes were glued to their sensor display as autotrackers positioned cross hairs on the still-distant, fuzzy images their INS computed as target positions. Beneath them, long jewellike strings of headlights could be clearly seen as automobiles streamed out of the besieged city.

Each pilot made scores of critical checks—and made them again. Were altitude, heading, and air speed correct? Was the computer in Attack mode? With a flip of the master arm switch, the weapons systems removed the locks that prevented accidental release of ordnance. "At ten miles, the pippers [cross hairs] covered two zip codes," said one pilot, but IR images of the targets were rapidly becoming more distinct as the Black Jets sped past the IPs. INSs were now running down in thousands of feet instead of miles, and individual buildings and streets were becoming clear. Target photos on leg boards were instantly scanned to ensure that what was on the sensor displays matched where the pilots were flying. A small jump in azimuth marked the transition from the FLIR to DLIR sensors. Each pilot intensely studied the glowing display screen in front of him in an effort to detect any minute moves in the cross hairs' position, then delicately moved the finger tip target "slew button" on the throttle back on the designated mean point of impact—the precise aim point where the LGB would do the most good.

Following cues from symbology on the MFDs and head-up display positioned above them, the pilots corrected for crosswinds that might cause just enough drift for their bombs to miss the targets. The stealth pilots agreed with the computer logic displayed, and depressed the red "pickle" buttons ten seconds prior to release, to give the weapons computers their "consent" to drop the bombs. The snapping open of one or both bomb bays was sig-

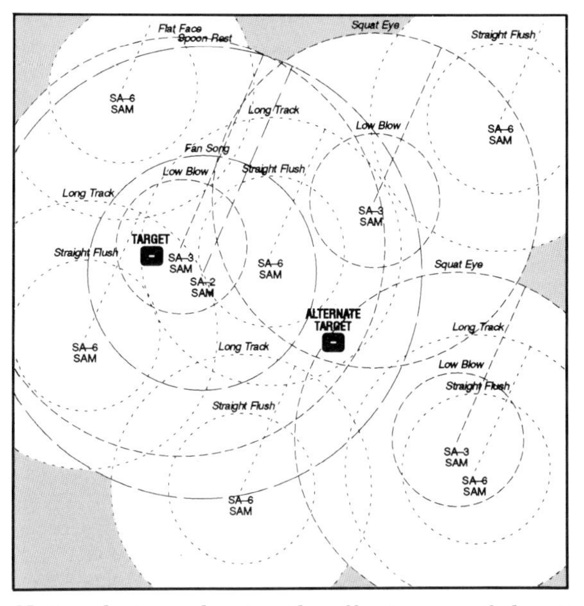

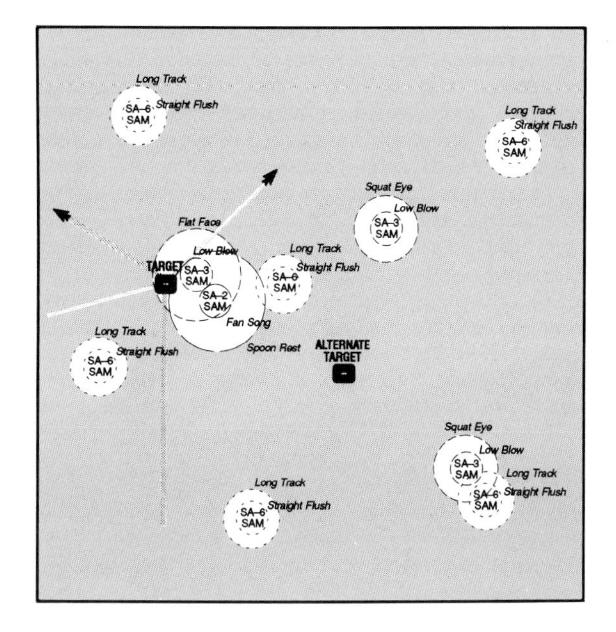

Notional views showing the effectiveness of threat radars in a 340km by 340km defense area against conventional aircraft (left) and the F-117A (right).

naled by the flash of the Door Open lights on the weapons panels. The planes began to vibrate, and wind noise picked up as the door or doors hit the air stream. A *ka-chunk* and a slight bounce of the now-2,000lb-lighter planes told the pilots that their bombs were on their way to the targets. Some pilots had depressed the Target Designator (TD) buttons to start the laser designators operating before the drops, whereas others only lased for the last few seconds of their bombs' roughly half-minute flight. The pilots kept the laser spots on aim points during preplanned turns from the targets, and poured on as much speed as their aircraft could take. "One thing is certain," Maj. Eskridge later said. "Nobody has ever been able to egress a target fast enough. Nobody. Ever."[23]

From their ninth-floor suite at the Al-Rasheed Hotel, correspondents Bernard Shaw and John Holliman of CNN were asking their colleague Peter Arnett, who had been a reporter in Vietnam, about what they'd witnessed over the last half-hour: Why hadn't the city's lights been blacked out? Would the US planes return for another attack? Had B-52s been flying so high overhead that they couldn't be heard? The discussion continued with millions of television viewers listening in, including some particularly interested parties in Washington, DC, and Riyadh. Shaw commented, "We haven't heard any planes yet, Peter," as the low, moaning tones of an air raid warning began to rise over the city. "Now the sirens are sounding for the first time," said Arnett. "The Iraqis have informed us—*SSSSSSSSSSS* ."[24]

At CENTAF Headquarters, Maj. Mark B. ("Buck") Rogers, who had been sent upstairs from the Black Hole to monitor the television, soon called back down: "Baghdad just went off the air!" Wild cheers immediately filled the windowless basement. Five hundred miles away at the McDonnell Douglas compound, off-duty airmen packed around the TV howled, "Absolutely!" and slammed each other on the back. In Washington, President Bush looked up from ABC News as the clock on the Oval Office wall struck seven times. He remarked, "This is just the way it was scheduled," to the few close advisers with him, and sent Press Secretary Marlin Fitzwater out to the press room to announce, "The liberation of Kuwait has begun."[25]

At precisely 3:00am Baghdad time, Marcel Kerdavid's LGB crashed through the dome of the Al-Kark Communications Tower, the space needle that rose 370 feet from the west bank of the Tigris in the

Pilot and ground crew ready their Black Jet for a twilight launch. USAF

very heart of the city. The bomb penetrated deep inside its bulbous, antenna-studded top to detonate among the delicate electronic systems that broadcast television signals to Iraq—and beamed transmissions from Western news agencies to satellites for relay to the United States and Europe. Only CNN, which had established an audio, land-line link through Jordan as a back-up, was able to continue live coverage, and that was minus the visuals.

Within seconds, Capt. Paul Dolson dropped a slender, thick-cased penetrator through the hardened roof of the 14-story Al-Karak skyscraper housing the main telephone and telegraph office directly across the river from the similarly named space needle; this facility was often referred to on strike plans as the "AT&T building." Capt. Mark Lindstrom planted another penetrator through a weak point on top of the new Iraqi Air Force Headquarters building, and Getchell headed for the National Air Defense Operations Center–SOC. The reawakened defenders of Baghdad fought back with a fury. From the cockpits of their Black Jet, the stealth pilots beheld a cloud of dense antiaircraft fire as it seemed to rise in slow motion from the broad expanse of the city, then climb to heights well above their attack altitudes—a mass of ordnance even more thick and deadly than it looked, since only about one in five rounds was manufactured to display a trace. All hoped they would not be the one struck by the Golden BB—the randomly fired round that could kill a person just as surely as one that was aimed.

Traveling through the fireworks one minute behind Capt. Dolson, Jerry Leatherman ignored the burning sky and focused on the looming target Dolson had just struck. The hole punched in the roof of the Al-Karak by Dolson's GBU-27A/B penetrator was the aim point for Leatherman's two standard GBU-10s. The GBU-27A/B and the GBU-10 were both 2,000lb weapons, but the GBU-10 had a thinner, traditional casing and thus contained more explosives for a greater blast effect.

Released seconds apart, both of Leatherman's bombs arced through the sky, carried forward by the momentum imparted from his aircraft. Closing on the target, their Paveway II seekers picked up the beam of laser energy directed from the Black Jet and tracked it "into the basket," where the bombs gutted the building's interior.

"You lase only the last few seconds," explained Leatherman, "mainly to maintain energy on the bomb, because if it's got a 30-second time of flight and you start lasing right away, the thing starts to see it and will start trying to guide. As it starts to do that, it starts losing its energy as it's going down, because of the porpoise effect. Whereas [if] you just let it go, the computer shuts off the laser at release, knows the bomb's time of fall, and fires the laser at the optimum time. Then those last few seconds, you start having a guide then, and [the bomb] impacts with a lot higher angle."[26] Once the LGB has struck its target, it's time to, as Col. Getchell put it, "get the hell out of there."[27]

Pulling away, Leatherman turned to look at the smoking skyscraper, and for the first time was able to get a good look at the mass of ordnance he was passing through. "There were greens, reds, some yellows, and you could see little white flashes all over—the airbursts. There were lots of reds," said Leatherman. "You could tell the difference between the triple-A and SAMs. You could see the rockets. As they'd go off, you'd see them move around as they were trying to guide on something, whereas the tracers would just move in a straight line. The 23mms—ZSU-23-4s—looked like pinwheels the way the Iraqis were using them. They've got four barrels on a chase; it looked like they'd just start firing and spin 'em around. When you looked down on them from the air, they looked like those red pinwheel fireworks."[28]

Long after that night, Ralph Getchell still marveled at the quantity of metal thrown into the air. "When you look at this kind of [strike] footage, it is easy to forget what is going on at the same time the bombs are falling. The pilot looks at an eight-inch screen, but there is a war going on outside. For example, that first night Jerry [Leatherman] and I were in the first wave of ten that hit downtown, the town lit up like Las Vegas. If you take every Washington 4th of July you ever saw with all the fireworks going up in the sky, that is what Baghdad looked like....It took a lot of concentration while the pilots were being shot at, to keep the crosshairs right on the target so we could destroy it."[29]

More command-and-control, leadership, and communications facilities were struck in the capital. One site that Gen. Schwarzkopf took a great deal of personal interest in—and was later able happily to state "had been annihilated"[30]—was Lee Gustin's target just east of Baghdad's international airport. Surrounded by a huge engineered lake, the palatial residence–command center was believed by some intelligence sources to be the most likely place to find Saddam Hussein that night.

After striking the capital, the stealth pilots peeled away from the deadly skies over Baghdad, and those who still carried a second bomb headed for their next target. Kerdavid struck the deep National Command alternate bunker at the North Taji military complex, but results were apparently less-than-hoped-for, since two more unsuccessful F-117 strikes would be made there in the coming weeks. The giant bunker would not be destroyed until the final days of the war when F-111F Ardvarks would drop two specially developed, deep-penetrating GBU-28s. Other pilots had better luck, however, destroying a telecommunications center at Ar-Ramadi and the SOC at Tallil.

The Black Jets' exit from the capital was followed by a half-dozen-or-so TLAM strikes that blasted government ministries and district-sized telephone exchanges between 3:06am and 3:11am. The strikes would continue sporadically over the next 24 hours as agog Western reporters and Iraqis watched the cruise missiles trundle along less than 100ft above the city's boulevards, making sharp turns at preregistered street corners and proceeding to their destination, where they exploded in midair. But in these first few minutes, through its outlying IOCs and the remaining national radars, Baghdad's still-operational SOC got its first good look at the two mammoth conventional strike packages converging on it—the long-awaited attack on the capital. The area's 76 missile batteries were poised and ready to take revenge for the Americans' assault on their homeland, and around 3:25am, began launching showers of SA-2, SA-3, SA-6, SA-8, and Roland missiles at targets that had moved beyond the protection of jamming aircraft.

What the ground radars had seen, however, were not strike aircraft but drones designed to give off the active and passive radar signatures simulating real planes. Most of these 137 tactical air-launched decoys (TALDs) released by Navy jets were successfully engaged by the missiles and were

A maintainer talks over the roar of jet engines to his crew chief. USAF

obliterated within moments. Unfortunately for the Iraqis, while the TALDs were soaking up their SAMs, the radars that controlled the antiaircraft missiles and searched for American aircraft were themselves marked for destruction by HARMs fired from F-4G Wild Weasels and F/A-18 Hornets. Over 200 HARMs were in the air simultaneously, homing in on the threat radars. Within a few minutes after 3:30am, most of the tactical radars in the Baghdad area were destroyed. At 3:35am, the lights finally went out in the capital, possibly because of TLAM and ALCM strikes on power facilities, but triple-A continued to fill the air in surges and the main telecommunications skyscraper was glowing from the internal fires that raged within.

As the Nightstalkers rendezvoused with their tankers, the Ghost Riders were pulling ever closer to their targets. For Al Whitley, who had chosen to fly with them, it was a sobering experience. "I've got to tell you," he said, "in retrospect I really wondered if it was a very smart decision. Because on that second wave—the weather was great that night—I can tell you that out there, at 100 miles plus, you could look out there following the horizon of Baghdad, and it looked like a charcoal grill on the 4th of July. It was just a red glow, and the closer you got, the brighter and brighter the glow got. I mean, I couldn't believe it, 100 miles plus and I could see the city. I wished like hell it wasn't what I knew it was, because I'd seen triple-A before."[31]

"That second wave [was also] complicated by the fact that as we went in, the guys from the first wave were coming out," said the colonel. "And remember, you're maintaining radio silence; you're not talking to these guys. It took a lot of planning to make sure everybody had precise routes to fly and precise altitudes, to be in a precise place at a precise time. There's nothing worse in a double reverse than having two guys run into each other."[32] Reaching Baghdad at 4:00am, just as hundreds of Coalition jets began their attacks on Iraqi airfields to the south, Whitley found that the skies over the city were as bad as they looked during the run in. "I could look all the way around my cockpit and it was a giant 4th of July display from the surface to 15,000 or 20,000 feet in every direction....Once the first bomb hit, they knew we were up there; they just didn't know where. It was kind'a like duck hunting before the sun comes up. You can hear'em and you know they're flying overhead. But you have a helluva time bagging your limit under those conditions."[33]

The Air Force Headquarters had been revisited, as had the National Air Defense Operations Center–SOC, in the capital. IOCs at Al-Taqaddum AB, in the lakes region of Iraq, and Ar-Rutba, in the west of Iraq, were struck, along with leadership and communications facilities from the Jordanian border to Kuwait. With the destruction of the three SOCs closest to Saudi Arabia, only the one at Kirkuk AB, far to the north and temporarily beyond the Black Jets' reach, remained on-line. For all practical purposes, Iraq's carefully built multibillion-dollar IADS had been neutralized. Repeat visits to these facilities and certain IOCs in the nights to come would keep it that way. The country's fantastic number of triple-A weapons would still make lower altitudes a deadly place to be, but the American and Coalition air forces could operate relatively unhindered over about 10,000 feet.

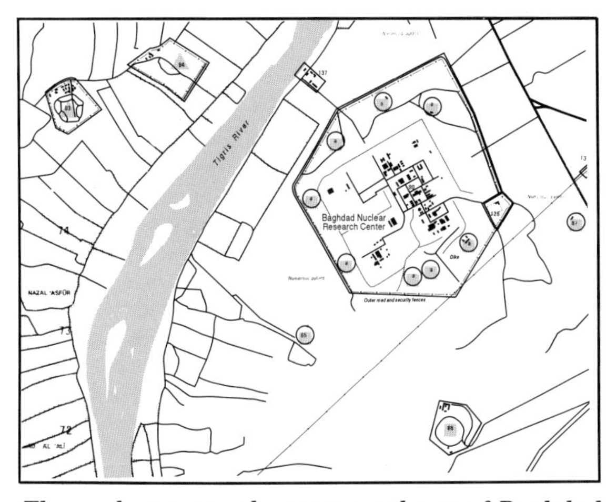

The nuclear research center southeast of Baghdad was nearly completely surrounded by a mammoth dike, which made even the largest structures it protected look like children's building blocks from the air. Built after a successful F-16 strike by the Israelis in 1982 that set Saddam Hussein's nuclear program back a decade, it was designed to make low-flying attackers pop up during the final run to the center's numerous targets, disturbing their aim and also making them more vulnerable to triple-A. The triangles on the map represent the locations of permanently sited SAM facilities guarding the complex, and the squares represent permanently sited triple-A batteries. The batteries within the perimeter road are atop the huge dike. Defense Mapping Agency

The Iraqis' dismal performance appeared to be a result of their having prepared to refight the air war over Vietnam. They, of course, knew about the F-117, but didn't anticipate the variety of ways it, or even the venerable old B-52s, would be employed. That HARMs would have vastly improved capabilities over the similar Vietnam-era Shrike missiles was apparently not anticipated, and the Iraqis' belief that ECMs would have only a limited effect on their IADS's ability to operate was typified by the comments made by an Indian Air Force vice–air marshal: "It should not come as a surprise that the first targets in this war were the radars whose operating frequencies were below about 500 MHz, eg., Knife Rest, Spoon Rest, Flat Face, Squat Eye etc., [since these could not] be jammed [and] nor could the anti-radar missiles be used against them."[34] That this was said months after the results of the Gulf War's ECM operations were widely known, seems remarkable and prompted one stealth pilot to comment, "Wow! Is that what the Soviets tell them? If they really believe that, they're going to get creamed if they get themselves in a war anytime soon."[35]

Untold numbers of Iraqi officers, some quite senior, lost their life after being stampeded into "impregnable" bunkers during the prolonged opening phase of the air campaign that preceded the actual attack on Baghdad. Gen. Charles Horner's counterpart, Gen. Muzahim Saab Hassan, was one of the few to escape death that night. According to Soviet officials, he was arrested and executed several days later when the extent of the damage to the IADS became fully known, and the hundred-plus infidel aircraft claimed destroyed were found to be mostly decoys.

Not all smart bombs had found their mark, of course, plus some very worthwhile targets had even been removed from target lists and put into the no-go category if the risk to civilians was considered too great. Thankfully, the nature of the F-117's precision munitions and delivery system kept both eventualities to a minimum, and for example, the stealth pilots were able to strike the main Baghdad telephone exchange even though it was located just across a wide boulevard from the Mustashfa Faydi, a hospital. Before they were kicked out of the country, Western newspeople caused much gnashing of teeth among the Iraqi leadership because of their filing of report after report describing how the only collateral damage around most attack sites was little more than a few broken windows. A 30ft crater blasted by a wayward LGB across the river from the presidential palace—containing sewer water and a capsized car—became a regular stop for TV cameramen, primarily because it was a rarity.

At least some of the misses that did occur were caused by laser locks being broken by thin layers of wispy clouds around 5,000 feet that aircraft found themselves passing over during the final, critical seconds of their attack run. Central Iraq was fairly clear during the first two waves, but elsewhere, spotty clouds were sometimes very heavy. A taste of things to come was obtained by Capt. Rob Donaldson, who found that he "was able to disregard the intense triple-A and SAMs" but complained, "the most frustrating part of it was that I couldn't find my target due to cloud cover."[36] Col. Whitley had brought along a Snickers bar for the return trip, but allowed himself only half because he knew that one of his bombs had missed its aim point. The night's third wave of eight Black Jets arrived just as a heavy bank of clouds rolled over Iraq, and scored only five hits. Weather during this time period normally resulted in about 13 percent cloud cover, but this winter turned out to be the worst in 14 years, with an average of 39 percent of the sky blotted out.

Of the 60 LGBs carried by F-117s that night, 11 were not released because the pilots were either not able to get a positive identification of the target or were not confident that their weapons would guide properly. Of 49 LGBs dropped, only 28 actually hit their aim point. Most of the misses were at outlying targets, where the extreme care exerted in heavily populated areas was less closely adhered to. Gen. Horner reported to his disappointed boss, Schwarzkopf, that whereas F-111s, flying below cloud cover, successfully attacked 70 percent of their targets, the Black Jets "dropped just 55 percent of their bombs on target."[37] Many of the sorties, however, were redundant strikes, to ensure that critical Iraqi sites were destroyed. The bottom line was that the stealth pilots had taken out the most heavily defended strategic sites and cleared the way for unstealthy Coalition aircraft to operate with some degree of safety. "I generally put the F-117s against the Baghdad targets," said Horner, "since those are the ones they could hit with relative—and I use the word carefully—with relative immunity; where we would have lost [conventional] airplanes."[38]

Winging their way back to friendly airspace, the stealth pilots believed that the cost of the night's victory had been high. They were convinced they wouldn't see the face of some of their friends when they landed at King Khalid. "I came out of there on that first night and went, 'Whew...I survived that one!'" said Capt. Donaldson. "But on the way back, I really thought that we had lost some guys due to the heavy volume of bullets and missiles that were thrown up in the air."[39]

As air crews have done since combat aircraft first took to the skies in World War I, the ones at King Khalid counted off the Black Jets as they landed. Miraculously, not only had all the stealth pilots survived, but none of their aircraft had even been nicked. Clearly, though, the times on target (TOTs) were going to have to be modified if unnecessary losses were to be avoided in future missions.

The original idea had been for follow-up aircraft striking the same site to hit at one-minute intervals in order to allow enough time for surface winds to push dust and smoke away from the aim points. This did not work out, as can be very clearly seen on the strike tapes of the second aircraft to hit certain targets. "The first TOTs were where we learned the big lesson," said Maj. Leatherman. "Let's put it this way: we didn't anticipate as dense a triple-A for so long. I'd been told that known triple-A pieces—and this was before they put them on every building out there—was somewhere around 3,000 pieces in Baghdad. Some crazy number. [In fact, the number of triple-A *pieces* in the Baghdad area was judged to be at least 1,267 at the onset of the air campaign. Located at 380 separate sites, many were twin- and quad-barreled weapons, which brought the total number of *barrels* to over 3,000.] So, after we did [one-minute intervals] the first night, we went back and changed the game plan. If somebody was going to have to hit a target after somebody else in the same area, we were going to vary the time. We figured it usually took anywhere from eight to 15 minutes for the triple-A to finally die down. As long as there's not explosions, they finally get tired of it and quit shooting. But they sure did it for a long time."[40]

The revamped sequencing was immediately initiated and proved its worth. "[The Iraqis] knew they were at war the second night and they had every gun manned," said Capt. Miles Pound. "They were more than willing to use them."[41] Col. Whitley firmly believed that "they wanted one of those Black Jets badly," and added, "they tried their best to get one of the F-117s, if nothing else, for political reasons and a morale boost....We all knew there is one airplane this man [Hussein] would have loved to have had. You can bet there was a great deal of effort going on to do whatever they could to get one of our black jets. I think the Iraqis realized they were in for a real tussle. This was not Vietnam. [We weren't] going to be spraying bombs all over the countryside....This was going to be precision attack."[42]

For the time being, however, the wretched weather that had flowed down from Turkey would take much of the "precision" out of the "attack." On the second night of the war, the wing launched 12 Nightstalkers in wave one and an equal number of Ghost Riders in wave two, although one of the 415th's planes suffered an air abort and had to return to base. Operating against a set of targets similar to those on the first night, the fighters experienced no-drops and misses that limited the number of hits to just 23, but these well-placed bombs went a long way toward further degrading the Iraqi leadership's command and control. A pilot from the

415th even bagged one of the Iraqi's three Adnan-2s, which were Soviet-built Il-76 transports converted into early warning aircraft by the addition of French-designed Tiger G radars.

Visibility continued to deteriorate. It was so bad on the third night of the air campaign, when the weather front stalled over Iraq, that the wing scored only six hits. Fewer misses and no-drops occurred the following night, as clearing skies allowed effective attacks against 17 targets. The stealth wing attempted better to profit from the steadily improving picture on the fifth night, by delaying the launch of both waves until after midnight. However, two 415th air aborts and a 416th ground abort, combined with "unreliable aircraft systems and target acquisition errors,"[43] all conspired to limit direct hits to 17 for the second time in a row. Interesting diversions from the normal target lists during this time frame were strikes conducted against twin SAM sites containing American-made Hawk missile batteries. These weapons had been captured during Iraq's invasion of Kuwait and were targeted on the third and fifth nights of the war respectively, by the Nightstalkers and the Ghost Riders.

Both squadrons were able to take advantage of excellent fighting weather on January 21–22, and sent streams of Black Jets north to give one of the wing's best performances of the war. Striking in the early morning hours, 14 aircraft of the 416th TFS registered 26 hits and two misses on a wide variety of targets in the Baghdad area, including the Ministry of Defense, the Air Force Headquarters, the GID (Internal Security) Headquarters, the presidential palace and presidential retreat, Hawk sites, telephone exchanges, and a biological warfare facility that the Iraqis later tried to pass off as a baby milk factory. Earlier that night, the 415th had sent up an equal number of aircraft but suffered two air aborts before strikes could be launched against the Air Force Headquarters and a potpourri of communications facilities, plus a command-and-control bunker at Abu Ghurayb. Eight of the squadron's Black Jets also made one pass each at what the wing's unclassified chronology of operations in the Gulf War blandly called "the nuclear research center in Baghdad,"[44] a site Gen. Buster Glosson identified as "one of the three most heavily defended areas in all of Iraq."[45]

The Baghdad Nuclear Research Center—which in some references was called or included the Osirak Nuclear Research Center, the Isis Reactor Building, and the Tuwaythas Research Facility—was located beyond the east bank of a wide bend in the Tigris River, just southeast of the Iraqi capital. It was well within the area covered by the ring of permanent SAM sites surrounding the city, and had its own dedicated SAM sites just across the river. A massive earthen dike protected the quarter-mile-square facility and its four reactors from periodic floods and attack by ground-hugging aircraft. This embankment was also home to an extremely large number of triple-A batteries. The barrier supported so many pieces of artillery, in fact, that Capt. Phil McDaniel, who served on the wing's mission planning cell, was only half-joking when he cracked that there was a gun "about every 30ft along the berm."[46]

Greatly encouraged by the damage inflicted on target and acquisition radars in the Baghdad area, CENTAF went for a full-fledged bite on Saturday, January 19. Seventy F-16s, escorted by F-15Cs and supported by EF-111As and F-4Gs, went after the research center and the nearby Daura Petroleum Refinery, located even deeper in the Baghdad defense zone. The result was two downed F-16s and almost no damage inflicted on the reactors. A combination of bad weather and dense defensive fires disrupted the attack. "When the first airplanes rolled in," said Gen. Charles Horner, "[the Iraqis] started up these smoke pots they had on the levies around the target. Within seconds the whole target was covered with smoke which contributed to the inaccuracy of the F-16 bombing."[47]

The Iraqis were not given a chance to obscure the target on the evening of January 21, when two of the three targeted reactors were destroyed, the third was heavily damaged, and key research facilities at the center were gutted. "The first time [the Iraqis] knew the [F-117s] were there was when the bombs were impacting," said Buster Glosson. "For the next week or so after the initial attack, [the stealth aircraft] would hit a target in Baghdad and then come back over that area to finish destroying the [site]."[48] Ralph Getchell simply commented, "We were very thorough."[49]

Chapter 8

Eye of the Storm

Intellectually, 37th TFW—P personnel knew that stealth worked. They had trained with it, they knew all the numbers, and the experts told them it worked. "Most guys had about 90-percent confidence in the F-117 going into the war, in terms of believing that it could do what they said it could do," said Rob Donaldson.[1] It took a few nights of pummeling Iraqi targets at will before the pilots felt comfortable believing it themselves. Even then, however, "there was always the sneaking, underlying suspicion," said Matt Byrd, "that Saddam [Hussein] had some big secret weapon or some ace up his sleeve that he was going to use—chem[ical weapon]s were a part of that, and Scuds."[2]

Hussein did his best to perpetuate this myth of invincibility, but, although it did have some effect on decisions made during the air campaign, the end result was still the same. Iraq's military infrastructure was systematically picked apart by Coalition air forces. Despite being hampered by the weather and other problems associated with massive human endeavors like war, the 37th TFW—P did its job extraordinarily well and was a central part of the war effort. By the end of the air campaign, stealth pilots had racked up over 40 percent of the Coalition's strategic sorties.

The night after the 416th's big strike against the Baghdad Nuclear Research Center, the squadron found itself having to cut four aircraft from the line-up when they were refragged to a new target from an operation that had already been planned, with less-than-ample time to perform the necessary mission planning. CENTAF was also unable to supply appropriate target photos, which must include shots of not only the aim points but also the run to the target from certain angles. The remaining ten Ghost Riders took off on schedule at midnight to pound the main signals intelligence station and transportation facilities in the capital, a VIP residence at Abu Jahish, missile handling facilities, and other targets in Iraq.

Earlier that evening, 14 Nightstalkers had launched at dusk for a mass strike at Balad Southeast AB north of Baghdad. Although one 415th pilot was forced to divert to an alternate target, his buddies saturated the airfield with 21 direct hits before heading for home. The success at Balad Southeast, however, was not what it seemed.

"The airfield had what we called third-generation aircraft shelters," said Jerry Leatherman. "I think intel said they were built by Yugoslavians. Anyway, they were very similar to the shelters that we were living in down at Khamis. They were top quality. We went there one night to blow them up because the Iraqi aircraft had gone underground, but we didn't drop our penetrators, our 'hard' bombs; we dropped [GBU-]10s, which are 'soft' bombs. Well, those babies bounced off like tennis balls."[3] Why were GBU-10s used when mission planners at Checkmate, the Black Hole, and King Khalid all knew that these facilities weren't typical "10 meat"—half-moon-shaped shelters with eight inches to perhaps a foot of concrete applied over curved, corrugated metal sections? These were the Big Wahines, designed to withstand even nearby nuclear detonations. The answer had less to do with air operations against Iraq than it did with what was being broadcast every day, indeed every hour, on television.

Reporters, hard pressed for unique stories,

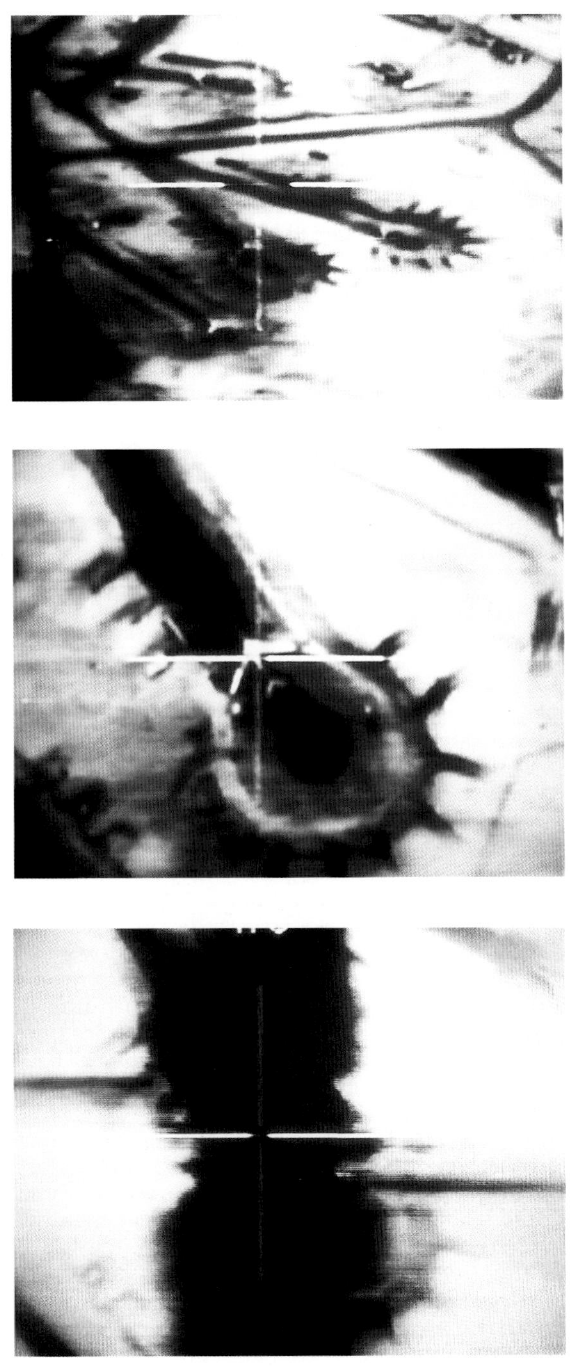

Iraqi Badgers spotted in open revetments, pipper's on target, and boom! USAF

quickly began to be frustrated by a pace of events that did not conform to evening news and morning paper deadlines. When nothing the pack considered to be decisive occurred between the opening Thursday night bombing and Sunday, the inevitable "War Drags into Second Week" stories began to appear. The hard news that had dominated the first few days was generally supplanted as the opinions of pundits and "experts" were pushed to the fore. One prime theme of this discourse revolved around a single burning question: What is the Magic Bullet— the war-winning miracle weapon—that will bring victory to Saddam Hussein or to the United States and its Coalition allies? The elusive Scud missile, or its Yankee nemesis, the Patriot missile? That scourge of trench warfare poison gas, or advanced American technology?

In the developing climate, certain weapons systems took on almost mystical qualities, and any perceived weakness—especially if it was with a US weapon—was sure to be jumped on as a sign that its owners might as well cash in their chips because the war for them was as good as lost. Although such bizarre notions don't track well with reality, they can certainly affect public opinion if the drumbeat is loud and long—encouraging Hussein and his supporters to try to outlast his enemies while simultaneously pressuring those same enemies to leave Hussein with his ill-gotten gains. Much as the stealth pilots might have wanted to get on with their job in the most efficient manner possible, the wider realities of flying a "wonder weapon" were bound to have an effect sooner or later.

At the time that pilots of conventional Coalition aircraft found CENTAF lowering their minimum safe altitude from 15,000 to 12,000, then 8,000ft, the Black Jet's minimum was actually raised, even though its best weapons, the GBU-27–series bombs, could be employed most effectively from medium altitudes. "After about a week," said one stealth pilot, "they really started to worry about somebody getting hit by all that triple-A. We could accurately drop 10s[, which had longer tail fins,] higher than 27s—and that's okay some of the time—but sending a dozen or more guys to those shelters with 10s is pointless. You just waste a bunch of sorties that could have done some good, and turn 'em into a training mission with live bullets."[4] Another pilot remarked that "it became quite an argument. Riyadh tried to convince us—and I think themselves—that the 10s would work."[5]

Maj. Leatherman admitted that CENTAF "started to get a little antsy because nobody had

Nerve-agent–filled gas bombs built for the internal bay of Soviet- and Chinese-made Badgers. These bombs were uncovered by UN inspectors at Al-Walid AB, Iraq. Wing-mounted aerial gas bombs made for the weapons pylons of Iraq's fighter-bombers were more aerodynamic than these bombs and looked similar to the US Mk-84. UN

been dinged," and that "they basically ordered us to drop 10s on Balad." The following day, he continued, "we said, 'Hey, those things didn't work.' They refragged us to go back there and let us pick the weapons. We picked the penetrators." Leatherman soon found that the failed strike had an unexpected up side. The Iraqis had also paid close attention to the results of the strike. "Evidently," said Leatherman, "because those 10s bounced off of there, the Iraqis thought those shelters were good. They started getting more airplanes and hiding them in there. Then we went back [on night 12] and blew the piss out of all those places, with the penetrators." From that point on, the ATO conveyed all the same information as before but did not specify how the stealth wing was to carry out its attacks. "That was the last time," noted Leatherman, "that they tried to tell us what weapon to put on a target."[6]

The Black Jets continued to operate freely against Iraqi gunners who fired aimlessly in the air, but on numerous occasions, planes had to fly near moonlit clouds, making the aircraft very unstealthy, very fast. "That did happen," said Leatherman, "but it didn't really amount to anything. What we worried about more than the ground stuff [seeing them under the clouds] was if they still had the air threat. If you're just above a cloud deck, with the moon reflecting off it, you can really stick out.... I saw one of the Black Jets one night as our routes were converging. I just happened to look outside because I knew what the attack plan was. I knew there was going to be a guy coming across and just slightly above me. So, I was looking out there just to see if I could see him, and I saw him. It would have been harder, though, if you didn't know where somebody was supposed to be."[7]

As if to emphasize this point, Col. Al Whitley recounted that when one stealth pilot saw what appeared to be an Iraqi Mirage F1 slowly closing on him, a turn of just a few degrees ensured that the threat aircraft's radar would not pick him up. The stealth pilot "felt" that the threat aircraft was being "guided toward him" and was even shining what appeared to be a bright forward landing or dogfighting light in a futile effort visually to detect the Black Jet. This was the only time during Desert Storm that an F-117 was threatened by an Iraqi fighter, and the stealth fighters continued to strike targets with little fear from the air.

Throughout the campaign, the 37th TFW—P returned again and again to chemical and biological warfare targets such as the research laboratories at Salmon Pak and the bunkers at Samarra and Habbaniya where gas-filled artillery shells and chemicals were stored. According to Gen. Glosson, one set of bunkers was the recipient of over 50 Black Jet sorties, and particularly deep bunkers would sometimes require four bombs striking exactly the same spot, one after another, to penetrate down to the munitions. Reviewing the IR video from one such attack, Leatherman pointed out some of its more interesting features: "Here's the hot spot from three other bombs that have impacted this ammo storage bunker. We are sending our fourth guy across here, and it is pretty spectacular results there. He felt that one in the airplane."[8] Attacks were timed to occur just 45 minutes before dawn because whereas darkness was needed to mask the F-117's dash to Saudi airspace, sunlight and increased daytime temperatures would decrease the lethality of both biological spores and poison gas.

The most unique strike against the Iraqi's chemical warfare assets came on the eighth night of the war, when the 416th was refragged at the last minute to attack at Al-Taqaddum, the air base where Chinese- and Soviet-built Badger medium bombers sat in open revetments because they were too large for any of the Iraqis' hangars. "Riyadh got intel reports back that they were loading the Badgers with chemical munitions," said Leatherman, "and was worried that they were going to use them on the guys sitting down there on the line. So, we switched a bunch of guys around and sent them over to Taqaddum. Sure enough, they caught a bunch of 'em just sitting there. Fueled up, for sure, and a lot of vehicles all around them like they were getting ready to launch at first light. We bombed them just before sunrise."[9] When recalling how the big, fully fueled aircraft turned into giant fireballs when struck by GBU-10s, a wistful look came across Capt. Byrd's eyes. "Boy," he said, "those blow up nice."[10] Three of the eight bombers were destroyed, and a raid the following day by conventional jets mopped up three more.

The following night found the 416th ranging across Iraq to strike targets it had never expected to find on its lists: bridges. "We blew up a hell of a lot of bridges," said Leatherman. "We got asked to do the bridges because when the weather was bad in Baghdad, a lot of times it was good over Kuwait. We were an available asset. Only one of the bridges in Basra had been dropped by the guys that were trying to do that, and so Riyadh asked us if we could hit them."[11]

The wing had already taken out a few bridges in Baghdad, primarily because the Iraqis had run fiber-optic cables along them instead of laying the cables across river bottoms where they would be less vulnerable—but the quantity of bridge busting on the ninth night of the war, January 24–25, was considered a bit unusual. The 415th had tried to perform the same mission the previous night, but foul weather forced a squadron record of 23 no-drops. The weather cooperated with the Ghost Riders, though. "They gave us ten guys to go after ten different bridges that were all along the Tigris and Euphrates around the Basra area," recalled Leatherman. "Of the first ten guys, I think six had dropped spans in the water. Then, it was kind of like, 'Hey, you guys can do this?' After that, Riyadh sent us after bridges, and as secondary targets too.

Fiber-optic cables dangle from one of the dozens of bridges destroyed by Team Stealth. US Army

A US soldier examines the hole punched in a hardened roof by an LGB. US Army

If you're weathered out going through Baghdad, any bridge in Iraq is fair game."[12]

The night of January 24–25 also was the first time CENTAF felt secure enough with its control of Iraqi airspace along the Saudi border that it allowed tankers to travel north over Iraq. Coordination problems forced one Black Jet to return to base because of a lack of tanker support, but carrying out the refuelings farther north allowed the first wave of Black Jets enough range to reach out and bomb hardened shelters at Kirkuk and Qayyara West airfields, located well above Baghdad, where Iraqi aircraft had taken refuge from the intense Coalition attacks in the south. A mixed package of ten aircraft from the 415th and 416th squadrons formed a third wave, for the first time since D-day, which was also directed against hardened shelters. Unfortunately, the good luck the wing had been having with weather over the last few days ended abruptly. The wave turned out to be a bust with 19 no-drops and one miss.

The Black Jets were flying more than anyone had anticipated before the war, but CENTAF was compelled to employ them more frequently for a number of reasons: First, the F-117s were needed to help destroy as many Iraqi aircraft as possible before they could flee to Iran. Second, the continuing hunt for Scud mobile missiles had siphoned off other aircraft that would have normally performed that task, such as F-15Es. Third, the wretched weather had disrupted the bombing campaign's original timetable. And, fourth, CENTAF planners, who were primarily from the Ninth USAF instead of the Black Jet's parent Twelfth Air Force, found that the recently declassified plane was much more capable than they had expected.

Adding a third go meant the wing could realistically aim at launching 34 sorties a night, instead of a maximum of 28 sorties when only two waves went up. Originally, the missions were arranged in squadron sets: 415th Nightstalkers—first go; 416th Ghost Riders—second go. Most stealth pilots would have liked to maintain this setup, with previously readied aircraft and the cleanest aircraft from the first go being turned around for the third, but the crush of operations rapidly made this impossible, and for the balance of the air campaign, mixed-squadron packages were the norm. Most of the Black Jets in the Gulf flew "thirtysomething" combat missions, with the Nightstalkers' unnamed number 812 flying a remarkable 42 sorties. Only one aircraft, the Ghost Riders' *Spell Bound*, number 797, never got out of the single digits, finishing the war with eight missions. Even the ground crew of the 416th's bad actor, *Christine*, was able to work its aircraft up to an excellent finish of 39 sorties. The hard-working maintainers, who commonly put in 12–18-hour days as the pace of operations increased, also were able to lever the average turnaround time on the first-go aircraft down to just an hour and a half, enabling earlier launches for the third wave.

CENTAF probably would not have even considered sending over a third wave on more than a sporadic basis if the combat squadrons at King Khalid AB had not been beefed up by the addition of more aircraft from Tonopah. As the 415th TFS prepared for its late-afternoon launch on the second day of

The 416th TFW's AMU aircraft, Magic Hammer, *number 838, is towed from its bay. It finished the war having flown 36 combat missions. Note that although the Ghost Riders' facilities are precisely the same as the Nighthawks' on the inside, they do not have tons of earth and rocks across their top to provide an additional layer of protection and a semblance of camouflage.* USAF

the air campaign, eight aircraft from the 417th TFTS took off from their Nevada home for Langley AFB, where they could be easily staged to Saudi Arabia as "attrition reserves." There was, of course, no attrition. For about a week, the pilots waiting at Langley closely monitored operations out of King Khalid, and the air war as a whole, while doing a little flying to maintain proficiency. CENTAF's increasing reliance on the Black Jet was clearly putting more strain on the forward-deployed assets, however, and about the time the wing was given a heads-up to expect three-wave taskings, the stealth pilots cooling their heels at Langley were told to get themselves ready for a trip to "a hot sandy place." Six aircraft were assigned to the 416th TFS "for maintenance and management,"[13] and lifted into the sky for the long flight east on the same day the wing added a third go. Eventually, the need for more "shooters" at King Khalid necessitated that nearly every current stealth pilot be deployed across the big pond, including many of the trainers and even the commander of the 417th TFTS, Lt. Col. Robert J. ("Bob") Maher.

The make-up of the squadrons was shuffled slightly after the arrival of the supplementary pilots and planes, and the wing was now able to ready as many as three to five extra planes a night, with an additional pair maintaining a contingency alert. Having the spares relieved a lot of pressure but, naturally, did not guarantee full 34-sortie nights. One evening in particular, the gods of war took pleasure in tormenting a flyer who was whisked from plane to plane trying to find one that would work. With time running out—and having performed three sets of walk-arounds, cockpit checks, and so forth on three different Black Jets—he became so frustrated and angry that he flung his $300 custom-made black helmet to the ground, cracking it.

Meanwhile, back at TTR, the depleted training squadron continued to do its job, although at a somewhat attenuated pace. The course had to be lengthened by two months, and the current class was smaller than it had been in years, since some officers were able to delay their scheduled entry into the 37th in order to fight the war with their current unit. For example, instead of going directly to Tonopah, Capt. Tim Veeder put off his port call date and headed for Incirlik AB, Turkey, instead, and "played tag with SA-6s" in his Wild Weasel.[14]

The increased sortie rate in the Gulf, owing to the additional go, at first took its toll on aircraft availability; Gen. Glosson later remarked, "It dipped a little bit toward the middle, but basically we were within a few percentage points of the goal we shoot for in peacetime, about an 85-percent mission capable rate. Toward the end of the war, strangely enough, when we were flying more sorties every day—the airplane likes to fly—that rate went up."[15] By early February, 34 sorties a night was more than just a goal, it was commonplace when weather did not force the cancellation of entire waves or occasional air aborts did not occur. On the night of February 11–12, the 27th of Desert Storm, the wing squeaked up the number of sorties to 35, and it sent aloft 37 Black Jets on the nights of February 21 and 23. As the air campaign reached its climax with the Coalition's assault into Kuwait and southern Iraq, the wing geared up to launch two massive 32-plane waves each night.

After about the first week of combat, the pilots were fully settled into the routine that would carry them through the war—a routine that the British Lancaster bomber crews, who flew nightly missions over Germany in World War II, would find oddly familiar. "Typically, you're pretty tired." said Capt. Byrd. "By the time you got up; got a bite to eat; went to the briefing, which took a couple of hours;

Ground crew check to the left for traffic before pulling their charge beyond the canyonlike taxiway between two sets of four-bay hangars. The white minibus is part of the shuttle system that runs Team Stealth personnel between King Khalid AB and the McDonnell Douglas compound. USAF

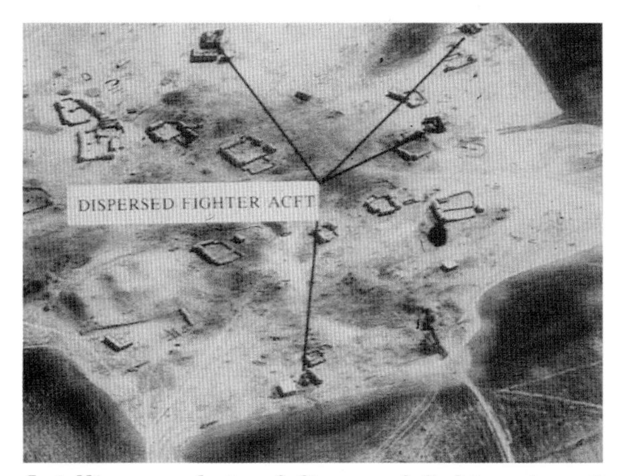

Intelligence photo of dispersed fighter aircraft placed among village houses north of Qayyara West Airfield, February 13, 1991. DIA

stepped, two hours prior to your takeoff, to your airplane; and you got in the airplane and took off—you've already been up for five or six hours. You fly a six-, six-and-a-half-hour mission; you come back and land. By the time you get away from the airplane, it's another hour, so that's seven and a half. By the time you end the debrief with intelligence, review your tape, and fill out the paperwork you've got to do, that's a 15–16-hour day right there. And it's been through some fairly strenuous activity—like getting shot at."[16]

Although it was not unusual for aircraft to be used twice, pilots never flew more than one mission a night. Other than very rare situations where a pilot might go up voluntarily two nights in a row, every other night the pilots would be either off or "pulling a sortie" with Leatherman's crew in the mission planning cell. Consequently, most flyers finished the war with about 20 or 21 combat missions, and those having additional duties on the ground—like Lt. Col. Getchell and Col. Whitley, who both flew 19 missions—or bad luck with the weather ended up with fewer. The pilot with the greatest number of combat sorties was Capt. Rob Donaldson at 23. Pilots could fly any Black Jet in the squadron they were assigned to, and in a pinch, the wing.

Stealth pilots were justifiably proud of their ability both to save the life of other Coalition airmen and to keep down civilian casualties. Some Iraqi activities were clearly designed to entice the forces arrayed against them into performing operations that could be trumpeted as "crimes against the Iraqi people," such as bombing jet aircraft placed among civilian housing or the country's priceless ruins dating from the dawn of civilization. "Hey," said an airman who returned to Iraq's hostile skies time and again, "we weren't blind. It was obvious this guy Saddam was trying to sucker us so that he could do the 'poor, poor, pitiful me' routine....And herding civilians into a com[munications] bunker," he said, angrily referring to the facility the Iraqis called General Shelter 25, "'For protection,' my ass! We were putting bombs through those things like they were made of cheese. The safest place to be, for Christ's sake, was *anyplace* but a bunker. Saddam certainly knew that. That's why him and some of his top guys started living out of Winnebagos."[17] For example, early in the morning of Wednesday, February 13, 1991, a pair of aircraft from the night's third wave dropped one bomb each through the roof of a communications bunker that had reactivated after similar structures had been destroyed. According to Iraq's Foreign Ministry, as many as 400 people were killed in what it called the air raid shelter, many of them women and children. Said Gen. Norman Schwarzkopf, "That was a terrible moment [but] it wasn't a mistake at all to bomb it....It had always been on our target list. Intelligence had confirmed that it was an operating military headquarters both before and after....Every investigation that's been conducted since then has confirmed that it was, in fact, a military target."[18]

The air war moved through its second, third, and fourth weeks with the Black Jets continuing their systematic dismantling of Saddam Hussein's war machine whenever the weather would allow accurate targeting. Many sites had to be revisited time and time again, such as when Black Hole planners had designated more aim points critical to the facilities' function than could be effectively taken out in a single raid. Some target sets simply contained a very large number of things to hit. For example, the dozens of primary and dispersal bases spread throughout Iraq contained 594 aircraft shelters protecting the sixth-largest air force in the world. By the end of the war, 375 of these would end up heavily damaged or destroyed, something that could only be accomplished one shelter at a time. Said a young captain who regularly "visited" Iraqi bases during the war, "They tried to paint bomb damage on some of them, but that was kinda pointless. I'd mark off the ones that had been hit on my [intelligence] photos so I wouldn't plink one

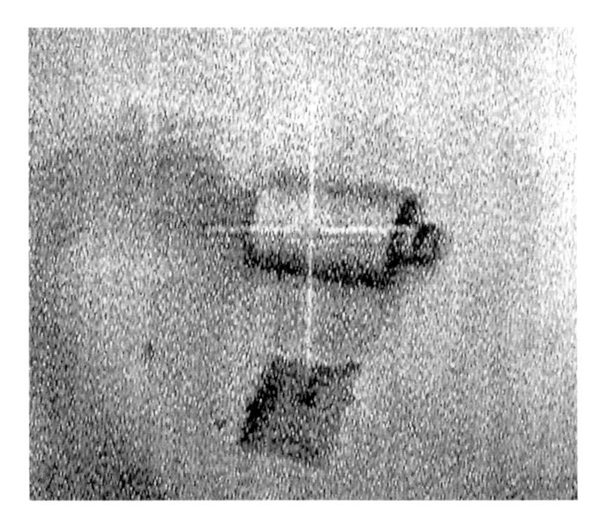

twice. That's what we called it: plinking."[19]

Another type of target suitable for plinking was the extensive network of hiding places for Scud missiles that the Iraqis had constructed in the western part of the country and particularly along the main highway to Jordan. Leatherman found that they "had built what looked like drainage ditches, except that they were large fake concrete culverts built specifically to hide Scud [mobile] missile launchers. They'd just back them right in there. We had targets on , but I can only remember one or two times when we actually had bombs go in and you could see secondary explosions. Hard to tell about those because [the Iraqis] had hundreds of them."[20]

Less ambiguous for the stealth pilots was the huge number of combat sorties that, day by day, they were steadily piling up in a very hostile envi-

An Iraqi HAS targeted for destruction, and the end result of several very thorough goings-over.

ronment, without a single Golden BB even nicking a Black Jet. Then, one night, a Ghost Rider aircraft landed with apparent battle damage. "I wasn't there when it came in," said one pilot, "but I understand people got real excited and were actually *disappointed* to find out that it was just some RAM that popped off during the flight. And I can understand that.... It was something we all expected to happen—to somebody else, of course—but wasn't happening at all. When they thought it finally did happen,... [i]t was like, 'Well, we've gotten this out of the way and nobody got hurt.'"[21]

Col. Whitley remembered that "everybody's first reaction was, 'Oh, my God, the airplane's been hit!' Of course, when you looked at it, that didn't make sense. It just popped. A portion of a fixed surface on the bottom part of the tail had delaminated. It's characteristic of what happens when you go a little too fast, and, it turned out, if you go back and look at the records of the airplane that was produced before it, and the airplane that was produced after it, both of them had the same problem happen over time. So we suspect that somewhere in the production cycle, when those components were constructed, that maybe there was some curing problem or something like that which contributed to problems with the structural integrity."[22]

This is not to say, however, that a number of aircraft weren't put out of action through various mishaps, accidents, and technical problems. Usually it was something common but time-consuming to fix, like a fuel leak that might have maintainers scratching their head for five or six days. On other occasions, it was simple human carelessness. "You're supposed to have a fire truck when you're doing a certain procedure," said Whitley, "and one night, some kid inadvertently hit a switch which filled the cockpit with water. It was no biggie, but the plane was down for two or three days until they dried everything out."[23]

Finally, on the 24th night of the war, the 37th Component Repair Squadron (CRS), the old F-Unit, got a job it could sink its teeth into. The third wave was landing after conducting a ten-plane attack on

One of several different leaflets featuring the Black Jet. They were produced by the Eighth Psychological Operations Task Force in Riyadh and scattered by F-16s at certain Iraqi air bases. The inscription on this one reads, "This location is subject to bombardment! Escape now and save yourselves!" Another leaflet, dropped after a strike, said, "Too late!" 18th Airborne Corps and Fourth Psychological Operations Group, USAF

Team Stealth's "bomb guys" were very proud of their craft. The stenciled inscription on this Mk-84 reads, "Bombs 'R' Us. Made in America. Assembled in Saudi. Detonated in Iraq." T/Sgt. Hans Deffner, USAF

the Samarra chemical bunkers when aircraft number 790, the *Deadly Jester*, blew a nose wheel on landing. Luckily, the pilot was unhurt and the aircraft was moving slow enough that only three probes were damaged on its delicate snout, in addition to the right E-bay panel, which was struck by pieces of the tire. If a similar accident had happened at TTR, with thirsty Black Jets stacked above and only one runway below, more damage may have been done to the multimillion dollar obstruction in an effort to get it out of the way quickly. King Khalid AB, however, was blessed with two runways, and the orbiting aircraft were simply diverted. The *Deadly Jester* was quickly put back into service, and made roughly ten more trips over Iraq, to end the air campaign with an even 30 combat missions.

The component repair squadron received no more customers with this degree of damage. The Iraqis' failure to hit any stealth aircraft during the war is even more remarkable than is first apparent, since the threat from triple-A did not appreciably diminish. Axel Foley of the 415th TFS was amazed at the continuous, thundering response from the Iraqi gunners. "You couldn't believe you were flying through such heavy defenses and weren't getting hit," he exclaimed. "It's amazing that this stuff's flying all around, and you're just cruising through it trying to hit your target....I'm still amazed."[24]

The steady triple-A made it difficult for the pilots to focus on their mission. "A couple of nights I felt the explosions, and the plane would move," said Capt. Don Chapman of the 417th TFTS. "I'd try to concentrate on the target, and on avoiding collateral damage. I didn't want to hit civilians. Sometimes I'd climb off the target after a successful mission and look over my shoulder and think 'What am I doing out here?'"[25] Miles Pound, Foley's squadron mate, found that manipulating his position in the cockpit helped keep the deadly triple-A from his sight. "My own technique," he said, "was to run the [ejection] seat down, so I wasn't distracted by what was going on outside. The lower you get in the cockpit, the less you can see outside. I would reduce the amount of distraction to the absolute lowest level and just concentrate on my target."[26]

"One thing that surprised me," said Leatherman, "was they didn't run low on ammunition." But, after a while, Iraqi defenders did try to conserve ammunition by firing more selectively and engaging in barrage fire in specific areas called "boxes" or sectors. After one mission, Capt. Rich Treadway remarked, "The first night, the entire city and everything near Baghdad was constant fire. You could nearly walk on the bullets. Over the past couple weeks, the threats have been dying—or not dying, but at least reduced considerably. Until tonight. For some reason tonight, there must have been a 'half-price sale' on 37- and 57-millimeter ammunition. You could tell where a bomb went off because the entire sector would be engulfed in tracers. Fortunately," said the 416th pilot, "most of it went up as we were leaving."[27]

At one point, the Iraqis hit upon a new idea, and were so convinced they would be able to bring down a Black Jet that they prompted Jordanian reporters to be ready to get good pictures. Gunners would keep strict fire discipline so that they could clearly see the glow of the F-117s' afterburners when the planes attempted to escape from the target area. Then they would open fire on the glowing targets.

The Iraqis had a long wait. Not only do stealthy F-117s not use afterburners, but the rear of the engines is shielded from direct viewing. Apparently, our old friends Whitley and Leatherman were the men the Iraqis tried their idea out on. Said Leatherman, "There was one night I went across Baghdad, and Col. Whitley was my wingman. We both went across at the same time, and it was eerily quiet—even after our bombs hit. This was maybe three weeks, four weeks or so into the war. That was the only time that I thought that maybe they're running out of bullets. But the next time I went back, it was just as bad."[28]

F-117As pulling out to the flight line. USAF

"[The flak] got close enough that I could hear it," recalled Whitley. "If you're smokin' along there at 480 knots [over 550mph], and you can hear the stuff going 'Pop, Pop, Pow,' through the canopy, with your helmet and mask on, you know it's right out there. You can't alter your course or you're not going to hit the target. The guys just grin and bear it, and say 'Hey, this is what I get paid to do.' But they'd be the first to admit that fate was good to us."[29]

The intense defensive fires necessitated that the detailed planning and execution of missions not be allowed to slip. Precise timing of the bomb drops was crucial to survivability during multiship attacks, and TOTs were planned within two seconds of each other. Col. Whitley related that at the beginning of the air campaign, Black Jets arriving either too soon or too late stretched this interval to a dangerous average of about ten seconds—more than enough time for gunners on the ground to react. The Black Jets in the Gulf had an autopilot to hold altitude and speed, but no autothrottle, which would have made speed adjustments. This meant that although the mission computer could program the speed required to approach a target at the appropriate time, it was up to the man himself to make the minor adjustments in speed to maintain the split-second schedules.

Lt. Col. Miles Pound remarked that "if another pilot's bombs were to hit a specific target at a specific second, I counted on his bombs exploding then. My airplane may have been going through the same airspace where those bombs would have been three or four seconds earlier. That pilot had to be on time, on target; I had to be on time, on target."[30] If a stealth pilot struck too early, that could provoke concentrated triple-A at follow-on aircraft. If a pilot was trailing too far behind the first attacker, the pilot would become the target. "Five seconds makes a big difference," said Whitley. "You'd better not be early or your buddies will let you know it. And you better not be late or you'll suffer the consequences."[31]

By the end of the air campaign, some missions called for such a high degree of precision that the remarkable opening-night attack on Baghdad seemed almost simple by comparison. Capt. Rob Donaldson described one strike video from a mission against the Ba'th Party Headquarters in Baghdad where "you can see two F-117s pass through the field of view and you can see bombs going off." With obvious pride, Donaldson maintained, "It's an illustration of the fact that we could take a lot of F-117s into a highly defended, dense area—using simultaneous attacks in a very small airspace—and successfully complete the job." Most of the time, the Iraqis didn't know they were under attack until the bombs went off, by which time, said Donaldson, "we were half-way out of Dodge."[32]

Watching the strike videos became quite a popular pastime in both CENTAF Headquarters and King Khalid AB. "We'd have to send in a composite of everybody's tapes from the missions the night before," said Leatherman. "A C-21 would pick those things up about 10:30 in the morning after the night's missions and take them to Riyadh. For the guys in the TACC, that was the big highlight of their day—when our tapes would come in. They'd all sit there and watch them. The generals would get to watch them first. It would take awhile for them to filter down, but I heard everybody had a blast watching our tapes."[33]

Appropriately, though, the maintainers who launched the planes saw the IR videos first. "They were really ecstatic—no kidding—when you told 'em you got a solid hit," recalled one stealth pilot. "During part of the debriefing with the intel folks, we'd go over the tape, and the crew chiefs and all the guys that worked on the planes would come in and watch too." Laughing heartily, he remarked that "sometimes they'd even bring popcorn with them! We had a great time."[34] Said SM/Sgt. Gary Martin, "We had a tremendous group of people—the pilots who flew our airplanes were really good heads, and there was a lot of camaraderie. They cared about the maintenance people."

Crew chief David Owings helps Joe Bouley settle into the cockpit. Sgt. Kimberly Yearean, USAF

"We had one of our pilots, Maj. Farnham, who when he had a significant event, he would go so far as to buy apple pie and ice cream out of his own pocket for over 200 maintenance folks. That's a pretty fair expense," said Martin. "He did it twice. I remember one time was when he was just promoted lieutenant colonel. I don't remember what led up to the other one. One of the things he always did was when he came back, if he had a good night's flying, he went and had apple pie a la mode, so that was his kind of greeting to us. When he came into debrief, he walked through the door with apple pie a la mode, so you knew that he had a good night."[35]

When Maj. Leatherman returned to base after gutting the AT&T building, he gave his crew chief a prized memento from that first, historic operation. "The bombs, they have little lanyards that pull the pins open, arm the fuses, and stuff like that. It's all that's left of the bomb afterwards. I kept one," said the major, "and gave one from the second bomb to him."[36]

Many of the maintainers, as well as friends and relatives back home, were anxious to have souvenirs taken aboard the Black Jets during combat missions. American flags were, hands-down, the most popular items, but "it was a frenzy," said Axel Foley. "We flew everything from Bart Simpson dolls to footballs."[37] Martin remembered the happiness of one of his crew chiefs, S/Sgt. Brad Bowers, when he received a fluffy stuffed animal. "That was 'Geronimo Bear.' He got it out of Any Serviceman's Mail, and every time his airplane flew, [that bear] went over Baghdad or wherever they were going. Last I heard, he told me that he was going to send it back to the girl who had originally sent it."[38]

Gen. Schwarzkopf never sent his own little brown teddy bear on a ride over Baghdad, but was clearly intrigued by the Black Jet's ability to strike critical targets with apparent immunity. "I know Gen. Schwarzkopf was always interested in where the F-117 was going tonight," said his air chief, Gen. Charles Horner. "We briefed him about tar-

S/Sgt. John Pennell presents an unofficial mascot of the 37th TFW—P to Secretary of Defense Dick Cheney during Cheney's visit to King Khalid AB on Saturday, February 10, 1991. Pete Williams, DOD

gets for tomorrow every night and he paid attention to targets we were hitting with the F-117."[39]

The aircraft was essentially a strategic asset, and its unanticipated versatility led to its being used in ways that had barely been touched on before the war. The lack of a common knowledge base of both the weapon's capabilities and its requirements did, however, on occasion lead to understandable misuses of the aircraft. For example, when planners realized that the Black Jets could be sent against a last-minute target with just a few tankers and the occasional EF-111—instead of a legion of strike aircraft with the attendant jammers, suppression aircraft with HARMs, and CAP aircraft, all supported by a host of tankers with their own CAP—they tended to follow the line of least resistance with the ATO. Instead of refragging perhaps 40 to 60 planes, the simple solution was to latch onto about one-tenth as many Black Jets and tankers and assign the target to them.

The problem with the simple solution was this: The F-117-as-weapons-system required an extensive period of mission planning and appropriate weather before it could operate effectively. The end result was an inordinate amount of false starts and, often, canceled missions on any target for the affected aircraft. Even when aircraft were not refragged with little notice, changing weather patterns over target areas would mean that the ATO could not be implemented as written.

Throughout the war, hardened 2,000lb BLU-109B and trusty old 2,000lb Mk-84 bombs, both combined with laser guidance kits, were the standard ordnance of the 37th TFW—P. Other weapons were used but only on very rare occasions, as when 500lb GBU-12s (Mk-82 bombs with Paveway II kits) were dropped on key elements of the fire trench system that ran along the Kuwaiti border

The early-morning sun shines dully off the forward panels of a third-wave aircraft from the night of February 9–10, landing after strikes at Kirkuk and Qayyara West Airfield ammunition depots. Some of the second-wave aircraft that night had helped soften up SAM sites before the large B-52 raid on Al-Taji. T/Sgt. Rose Reynolds, USAF

and was supposed to foil the Coalition's attempt to retake Kuwait in a ground invasion. Targeting distribution points, T-junctions, and pump stations in this attack, on February 15, the 31st night of the air campaign, the stealth pilots in the second wave found themselves having to identify some aim points from sketch maps because intelligence photos were not available. Col. Whitley described the bombs as "quite adequate" for the job, and 24 of the 27 released found their mark.[40]

A week earlier, on the night of February 9–10, the wing had wanted to use cluster bomb munitions (CBUs) when six of the 14 second-go aircraft struck SA-2 and SA-3 missile sites as a prelude to a massive B-52 strike on Al-Taji military-industrial complex just north of Baghdad the following night. "The guys flying A-10s and F-16s had all the CBUs and were using them against area targets," said Leatherman. "We were way down south, and it would have taken a major-league effort just to get the ordnance to us."[41] The next night, ten Black Jets paved the way for their big buddies to pummel the huge installation nicknamed SAMs' Town by planners in Riyadh. "We dropped [GBU-]10s on 'em—on the radar vans so they'd have to fire ballistic," said one stealth pilot. "They could always haul in new ones, but by that time the [B-52s] were long gone." The 37th TFW—P had been periodically attacking key nodes within that roughly four- by three-mile site since the first night of the war, but the number of aim points was so large that, the pilot joked, "we could have been going back there for, oh, about a year."[42]

"The amount of tonnage that it takes to destroy that type of complex is enormous," said Gen. Buster Glosson. "As you can appreciate, it was about the third week before we eventually were able to put B-52s into that environment. The F-117s would go in

A common sight in Baghdad: two 57mm S-60 antiaircraft guns in firing positions atop a civilian apartment building. DIA

and strike the critical targets in the complex, two or three buildings in each complex area, but all the storage areas, filling, production, etc. that was not critical to research and development, we delayed striking because of the tonnage problem and the significance of other targets we had to hit with the F-117s...."[43] "Before they made their strikes these guys, sixteen of them went to Baghdad and they took out every SA-2 and SA-3 from south of the city of Baghdad to Tikrit. Later that night we put in 24 B-52s without a problem. We would have lost several B-52s without the F-117s taking the SAMs out."[44]

Misses were inevitable. When viewing a strike tape showing an untouched bridge, Leatherman remarked, "I was the first to go in and attack this bridge, and I missed by about seven feet." With bridges, of course, 7ft from the aim point might as well be 7mi. "My wingman is coming here eight minutes behind me," the major continued. "Fortunately, we decided to double target the bridge because he will nail it and the whole bridge drops into the water."[45] On cue, the center of the screen suddenly turned black as an LGB struck home. Another site was so hard to miss that neither the Paveway III nor the older Paveway II guidance system was attached to the ordnance. The targeting of this particularly voluminous factory with 2,000lb dumb bombs came at an opportune time in that F-117 operations were using up the limited supply of unique GBU-27 tails at a steady clip. As one stealth pilot noted, "when you've got something that big, and intel can't actually give you much on where to aim, why waste a[n LGB] kit?"[46]

Stealth pilots had nothing but praise for the 37th TFW—P's weather and intelligence personnel. And for good reason. "I'll tell you this," said Jerry Leatherman, "the people in our wing who did the weather [Detachment 8, 25th AWS, under Maj. David S. Hadley] knew our requirements because of IR sensors and things like that. They were great. I don't want to piss the guys off in Riyadh, but our weather people knew where the weather was good and where it was bad better than they did. I trusted them more."

Despite their fatigue and their concern about the weather, the pilots kept going. Even when the weather was poor, planners were able to work out the TOTs in such a way as to have at least a few Black Jets hitting targets in Baghdad every night during projected holes in the weather. This could be successfully pulled off only a limited number of times, however, and desired strikes on some targets were pushed back further and further. For example, foul weather had forced the cancelation of missions against one HAS three times. Located at Al-Rashid, an air base between Baghdad and the nuclear research center, it was believed to house a remote-control MiG capable of dispensing chemical munitions. "We saw some activity around the hangars," said a naval officer, "and thought they were readying this aircraft for a desperation act like dispensing chemicals on our troops. This was just before the ground campaign started."[47] With time perhaps running out, and no way for the Black Jets to attack until well after dark, CENTAF directed that the Navy use its unmanned TLAM-C Tomahawks. Five of the six cruise missiles struck the hangar, destroying it.

The rough weather also made locating and refueling from the tankers a rather dicey business, but even in good weather, it had always been a matter of great concern to stealth pilots, since they were often very low on fuel after leaving Iraq. "Even after a successful mission," said Capt. Wesley Cockman, "you still had to worry about getting back and finding your tanker out there, or you'd find yourself landing in some strange land."[48]

"When [the F-117s] came back out [of Iraq]," remembered T/Sgt. Mark Sletten of the Beale Bandits, "they wanted gas right away. We had a small floodlight on top of the tail. The F-117 was a black plane and it would come at you out of the black night. Suddenly, one would just be there, visible out of my rear window in the dim glow of the floodlight.

I'd signal him into proper position by flashing the pilot director lights and then fly the boom down to his inflight refueling receptacle. Once the boom made contact in the receptacle, I could talk to the pilot on the intercom. Usually, he'd say he was glad to see my tanker. He'd get his gas and the boom would automatically disconnect. By that time, his wingman would have arrived, and I'd fill him up, too. They always sounded relieved to get that gas."[49]

With anywhere from 150 to 600 aircraft in the air at any one time during combat operations, dozens of refueling operations might be going on simultaneously. While flying seemingly endless racetrack patterns at staggered altitudes, tankers turned regularly, often banking as much as 15 degrees. For a tired stealth pilot, this type of motion could easily play havoc with the senses of balance and motion. "Needless to say," said Capt. Don Chapman, "that is a big concern of ours in the night environment. And when you put the weather with that, spatial disorientation could be your most dangerous enemy. It's not the SAMs, it's not the triple-A, it's not other aircraft. It's spatial disorientation. There's a lot of concern about flying at night and in the weather."[50]

Cockman agreed. "Our biggest concern in the last two weeks, at least in mission briefings, was not where we were going, or what we were going to do that night, but what the weather was in the tanker tracks." He explained, "We felt so comfortable with what we were doing and what we were up against, that the defenses were not as much concern as the weather....The rendezvous and departure with the tanker, that was our biggest concern. You wanted to make sure you got your gas and got home. You had to stay with the tanker for a fair amount of time. Anytime you're flying on the wing of an aircraft, and you're going through serious weather, in turbulence, it's not easy to do. There were times I'd be right under his wing, and there's very little separation. If I'd have gone up I'd have hit him. I had to really get tucked in there because the weather was so thick at times. If you lost him, your chances of getting back weren't always the greatest. There were other aircraft out there and you had to really be careful you didn't get off a particular altitude or you might hit somebody."[51]

Concurrent with the steady decline in the weather over the last weeks of February was a noticeable increase in business that the wing was receiving from the daily ATOs. US ground units were already aggressively probing Iraqi defenses, and the ground invasion was slated to begin as early as Thursday, February 21, 1991. When the time came to cut off the Iraqi army "and kill it," things would move very fast indeed, and CENTCOM believed that the war could be over by Monday the 25th. The last two weeks of the war," said Capt. McDaniel, "the tempo really picked up. It was like, 'Oh, oh. There's too many targets and not enough time.'"[52] The commander of the Joint Strategic Target Planning Staff, Gen. George Lee Butler, later stated, "I was utterly astonished every day as I looked at Iraq—and looked at bomb damage assessment and what was left after we conducted our strikes, the country was literally an armed camp. It was an extraordinary array of facilities, capabilities, and that is one of the things that made them the fourth largest army in the world and the sixth largest air force."[53] Said Leatherman, "The whole country was one big ammunition dump. They were calling us and giving us new targets all the way to the end."[54]

A several-day delay in the opening of the ground campaign bought planners a little more time to target facilities critical to Saddam Hussein's war-making capabilities, but 34 vital sorties were scrubbed in one fell swoop on the 41st night of the air campaign, February 25, because of poor weather across virtually all of Iraq. The breather was most welcome by pilots and maintainers alike, but they were in for a shock. The following night, the wing was ordered to schedule two massive waves of 32 aircraft each.

"That night, we really worked our asses off to get that to happen," said Leatherman. "The problem was that we knew the weather really was not much different than the night before, when we got canceled."[55] The mission planning was intense. Life support personnel picked up hot food to go, and brought it to the operations area where pilots hung around after the briefing and discussed how they were going to pull it off.

For the first wave, the Nightstalkers managed to launch 14 of the sixteen aircraft they were to contribute, but lost two more sorties when the tankers—which were, themselves, launching an extraordinary number of aircraft—suffered an abort. The Ghost Riders launched 15 of their aircraft in spite of several ground aborts. They had readied nearly all the 22 Black Jets assigned to their squadron, and when a problem developed, the stealth pilots simply pulled out their EDTM, gathered up their helmet bag, and switched to other waiting aircraft. A mass of 27 birds were airborne and on their way to Iraq, more than the wing had been able to launch in an entire night at the beginning of the war. They dropped a total of two bombs, which missed when their laser locks were broken by clouds, and brought the rest home. The second go also fell five sorties short of a 32-plane wave, but eight clear shots resulted in eight direct hits. Again, however, most ordnance stayed tucked up in the bomb bays.

"There were big thunderstorms right over the top of Baghdad," recalled Leatherman. "We had our weather back-ups set for coming in lower, under the weather, to try and get to the targets. I can remember one of the waves had something like 30 guys in it, where nobody dropped a bomb on Baghdad. All these guys flew up there, and there was just thunder and lightning everywhere. People couldn't see the target and started to leave Baghdad. In holes in the overcast, you could see red tracers. When we came back, we weren't too happy about that. That was one of the points where, I couldn't say morale was bad, but you'd heard a lot of guys saying things like, 'What the hell did we do that for?' And we'd told [Riyadh] that there would be problems. So everybody was a little bit torqued—that we would all be exposed for no gain."[56]

Sites targeted that night included a Tarmiya rocket facility; a fuse factory at Narawan; the Al-Musayyib rocket motor production works and Shahiyat rocket test facility; a terrorist camp at Salmon Pak; an artillery plant in Habbaniya; Muthenna Airport in Baghdad; and, finally, a site that would be targeted in a big way the next night, the Ba'th Party Headquarters.

One pilot in the second wave had trouble during the landing approach. "Coming home, I was pretty bushed, but that was par for everyone then. There were a lot of planes up, and I waited my turn to come in. I didn't think I was as tired as I actually was. My approach was normal, and so I'm coming in. But here's the thing: when you're coming in to land at night, you get a kind of reversed image of the runway coming across the top of the canopy. It's not distracting, really; it's there, and you know it's there. Just a vague optical illusion as you're looking outside to land. That night, even though I wasn't looking at it, I'd started paying attention to it. There was the sensation that the elephant ears [movable side glareshields] were kind of stretching back to the rear. I realized I was flying the plane into the ground. I shook it off and made a normal landing, but, Jesus, that scared me. As I was taxiing in, I thought my heart was going to pound out of my chest. What a way to end the war.

"The debriefs went pretty fast that night—at least, I think mine did. I didn't volunteer what had happened. I guess I was still trying to sort it out in my own mind. My crew chief could see something was wrong. He looked at me for a long time and asked if I was okay. I said yeah. You know, the optical illusion really isn't much of anything. I don't know how many times I'd seen it before—and since. Anyway, there was no way I could sleep, so I talked with ——— and Capt. ——— for a long time, then finally crashed out for a long time, a real long time. After I woke up, they told me the last go [on night 43] had been canceled. I didn't know the war was over. I just thought it was the weather."[57]

On that last night of the air campaign, February 27, 1991, the wing launched 20 aircraft in its first go. A few Black Jets headed for Muthenna, the capital's old airport located just off downtown, and the Salmon Pak chemical-biological research facility. Most, however, were sent to just one spot. "Riyadh wanted the Ba'th Party Headquarters eliminated," stated Leatherman. "If you've ever had a chance to see pictures of this place, it's amazing. It's like a couple of city blocks of offices and structures. We were sending the guys up there to drop them."[58] In an attack often described as "the pick-a-window mission," the stealth pilots devastated large portions of the complex. Ten aircraft in the second go then struck the Al-Musayyib rocket-motor test facility and the Al-Athir missile research, development, and production complex only recently discovered by US intelligence assets. The latter site was the recipient of the last bomb dropped by an F-117 during the Gulf War.

"We didn't know [that night] was going to be the last one, obviously," said Rob Donaldson, who described his final mission to the Ba'th Party Headquarters as "a real satisfying ending mission." At 11:30 that evening, said Donaldson, "CENTAF cancelled the wing's third wave and told Col. Whitley to put future attacks on Iraqi targets on hold, but to stand by in case events dictated a renewed assault."[59] As it turned out, no renewed assault would come for almost two years, long after Col. Whitley and the current group of pilots had left for home. The wing, however, was still largely unaware that hostilities were at an end. Said Donaldson, "I came back and landed, went to sleep and heard all this racket at 7:00 in the morning. Someone said that President Bush said [there'd be] no more fighting. I didn't believe it until I heard it for the third time and then I started hooting and hollering too."[60]

Epilogue

"During the war, I ate, I slept, and I flew," said Capt. Matt Byrd. "You couldn't go to town or off to the mountains. Not allowed to do that. We had a joke back then: 'The only time they let you off base is to go bomb Baghdad.' On the days I wasn't flying, I'd try to work out—try to ease my mind—but there wasn't much time. After the war, [while the wing remained stationed in Saudi Arabia,] there were plenty of opportunities to work out, and a lot of the guys took it as a chance to really get in shape. There was no alcohol there, the food was very bland, so people just tried hard to get their bodies in shape. We called it Club Saudi."[1]

Gen. Buster Glosson addressed the personnel shortly after the cessation of hostilities and confirmed many of their suspicions of what had been going on during the last few weeks of combat. The stealth pilots were already well aware that CENTAF "didn't have to refrag half the shooters and tankers to get the job done," if late-breaking targets were given to them instead of nonstealthy assets. What they were more curious about was the frequency of non-weather-related changes that had been disruptive to the point where numerous sorties, and even whole waves, had been canceled. It turned out that disagreements over the BDAs—or a simple lack of communication—within the intelligence community had been much greater than the pilots had suspected. Col. Bernard Harvey, of Checkmate's Strategic Assessment Section, regularly convened a small group representing national security agencies, but little ordering of priorities had occurred between the Central Intelligence Agency (CIA), Defense Intelligence Agency (DIA), NSA, National Security Agency (NSA) air staff, and even State Department, all of which were putting forth targets they insisted "had to be hit right away."[2]

After the war, critics complained that the armed forces had inflated the effectiveness of certain weapons systems. An argument took place, for example, over how much support the F-117 did, or did not, have from other aircraft, a controversy that genuinely amazed airmen from stealth pilots to the chief of staff. Said McPeak, "They did benefit from the fact that there was a lot of confusion in there. We created pandemonium but some of the stories I've read would make you think we had Wild Weasels on one wing and the EF-111 on the other and a Compass Call at six o'clock [astern] to get those guys across Baghdad. That is absolutely untrue. [The F-117s] were the only aircraft that we fragged into downtown, inside the city limits—the only one we could do that with because the threat down there was genuine."[3]

Early on, the USAF had presented the F-117 as achieving a 75 percent success rate based on its combat record of 1,669 direct hits and 418 misses. Naturally, when pundits found out that the aircraft also had nearly 480 no-drops, a howl went up that the "true figures" showed the Black Jets hitting their targets "barely half the time." Weapons systems limitations associated with weather were the cause of nearly all no-drops. "This is, perhaps, the thing that hurt us the worst," said the USAF chief. "This was certainly the poorest weather in 14 years in the Baghdad and Kuwait area. We lost a lot of Iraqi targets, especially [for] the [F]-117s, where low cloud cover prevented them from acquiring the targets."[4]

But no matter how much effort is made in some quarters to explain away the victory in the Gulf, a victory it was, and one that was obtained with remarkably little loss of life on both sides. "You know, the Army says, 'A plan never stands in contact with the enemy.' Ours did," said Maj. Leatherman. "And it did it for 43 days. For me, there was great personal satisfaction that something I had worked on, and the rest of the guys in the mission planning cell had worked on for five-and-a-half months—not taking any days off and basically getting real nit-picky with what would be considered minor details—worked every night."[5]

The first returning contingent of the wing arrived home on Monday, April 1, 1991, when eight 415th TFS jets and two KC-10s, containing 130 support personnel, touched down in front of a cheering crowd of 25,000 at Nellis AFB. "I've never had an experience like this before," said Col. Al Whitley, as he gazed out over the throng. "I've been in combat three times and the last two I just kind'a sneaked into the airport." He later recalled, "When I pulled into the chocks at Nellis to lead those eight Black Jets back home, and looked out there and saw thousands of people from throughout the community, I told my wife, 'I really don't know if this is for us or for you, or for all of us.'" Reliving the emotions of his homecoming, Whitley said, "Isn't it great that our kids can see all this? Isn't it great that our youth can see the value of a team effort? Isn't it great that our youth can understand what commitment means...that our youth can see what happens when this country unites in a common cause?"[6] Said Maj. Bob Eskridge, "The greatest feeling was to kneel down there on the ramp and to be greeted by three blondes—my wife and two daughters!"[7]

Returns from King Khalid AB continued through July, but not all the Black Jets came home. Six to eight aircraft and key support equipment stayed on in Saudi Arabia as the stealth component of a US presence of approximately 100 tactical, reconnaissance, and support aircraft taking part in Operation Southern Watch. A three-month rotational cycle was established for roughly 200 pilots, maintainers, and other appropriate personnel until the ongoing tension between Iraq and its neighbors subsided. A one-month training rotation for these people was also established to TAC Headquarters, at Langley AFB. Meanwhile, at Tonopah, the wing began preparations for its move to Holloman AFB near Alamogordo, New Mexico, a superb facility abutting the huge White Sands Missile Range, and got down to the serious business of incorporating the hard-learned lessons of the Gulf War into its training program.

Obviously, however, not all the high standards reached during the war could be maintained in a peacetime environment. "I used to have a lot of fun with this," said Leatherman, "because I'd ask the maintenance guys, 'Well, wait a minute. How come in war, we're flying the tits off these airplanes, then during peace, when we want to get just a couple more sorties...?' The airplane was never really designed to fly like it did in the Gulf."[8] A grinning Sgt. Gary Martin explained, "The individual technicians knew what we were up against and what needed to be done. They all went that 150 percent. They set standards for themselves. There was a component in the fire control system that in peacetime would normally take four to six hours to change. I had guys do the same task in less than two hours. So, now I go back to peacetime, the pilots want to know why things can't still be done as fast. I can't expect [my crews] to change it in less than two hours"—the senior master sergeant chuckled, then added, "but [the technicians] don't get the six hours anymore, like they used to have."[9]

The long-awaited OCIP (offensive capabilities improvement program) was finally begun, and aircraft were rotated like clockwork through Lockheed's Palmdale facility at Air Force Plant 42. Although certain proposed modifications to the F-117's airframe were judged to be unnecessary, the plane underwent important changes to its navigation and weapons systems. Engineer Richard Silz of Lockheed commented that the Black Jet's useful weapons delivery envelope was expanded "far beyond anything ever envisioned at the beginning of the program,"[10] and Col. George Zielsdorff, program director for GPS, stated that targets were able to be identified "from at least 50-percent farther out" than they were during the Gulf War.[11] Congress even briefly toyed with the idea of reopening the F-117 production line, and Lockheed officials floated proposals to use the stealthy bird for reconnaissance or to suppress hostile air defenses, saying "it would make a great Wild Weasel."[12]

Although these ideas were good, they were also a little too late to be used on this platform. Said Gen. McPeak, "The technology is rather old...so I wouldn't spend any money on what amounts to obsolete technology."[13] As for the existing fleet of Black Jets, it was planned that they would continue to perform their current mission well into the 21st century, and stealth pilots returning from the war increasingly found themselves taking part in new exercises, including brief deployments to Korea by the 416th and to Europe by the 415th, as the USAF accelerated its policy of mainstreaming the F-117A. Since the aircraft was no longer completely black, the pattern of edging some of the training hours into the late afternoon, established before the war, would also continue. Once the stealth unit settled in at Holloman, the availability of more and better training hours plus the ability now to live with their family for more than one bleary-eyed weekend at a time would greatly reduce the stealth pilots' traditional end-of-the-week fatigue as well as the stress on their family life. The minimum number of hours needed by prospective pilots was reduced from 1,000hr to 700hr

For the time being, though, the airmen were still living on "Tonopah time," and, as anticipated, the remote location of the facility, which had been an asset during the secret development of the plane, now imposed an unnecessary burden on the training schedule. "For the pilots," said Leatherman, "normally you'd get up [to Tonopah from Nellis] some time after noon—it varied depending on when nighttime was—but you'd get up there anywhere from noon to four o'clock on Mondays. They'd move the Key [Airline] schedule around on Mondays; they'd run about every half hour. In the morning, all the normal support people would be going up around ten to two o'clock." Of course, ferrying over 2,500 personnel back and forth between Nellis and Tonopah every week on 75 chartered flights was also a fantastically expensive proposition, and earned the wing's terminals the dubious distinction of being two of the three busiest in the USAF. "And that's part of the reason why they're moving to Holloman," explained Leatherman. "The contract with the airlines runs in millions of dollars just to get people to work every week."[14]

The stealth unit was getting more than a new home—it was getting a new name as well. In the post–cold war period, the USAF, like all the other armed services, had to plan for a steady downsizing. Older aircraft were retired from the inventory, and the assets and personnel of some organizations were consolidated when their parent units were inactivated. The names of the reorganized units were generally determined by which one of their component pieces had the most substantial historic lineage. Efforts were made to keep the 37th TFW designation when the F-117s went to Holloman AFB, but the combat history of the facility's 49th TFW was much more substantial and won out in this survival of the fittest. The 37th's three squadrons had, however, seen much action in both the Second World War and Vietnam—under other parent units—and had little trouble keeping their designations, especially since they at one time were night fighter squadrons flying P-61 Black Widows.

On October 1, 1991, the 415th TFS, the 416th TFS, and the 417th TFTS under, respectively, Lt. Cols. Bruce E. Kreidler, Greg Gonyea, and Barry Horne, were each redesignated as a fighter squadron (FS), and Tactical was likewise dropped from the name of the 37th and other USAF wings, including the 49th. The following month, an operations group under Col. Raleigh ("Tom") Harrington was organized to help facilitate the move to New Mexico. The transfer of F-117s to their new home was begun in May of the following year. During a ceremony at Holloman AFB on Wednesday, July 8, 1992, the 37th Fighter Wing (FW) was officially inactivated and Col. Whitley passed control of his beloved Black Jets to Brig. Gen. Lloyd W. ("Fig") Newton, the Stealth Bandit commanding the 49th FW. In what is likely to be a growing trend in the post–cold war USAF, the 49th FW coordinated the efforts of a large number of squadrons. In addition to the trio of stealth units, the 7th FS and the 8th FS carried on the wing's previous training functions with their AT-38Bs, and the recently arrived 9th FS from George AFB provided F-4 training to German Luftwaffe pilots.

Less than a month after the ceremony at Holloman, the stealth pilots were reminded that flying is a dangerous business, even when no war is on. Capt. John Mills was the 253d tactical pilot to qualify on the Black Jet, and a new member of the Ghost Riders. At 9:20pm on Monday, August 3, 1992, his aircraft crashed and burned just 8mi northeast of the base. Almost immediately after takeoff, his Black Jet had gone into an uncommanded roll and quickly caught fire. As it streaked out of control across the sky, the captain managed to eject safely before the plane exploded and plummeted to the earth. The former A-10 pilot landed 1/2mi from the crash site. Before hitching a ride back to Holloman with a highway patrolman, he found that he had sustained only a cut on the chin and a few bruises. His aircraft, number 810, had flown 19 combat missions over Iraq without so much as a nick from triple-A, but was now a $42.6 million pile of junk spread across the desert floor. Crash investigators believed that improper reinstallation of a bleed air duct before Capt. Mills' flight caused malfunctions in the Black Jet's hydraulic and flight control systems.

Stealth pilots were soon given another chance to prove they could be the first into a hot defended area, perform their mission, and exit unscathed. A long series of Iraqi evasions of cease-fire agreement provisions had gone relatively unpunished by the US and its Coalition allies, and finally led an emboldened Saddam Hussein to step a little too far. Toward the end of President George Bush's term in office, when it was believed he and his administration would be more concerned with leaving Washington than with world affairs, Iraq's periodic cross-border incursions into Kuwait escalated, as did threats to Coalition aviators enforcing no-fly zones over northern and southern portions of Iraq. No longer content with just locking their radars onto Coalition aircraft, Iraq planes and triple-A now felt they could fire with relative impunity.

Almost two years from the opening of the Desert Storm air campaign, a GBU-27A/B crashed through the roof of Al-Amara IOC on Wednesday, January 13, 1993, at 9:15pm Baghdad time. The center was extensively damaged, but five other Black Jets, carrying one bomb each, generally met with less success, with the stealth pilot's old nemesis, the weather, intervening. The strikes had, in fact, been scheduled for Tuesday night and delayed 24 hours because of cloud cover. The 49th's Saudi detachment still had intermittent clouds at 2,000ft to deal with when the attack was mounted, and the stealth pilot targeting the rebuilt Tallil SOC was unable even to find it. The mission of the other four Black Jets was reminiscent of the attacks that paved the way for the massive B-52 strike on Al-Taji during the war, with each stealth pilot going after an SA-3 SAM site's Spoon Rest D-radar.

The radar at Ashshuaybah was destroyed, but the uncooperative weather, which one pilot described as "ungodly,"[15] caused both bombs zeroing in on Spoon Rests at Nasiriya to break their laser locks and fall short, and probably contributed to a stealth pilot heading toward Basra's site misjudging his turn point and sending an LGB into a large single-story farmhouse a mile from the radar. Only two aim points were struck by the stealth fighters, and results from conventional aircraft were also mixed. The accumulative effect of the raids, though, had so seriously degraded the southern sector's laboriously rebuilt IADS that conventional aircraft were able to make a return visit—in broad daylight—several days later and finish the job.

Some stealth pilots worry that the ease of their recent victories may breed a complacency among their fellow citizens. The man who, more than anyone else, was responsible for the development of the F-117, Head Skunk Ben Rich, articulated what many in the military have come to call the Gulf War syndrome, an ironic twist on the Vietnam syndrome, which for many years poisoned American politics and encouraged terrorists and foreign dictators alike to confront the United States. Rich feared that "the American public will think that every war will be like *Desert Storm*, over quick, with low casualties. It's because we got air superiority in two days. The F-117 was critical to that. We knocked out their eyes....But I wouldn't want the public to think that every war was going to be that easy. We're cutting back in research and development," Rich said. "Everything that we used in *Desert Storm* was at least ten years old. The Patriots, the AWACs, the F-117s, all ten years old. Nothing was new. It takes time to get those. Yes, we're cutting back on [research and development money]. We're eating our seed corn."[16]

For the time being, weapons like the F-117A have bought the United States a little breathing room, which is particularly fortuitous because the post–cold war downsizing of the defense establishment has delayed the development of a new stealth platform to replace the Black Jet until after the turn of the century. It seems that like the venerable B-52 bomber, which was fielded before most of the current crop of stealth pilots were born, the Black Jet is destined to prowl the night sky for a long time to come. One former airman noted that the USAF Red Team had "studied more than 40 counterstealth concepts since being formed in 1981," and that "it [had] found no Achilles' heel that would negate the value of stealth technology in the foreseeable future."[17]

After returning from the Gulf War, Capt. Wesley Cockman stated flatly, "Stealth technology saved lives. It saved not only our lives, as pilots, but also shortened the war due to our ability to destroy targets at a quicker pace. And it saved the lives of others because of the targets we destroyed. If we didn't have Stealth technology, it would have been a totally different war. It will also serve as a deterrent for future actions by other countries. We can be thankful our country was involved with it first, rather than somebody else employing it against us."[18]

Capt. Matt Byrd was one person who had good reason to be thankful the United States had developed stealth. Several weeks into the war, Byrd was flying *Habu II*, number 837, on yet another mission through Iraq's hostile skies. "Coming north to south through Baghdad," recounted Byrd, "I'd already hit one target and now I'm going to hit another one. I'm doing what I need to do to find my target. It's the two minutes of concentration that are important here. I'm about 30 seconds into my two minutes. There are two bright white flashes off my right wing; my tape is running. I look down, and at extremely close range, two SAMs were launched at me nearly simultaneously. I felt that they were firing at me.

"I'd been targeted. By what means, I don't know. What I assume is noise. I think these were radar-guided SAMs, because I came back and talked to the intel folks, and we plotted out where it was, and we believe it was an SA-3 battery. It was so close that I could see the burner flame from the exhaust lighting up the ground and the vans around it. At that point," said Byrd, "you do not know for sure if stealth works. But once those missiles were launched, they never saw me. They're in the air; they went to my six o'clock; they came out my left side; and they exploded. It was that quick. I had it all on tape and talked my way through it: 'I've got two missiles launched at me right at three o'clock,' and then they exploded. I was able to hit my target because of this airplane. Stealth works."

"Go back to World War II and those Lancaster bombers you were talking about. To take out a specific pinpoint target, a high-value target, you needed to send hundreds of Lancaster bombers across, and look at the crew that are on those Lancaster bombers. Put a price on those lives, and the hundreds of sorties, and the hundreds of men's lives, which were put in harm's way, compared to a couple B-2s which can do the same job today. Money is buying technology, which saves lives. That's what America is all about. That's what our social system, our education system is about: bettering human rights, individualism—promoting the individual because we put such a high value on individuals in this country. We can use technology and know-how to keep people out of harm's way, that's what it's all about."[19]

Footnotes

Chapter 1

1. James P. Coyne, *Airpower in the Gulf*, Air Force Association, Arlington, Virginia, 1992, p. 69.
2. US Congress, House Subcommittee on the Department of Defense, *Hearings before a Subcommittee of the Committee on Appropriations*, 102d Congress, US Government Printing Office, Washington, DC, 1991, p. 468 (hereinafter cited as *Hearings*).
3. "F-117 Probe Is Inconclusive," *Defense News*, December 2, 1991, p. 2.
4. "Czechoslovakia Says System Sees Stealth," *Washington Times*, June 19, 1991, p. 9.
5. Daniel Plesch and Michael Wardell, "Stealth Fighter Uncloaked," *Los Angeles Times*, May 1, 1991, p. B-5.
6. John R. Kasich and Ronald V. Dellums, "A Bomber We Don't Need," *Washington Post*, May 22, 1991, p. op-ed.
7. Jeffrey Record, "Why the Air War Worked," *Armed Forces Journal International*, April 1991, pp. 44–45.
8. Ibid.
9. "Networks for Stealth: Can Our Radars Detect Stealth Aircraft?" *Commonwealth of Independent States: A Journal of Selected Press Translations*, Winter 1991–92, pp. 50–52 (first published in *Krasnaya zvezda*, January 31, 1991, p. 2).
10. Doug Richardson, "Soviet Fighter Radar: Leaving the West Behind," *Defense and Diplomacy*, August–September 1991, pp. 46–48.
11. Maj. Jerry Leatherman, Team Stealth interview.
12. Richardson, "Soviet Fighter Radar," pp. 46–48.
13. Ibid.
14. Capt. David P. Dilegge, US Marine Corps Reserve, "Soviet Lessons Learned from Operation Desert Storm," *Marine Corps Gazette*, February 1992, pp. 38–39.
15. Neil Munro and Barbara Opall, "European Officials: Electro-optics Will Counter Stealth," *Defense News*, June 24, 1991, p. 44.
16. US Congress, *Hearings*, p. 479.
17. Bruce B. Auster, "The Myth of the Lone Gunslinger," *US News and World Report*, November 18, 1991, p. 52.
18. Col. Alton C. Whitley, Jr., Team Stealth interview.
19. "Capt. Scott," Team Stealth interview.
20. David Evans, "Is the B-2 Bomber as Stealthy as the Air Force Claims?" *Chicago Tribune*, January 17, 1992, p. 19.
21. US Congress, *Hearings*, p. 520.
22. Robert Macy and Melinda Macy, *Destination Baghdad*, M&M Graphics, Las Vegas, Nevada, 1991, p. 14.

Chapter 2

1. "Lockheed Credits Soviet Theory in Design of F-117," *Aviation Week & Space Technology* December 16–23, 1991, p. 27.
2. Malcolm W. Brown, "Rival Designers Led the Way to Stealthy Airplanes," *New York Times*, May 14, 1991, p. C-1.
3. "Lockheed Credits Soviet Theory in Design of F-117," *Aviation Week & Space Technology*, December 16–23, 1991, p. 27.
4. Brown, "Rival Designers," p. C-1.
5. Ibid.
6. "Northrop's 1976 Stealth Fighter Proposal Featured Faceted Body with Overhead Inlet," *Aviation Week & Space Technology*, February 10, 1992, p. 23.
7. Brown, "Rival Designers," p. C-1.
8. Ben R. Rich, *Remarks of Ben R. Rich, F-117A Final Delivery Ceremony, 12 July 1990*, Lockheed press release.

9. Bill Sweetman and James Goodall, *Lockheed F-117A: Operation and Development of the Stealth Fighter*, Motorbooks International, Osceola, Wisconsin, 1990, p. 64.
10. Col. Alton C. Whitley, Jr., Team Stealth interview.
11. Jeffrey P. Rhodes, "The Black Jet," *Air Force Magazine*, July 1990, pp. 72–76.
12. Robert Macy and Melinda Macy, *Destination Baghdad*, M&M Graphics, Las Vegas, Nevada, 1991, p. 43.
13. "We Own the Night," *Lockheed Horizons*, May 1992, p. 13.

Chapter 3

1. Robert Macy and Melinda Macy, *Destination Baghdad*, M&M Graphics, Las Vegas, Nevada, 1991, p. 26.
2. Office of History, 37th Fighter Wing Headquarters, Twelfth Air Force, Tactical Air Command, *History and Lineage of the F-117A Stealth Fighter Organizations*, special study HO-91-2, 1991, p. i (see also Office of History, 37th Fighter Wing Headquarters, Twelfth Air Force, Tactical Air Command, *Nighthawks over Iraq: A Chronology of the F-117A Stealth Fighter in Operations Desert Shield and Desert Storm*, special study 37FW/HO-91-1, 1991).
3. Bill Sweetman and James Goodall, Lockheed F-117A: *Lockheed F-117A: Operation and Development of the Stealth Fighter*, Motorbooks International, Osceola, Wisconsin, 1990, p. 69.
4. Macy and Macy, *Destination Baghdad*, p. 54.
5. Col. Alton C. Whitley, Jr., Team Stealth interview.
6. Ibid.
7. Ibid.
8. Ibid.
9. Ibid.
10. Ibid.
11. David Gustafson, "Stealth Materializes at EAA Oshkosh '90," *Sport Aviation*, October 1990, pp. 58–63.
12. Capt. Matt Byrd, Team Stealth interview.
13. Capt. Tim Veeder, Team Stealth interview.
14. Bill Sweetman and James Goodall, *Lockheed F-117A: Operation and Development of the Stealth Fighter*, Motorbooks International, Osceola, Wisconsin, 1990, p. 35–36.
15. Macy and Macy, *Destination Baghdad*, p. 28.
16. Whitley, interview.
17. Ibid.
18. Maj. Jerry Leatherman, Team Stealth interview.
19. Whitley, interview.
20. Leatherman, interview.
21. Ibid.
22. Leatherman, interview.
23. "We Own the Night," *Lockheed Horizons*, May 1992, p. 49.

Chapter 4

1. Maj. Jerry Leatherman, Team Stealth interview.
2. Ibid.
3. Ibid.
4. "Capt. Courtney," Team Stealth interview.
5. Robert Macy and Melinda Macy, *Destination Baghdad*, M&M Graphics, Las Vegas, Nevada, 1991, p. 55.
6. Ibid., p. 73.
7. Capt. Tim Veeder, Team Stealth interview.
8. Macy and Macy, *Destination Baghdad*, p. 55.
9. Capt. Matt Byrd, Team Stealth interview.
10. Nick Cook, "In the Lair of the Black Jet," *Jane's Defence Weekly*, April 25, 1992, pp. 702–10.
11. Leatherman, interview.
12. Cook, "Lair of the Black Jet," pp. 702–10.
13. Leatherman, interview.
14. Ibid.
15. Cook, "Lair of the Black Jet," pp. 702–10.
16. David Gustafson, "Stealth Materializes at EAA Oshkosh '90," *Sport Aviation*, October 1990, pp. 58–63.
17. Jeffrey P. Rhodes, "The Black Jet," *Air Force Magazine*, July 1990, pp. 72–76.
18. Veeder, interview.
19. Cook, "Lair of the Black Jet," pp. 702–10.
20. "Capt. Scott," Team Stealth interview.
21. Eric DeRitis, "UK Pilot Takes a 'Psychology Lesson' at Controls of F-117A Stealth Fighter," *Armed Forces Journal International*, November 1991, p. 18.
22. Byrd, interview.
23. Veeder, interview.
24. Leatherman, interview.
25. Leatherman, interview.
26. Col. Alton C. Whitley, Jr., Team Stealth interview.
27. "Capt. Courtney," Team Stealth interview.
28. Bill Sweetman and James Goodall, *Lockheed F-117A: Operation and Development of the Stealth Fighter*, Motorbooks International, Osceola, Wisconsin, 1990, p. 80.
29. Gustafson, "Stealth Materializes," pp. 58–63.
30. Sweetman and Goodall, *Lockheed F-117A*, p. 80.
31. Leatherman, interview.
32. Sweetman and Goodall, *Lockheed F-117A*, p. 80.
33. "Courtney," interview.
34. "Scott," interview.
35. Sweetman and Goodall, *Lockheed F-117A*, p. 82.
36. Ibid., p. 82.

Chapter 5

1. "Maj. Brand," Team Stealth interview.
2. Maj. Jerry Leatherman, Team Stealth interview.
3. Robert Macy and Melinda Macy, *Destination Baghdad*, M&M Graphics, Las Vegas, Nevada, 1991, p. 32.
4. Capt. Tim Veeder, Team Stealth interview.
5. Robert E. van Patten, "Which Way Is Up," *Air Force Magazine*, January 1992, p. 80.
6. "F-117A: Mystery Fighter of the Gulf War," *Defense Journal*, Kuala Lumpur, Malaysia, 3d Quarter 1991, pp. 47–51.
7. Leatherman, interview.
8. Macy and Macy, *Destination Baghdad*, p. 32.
9. Maj. Jerry Leatherman, Team Stealth interview.
10. Michael A. Dornheim, "F-117A Uses Conventional Refueling Techniques for Mideast Deployment," *Aviation Week & Space Technology*, August 27, 1990, pp. 24–25.
11. "Brand," interview.
12. Capt. Matt Byrd, Team Stealth interview.
13. Leatherman, interview.
14. Bill Sweetman, "Stealth Comes of Age with F-22," *Jane's Defence Weekly*, January 4, 1992, p. 12.
15. "Brand," interview.
16. Commander Mark P. Grissom, US Navy, "Stealth in Naval Aviation: A Hard Look," *Naval War College Review*, Summer 1991, p. 14.
17. SM/Sgt. Gary Martin, Team Stealth interview.
18. Ibid.
19. Ibid.
20. Ibid.
21. David Hughes and Jeffrey M. Lenorovitz, "F-117A's Improvements Boost Wide Range of Improvements," *Aviation Week & Space Technology*, June 24, 1991, pp. 20–23.
22. Martin, interview.
23. Nick Cook, "In the Lair of the Black Jet," *Jane's Defence Weekly*, April 25, 1992, pp. 702–10.
24. Macy and Macy, *Destination Baghdad*, p. 54.
25. Eric DeRitis, "UK Pilot Takes a 'Psychology Lesson' at Controls of F-117A Stealth Fighter," *Armed Forces Journal International*, November 1991, p. 18.
26. Macy and Macy, *Destination Baghdad*, p. 57.
27. Cook, "Lair of the Black Jet," pp. 702–10.
28. Bill Sweetman and James Goodall, *Lockheed F-117A: Operation and Development of the Stealth Fighter*, Motorbooks International, Osceola, Wisconsin, 1990, p. 77.
29. Ibid., p. 78.
30. "Capt. Scott," Team Stealth interview.
31. Sweetman and Goodall, *Lockheed F-117A*, p. 77.

32. "Brand," interview.
33. David Gustafson, "Stealth Materializes at EAA Oshkosh '90," *Sport Aviation*, October 1990, pp. 58–63.
34. Leatherman, interview.
35. Jeffrey P. Rhodes, "The Black Jet," *Air Force Magazine*, July 1990, pp. 72–76.
36. "Capt. Courtney," Team Stealth interview.
37. Rhodes, "Black Jet," pp. 72–76.
38. Rhodes, "Black Jet," pp. 72–76.
39. Jay Miller, *Lockheed F-117 Stealth Fighter*, Specialty Press, Stillwater, Minnesota, 1991, p. 33.
40. William B. Scott, "USAF Expands Use of F-117A, Adds More Daytime Flights," *Aviation Week & Space Technology*, May 1, 1989, pp. 24–27.
41. "Pilots Describe USAF Stealth Aircraft as Highly Maneuverable," *Aviation Week & Space Technology*, June 18, 1990, p. 75.
42. Veeder, interview.
43. "High Tech, Proved in Gulf, May Not Work Everywhere, Aspin Says," *Aerospace Daily*, June 21, 1991, p. 489.
44. David F. Bond, *Aviation Week & Space Technology* March 5, 1990.

Chapter 6

1. Robert Macy and Melinda Macy, *Destination Baghdad*, M&M Graphics, Las Vegas, Nevada, 1991, p. 21.
2. Maj. Jerry Leatherman, Team Stealth interview.
3. Col. Alton C. Whitley, Jr., Team Stealth interview.
4. Ibid.
5. Macy and Macy, *Destination Baghdad*, p. 51.
6. Macy and Macy, *Destination Baghdad*, p. 22.
7. David Gustafson, "Stealth over Iraq," *Sport Aviation*, October 1991, pp. 54–57.
8. Gustafson, "Stealth over Iraq," pp. 54–57.
9. Lt. Gen. Charles A. Horner, "The Air Campaign," *Military Review*, September 1991, pp. 16–27.
10. James P. Coyne, *Airpower in the Gulf*, Air Force Association, Arlington, Virginia, 1992, p. 27.
11. Gen. Michael Dugan, "The Air War," *US News and World Report*, February 11, 1991, pp. 24–31.
12. Leatherman, interview.
13. SM/Sgt. Gary Martin, Team Stealth interview.
14. Capt. Matt Byrd, Team Stealth interview.
15. Whitley, interview.
16. Ibid.
17. "Capt. Courtney," Team Stealth interview.
18. "Maj. Brand," Team Stealth interview.
19. Gustafson, "Stealth over Iraq," pp. 54–57.
20. Macy and Macy, *Destination Baghdad*, p. 20.
21. Ibid., pp. 19–20.
22. Martin, interview.
23. Whitley, interview.
24. Martin, interview.
25. US Congress, House Subcommittee on the Department of Defense, *Hearings before a Subcommittee of the Committee on Appropriations*, 102d Congress, US Government Printing Office, Washington, DC, 1991, p. 484 (hereinafter cited as *Hearings*).
26. Rick Atkinson, "US to Rely on Air Strikes if War Erupts," *Washington Post*, September 16, 1990, p. 1.
27. US News and World Report, *Triumph without Victory*, Random House, New York, 1992, p. 4.
28. Bill Sweetman, "Catching up with Doctrine," *Jane's Defence Weekly*, June 29, 1991, pp. 1174–75.
29. James P. Coyne, "Plan of Attack," *Air Force Magazine*, April 1992, pp. 40–46.
30. Capt. Daniel L. Thomas, US Army, "Bombing Baghdad: Air Force Target Development," *Military Intelligence*, October–December 1991, pp. 14–18.
31. Coyne, "Plan of Attack," pp. 40–46.
32. Leatherman, interview.
33. Ibid.
34. Whitley, interview.
35. Whitley, interview.
36. Whitley, interview.
37. "Brand," interview.
38. Nick Cook, "In the Lair of the Black Jet," *Jane's Defence Weekly*, April 25, 1992, pp. 702–10.
39. Whitley, interview.
40. Whitley, interview.
41. Courtney, interview.
42. Whitley, interview.
43. Ibid.
44. Lt. Gen. Calvin H. Waller, address to the students and faculty of the US Army's Command and Gen. Staff College, Fort Leavenworth, Kansas, May 7, 1991.
45. Leatherman, interview.
46. Whitley, interview.
47. "Capt. Scott," Team Stealth interview.
48. Ibid.
49. Macy and Macy, *Destination Baghdad*, p. 81.
50. Whitley, interview.
51. Ibid.
52. Macy and Macy, *Destination Baghdad.*, p. 27.
53. "Brand," interview.
54. Whitley, interview.
55. Ibid.
56. "Scott," interview.
57. Leatherman, interview.
58. Whitley, interview.
59. Ibid.

Chapter 7

1. David Gustafson, "Stealth over Iraq," *Sport Aviation*, October 1991, pp. 54–57.
2. Capt. Matt Byrd, Team Stealth interview.
3. Col. Alton C. Whitley, Jr., Team Stealth interview.
4. Robert Macy and Melinda Macy, *Destination Baghdad*, M&M Graphics, Las Vegas, Nevada, 1991, p. 11.
5. Ibid., p. 29.
6. Maj. Jerry Leatherman, Team Stealth interview.
7. Malcolm McConnell, "They Went to War," *Reader's Digest*, September 1991, pp. 54–62.
8. SM/Sgt. Gary Martin, Team Stealth interview.
9. Leatherman, interview.
10. Macy and Macy, *Destination Baghdad*, p. 11.
11. Gustafson, "Stealth over Iraq," pp. 54–57.
12. Macy and Macy, *Destination Baghdad*, p. 30.
13. James P. Coyne, "Plan of Attack," *Air Force Magazine*, April 1992, pp. 40–46.
14. Macy and Macy, *Destination Baghdad*, p. 33.
15. S/Sgt. Kelly Godbey, Team Stealth interview.
16. John Simpson, "When the Cruise Missiles Came," *Harper's Magazine*, April 1991, pp. 73–78.
17. David C. Isby, *Weapons and Tactics of the Soviet Army*, Jane's Publishing Co., London, 1988, p. 307.
18. English-language radio broadcast from Baghdad, monitored in Israel, in late December 1990.
19. Marie Colvin, "The Enemy Above Was Unseen and Unheard," *Sunday Times*, London, p. 13.
20. US News and World Report, *Triumph without Victory*, Random House, New York, 1992, p. 233.
21. James P. Coyne, *Airpower in the Gulf*, Air Force Association, Arlington, Virginia, 1992, p. 7.
22. US Congress, House Subcommittee on the Department of Defense, *Hearings before a Subcommittee of the Committee on Appropriations*, 102d Congress, US Government Printing Office, Washington, DC, 1991, p. 480 (hereinafter cited as *Hearings*).
23. Coyne, "Plan of Attack," p. 10.
24. Cable News Network broadcast, January 16, 1991.
25. Coyne, "Plan of Attack," pp. 40–46, and US News and World Report, *Triumph*, pp. 228–29.
26. Leatherman, interview.

27. US Congress, *Hearings*, p. 480.
28. Leatherman, interview.
29. US Congress, *Hearings*, p. 460.
30. Gen. H. Norman Schwarzkopf, US Army, and Peter Petre, *It Doesn't Take a Hero*, Linda Grey, Bantam Books, New York, 1992, p. 415.
31. Macy and Macy, *Destination Baghdad*, p. 11.
32. Ibid., p. 30.
33. Ibid., p. 13.
34. Air Vice-Marshal (Retired) V. M. Tiwari, "Gulf War in the Fourth Dimension," *USI Journal*, New Delhi, India, October–December 1991, pp. 482–90.
35. "Capt. Scott," Team Stealth interview.
36. Gustafson, "Stealth over Iraq," pp. 54–57.
37. Schwarzkopf and Petre, *Hero*, p. 415.
38. US Congress, *Hearings*, p. 491.
39. James P. Coyne, *Airpower in the Gulf*, p. 8.
40. Leatherman, interview.
41. Macy and Macy, *Destination Baghdad*, p. 17.
42. Ibid., p. 12.
43. Office of History, 37th Fighter Wing Headquarters, Twelfth Air Force, Tactical Air Command, *Nighthawks over Iraq: A Chronology of the F-117A Stealth Fighter in Operations Desert Shield and Desert Storm*, special study 37FW/HO-91-1, 1991, p. 11 (hereinafter cited as *Nighthawks*).
44. Office of History, *Nighthawks*, pp. 11–12.
45. US Congress, *Hearings*, p. 490.
46. Capt. Phil McDaniel, Team Stealth interview.
47. US Congress, *Hearings*, p. 490.
48. Buster Glosson, interview
49. Michael A. Dornheim, "F-117A Pilots Conduct Precision Bombing in High Threat Environment," *Aviation Week & Space Technology*, April 22, 1991, pp. 51–53.

Chapter 8

1. David Gustafson, "Stealth over Iraq," *Sport Aviation*, October 1991, pp. 54–57.
2. Capt. Matt Byrd, Team Stealth interview.
3. Maj. Jerry Leatherman, Team Stealth interview.
4. "Maj. Brand," Team Stealth interview.
5. "Capt. Scott," Team Stealth interview.
6. Leatherman, interview.
7. Ibid.
8. Ibid.
9. Ibid.
10. Byrd, interview.
11. Leatherman, interview.
12. Ibid.
13. 37th Fighter Wing Headquarters, Twelfth Air Force, Tactical Air Command, *Nighthawks over Iraq: A Chronology of the F-117A Stealth Fighter in Operations Desert Shield and Desert Storm*, special study 37FW/HO-91-1, 1991, p. 9 (hereinafter cited as *Nighthawks*).
14. Capt. Tim Veeder, Team Stealth interview.
15. US Congress, House Subcommittee on the Department of Defense, *Hearings before a Subcommittee of the Committee on Appropriations*, 102d Congress, US Government Printing Office, Washington, DC, 1991, p. 483 (hereinafter cited as *Hearings*).
16. Byrd, interview.
17. "Capt. Courtney," Team Stealth interview.
18. Gen. H. Norman Schwarzkopf, interview with Barbara Walters on American Broadcasting Company's *Twenty/Twenty* news program.
19. "Capt. Courtney," Team Stealth interview.
20. Leatherman, interview.
21. Brand, interview.
22. Col. Alton C. Whitley, Jr., Team Stealth interview.
23. Ibid.
24. Robert Macy and Melinda Macy, *Destination Baghdad*, M&M Graphics, Las Vegas, Nevada, 1991, p. 18.
25. Robert Macy and Melinda Macy, *Destination Baghdad*, M&M Graphics, Las Vegas, Nevada, 1991, pp. 15–16.
26. Ibid., p. 17.
27. Time-Life video.
28. Leatherman, interview.
29. Macy and Macy, *Destination Baghdad*, p. 13.
30. Macy and Macy, *Destination Baghdad*, p. 29.
31. US News and World Report, *Triumph without Victory*, Random House, New York, 1992, p. 232.
32. Gustafson, "Stealth over Iraq," pp. 54–57.
33. Leatherman, interview.
34. "Brand," interview.
35. SM/Sgt. Gary Martin, Team Stealth interview.
36. Leatherman, interview.
37. Macy and Macy, *Destination Baghdad*, p. 30.
38. Martin, interview.
39. US Congress, *Hearings*, p. 462.
40. Whitley, interview.
41. Leatherman, interview.
42. "Scott," interview.
43. US Congress, Hearings, p. 478.
44. US Congress, *Hearings*, p. 489.
45. Ibid., p. 461.
46. "Scott," interview.
47. "Navy Striving to Update Aircraft Munitions Arsenal," *Aviation Week & Space Technology*, p. 56.
48. Macy and Macy, *Destination Baghdad*, p. 16.
49. James P. Coyne, *Airpower in the Gulf*, Air Force Association, Arlington, Virginia, 1992, p. 136.
50. Macy and Macy, *Destination Baghdad*, p. 32.
51. Ibid., pp. 31–32.
52. Capt. Phil McDaniel, Team Stealth interview.
53. US Congress, *Hearings*, pp. 537–38.
54. Leatherman, interview.
55. Leatherman, interview.
56. Ibid.
57. "Scott," interview.
58. Leatherman, interview.
59. Office of History, *Nighthawks*, p. 36.
60. Gustafson, "Stealth over Iraq," pp. 54–57.

Epilogue

1. Capt. Matt Byrd, Team Stealth interview.
2. Maj. Jerry Leatherman, Team Stealth interview.
3. Dudney, "Washington Watch," pp. 21–24.
4. Ibid.
5. Leatherman, interview.
6. Robert Macy and Melinda Macy, *Destination Baghdad*, M&M Graphics, Las Vegas, Nevada, 1991, pp. 68–69.
7. Capt. Jerry Winans, "Stealth Pilot's Flights Memorable," *Skywriter*, Wright-Patterson AFB, Ohio, July 5, 1991, p. 4.
8. Leatherman, interview.
9. SM/Sgt. Gary Martin, Team Stealth interview.
10. William Scott, "F-117A Design Presented Avionics Challenges," *Aviation Week & Space Technology*, February 8, 1993, pp. 43–44.
11. "USAF Seeks Modification of F-117 Upgrade Contract to Include GPS," *Inside the Air Force*, Dayton, Ohio, July 6, 1992, p. 3.
12. "Weasel Role for F-117," *Jane's Defence Weekly*, June 22, 1991, p. 1090.
13. Barbara Opall, "Nunn Urges Tactical Reconnaissance Role for F-117A," *Defense News*, August 12, 1991, p. 10.
14. Leatherman, interview.
15. David H. Fulghum, "Allies Strike Iraq for Defying UN," *Aviation Week & Space Technology*, January 18, 1993, pp. 22–25.
16. Macy and Macy, *Destination Baghdad*., p. 72.
17. Col. (Retired) Randolph H. Brinkley, US Marine Corps, "Future US Fighters at Cost/Technology Crossroad," *Armed Forces Journal International*, January 1991, pp. 49–50.
18. Macy and Macy, *Destination Baghdad*, p. 86.
19. Byrd, interview.

Index